SUPER BRAIN POWER

28 Minutes to a Supercharged Brain

DANE SPOTTS
WITH NANCY ATKINS

A LifeQuest Book/CD Experience

Published by
LifeQuest Publishing Group
SEATTLE, WASHINGTON

A LifeQuest Book/CD Experience
Published by LifeQuest Publishing Group
P.O. Box 1444
Issaquah, Washington 98027

LifeQuest Publishing Group
P.O. Box 1444
Issaquah, WA 98027
lifequest@usa.net

® *Brain Supercharger* is a registered trademark of Visionary Technology, Ltd.
Super Intelligence, Mozart Brain Boost, Mindscripting Technology, Neuro-Mapping, Neuro-Entrainment Matrix, are all trademarks of Visionary Technology, Ltd.
All rights reserved.

Publisher's Cataloging-in-Publication

Spotts, Dane.
    Super brain power : 28 minutes to a
supercharged brain / Dane Spotts with Nancy
Atkins. -- 1st ed.
p. cm.
Includes bibliographical references.
LCCN: 98-88027
ISBN: 1-892805-00-6

1. Self-actualization (Psychology) 2. Thought
and thinking--Popular works. 3. Mental efficency
--Popular works. 4. Success.   I. Title

BF431.S66 1999   153
                 QBI99-247

Printed in the United States of America
    3   4   5   6   7   8   9   10

This Book Is Dedicated To The "Mind Warrior."
Pilgrim Souls Leading Us Along The
Path Of Enlightenment.

Acknowledgments

I am deeply grateful to the people in my life who have contributed to this work and my own personal development in so many countless ways. To my writing buddy Nancy—who takes rough ideas and gives them wings. To my musical genius partner Rob—whose creative spirit breathes life into any project. To my talented daughter Athena—who not only designed this book but daily teaches me how to be a better person. To graphic designer Jeff—who knows how to "crank and rock." To media coordinator Miller—who connects the dots. To operations maestro Michael—who delivers the goods. To my wife Diane—who makes the magic. And to my parents Don and Carol who taught me one of life's most valuable lessons, "you can be whatever you want to be." — my thanks.

Contents

Preface

August 27, 1987. I hit a turning point. In a Southern California recording studio experimenting with sound, phasing various audio frequencies, I stumbled upon a combination that was mind blowing to say the least. Within seconds, I was sucked into a deep meditative trance unlike anything I'd ever experienced. Plugged into a Mind Mirror (an EEG machine that measures brainwaves as well as hemispheric synchronization), I was amazed to see bursts of Alpha and Theta activity. I was tripping into an altered state of consciousness...big time. I realized this was no ordinary self-improvement recording.

November 18, 1987. It was late afternoon when I finished laying down the final audio tracks of what was to become the *Brain Supercharger®* soundtrack. Walking out of that recording studio with masters in hand, I felt an inexplicable awe.

The flat afternoon sun washed everything in a surreal shade of twilight. An incomprehensible space seemed to open up among the people and cars crowding the streets...in that space, every sound was silenced into an utter stillness. Acutely aware of my surroundings, I felt connected to a greater dimension focused somewhere in my mind. I was alert and felt more alive than ever...a high level of energy surged through my body. I kept thinking to myself...

> **"If other people have the same experience I just did listening to the final cut of this soundtrack... it could change their lives."**

At that point, I had no idea how many people would be remotely interested in the concept of mind development, let alone willing to plug in their brains for 28 minutes each day to this soundtrack. But it was my passion, so I followed it. And I've been on this path ever since.

After the first *Brain Supercharger* ad appeared in OMNI magazine, I received thousands of calls from people wanting to try it, paying up to $50 for a single cassette tape. It was then that I began to realize the impact this was going to have on people. Even then, my wildest expectations could not envision the abundance of support I received from every part of the globe.

Since its debut in 1988, over 500,000 soundtracks incorporating the *Brain Supercharger* technology have been distributed throughout the world. Today, I believe the demand for mind development tools, meditation programs, and personal growth technologies is stronger than ever. The pursuit of self-improvement has gone **mainstream**.

This book is about **self-improvement**—the innate need we humans have to be more than we are. I will share my personal journey of self-discovery and my experiences developing and using the *Brain Supercharger* technology. I'll explore theories on the evolution of consciousness and how I believe, our future can be as wonderful as we want it to be. I'll also describe how my search for ideas that would allow **me** to develop my potential, evolved into a business whose mission it was **to develop technology and create tools to unleash the potential** in others.

The goal of this book is not about improving your IQ so you can score better on tests, or impress your friends with your intellect. It's about accessing a higher form of intelligence. Experiencing peak moments of enlightenment, flooding your mind with flashes of insight and wisdom that, in an instant, transform every aspect of your being. For in that moment of cosmic illumination comes a new kind of brain power, a kind of "super intelligence" that allows you to perceive the world in a new way. And once you experience that moment, you will never be the same again.

The CD enclosed with this book contains 2 powerful experimental soundtracks. The first is called *Super Intelligence*. Using the *Brain Supercharger* technology, this soundtrack is designed to alter your mind state and, through regular use, I believe will allow you to access higher states of consciousness.

The second soundtrack on the CD is called *Mozart Brain Boost*. It is designed to enhance focus, concentration, and learning by using a specific musical formula.

The technologies used in these soundtracks are based on scientific research, anecdotal evidence, and my personal experiences. I have included an extensive bibliography of references in the back of this book that I encourage you to explore.

What you're about to experience is unlike any other book or CD that's ever been published. Because this is more than just a book, and it's more than a CD. You don't just read or listen—you **experience**. This is a new media form. Designed not only to teach you new ideas or processes in an external sense, but to literally take your brain on a ride. An inner journey of self-discovery—to unleash a new power and way of thinking.

Read the book. Use the soundtracks. I believe an amazing universe of possibilities will open up to you. I will do the best I can to support you on your journey. Ultimately though, it's about you and your experiences. Enjoy the ride!

Dane Spotts
May 5, 1998

How to Use This Book

(Whether You Are Left or Right Brained...)

There are different approaches to moving through this book. If you tend to be more of a left-brained thinker—meaning you are more comfortable using logic when you process information—you will probably feel more comfortable reading the book quickly, in its entirety, and then re-reading it more slowly, doing the exercises and workshops in Part II as you go along. If you are more right-brained in your thinking—you tend to use intuition and emotion more than logic—you probably aren't even reading this and have gone immediately to whatever part of the book most appealed to you. If you are whole-brained—in that you use both the left and right side of your brain simultaneously—you will probably enjoy taking on Parts I and II at the same time, trying out the tools and workshops as you learn about the inner workings of your brain. The choice is yours!

The enclosed CD includes two soundtracks. While information about their development and use is included in Part I of the book, specific instructions for using them is covered in Part III as well as a brief introduction recorded onto Track 1.

The exercises and workshops included in Part II are in no particular order. You can begin anywhere you choose. The "How To Use This Section" at the beginning will give you basic information you need to get started, whether or not you have finished reading Part I. While the power of these tools is in their collective use, you will find that it's best not to try to absorb them all at once. Go gradually, being sure to do the exercises as you go along.

As you use these tools, you may experience uncertainty, discomfort, and be baffled by the doubts or anxieties that you feel. The process of transforming the energy in your brain is an exciting one, but like any growth process, it also requires work and may raise conflicting emotions in you. All this is a normal part of the transformation process.

Many people have experienced these same highs and lows. For that reason I've included a Question & Answer section in Part III to help answer some questions you may have as you begin your journey.

You will also find reprints of several letters from people who have gone through the experience of beginning their journey of self-discovery.

The purpose of this book is to provide information and guidance to help you along your path of mind development and personal growth. In the pages that follow you'll find tools that are designed to rewire how your brain is organized and adjust the way you view yourself and the world. These are powerful processes that can erase fear and stress, and replace them with confidence and vision to unleash your potential in the world. These processes are also experiential, and therefore must be **experienced** to be effective. Initially they may feel silly or uncomfortable because they conflict with your current thinking. I ask that you suspend your judgments until after you've read the book, gone through the workshops, and used your soundtracks on a consistent basis. Give yourself a chance to experience their benefits. See how they affect your life.

One of the major lessons to be learned in *Super Brain Power* is the idea of "letting go." This means to let go of any preconceived notions, analytical thinking, or negative beliefs that can prevent you from releasing the power of your intuitive right brain and experiencing whole brain thinking.

Give yourself 90 days of actively using these tools. By the end of this period you should experience, at minimum, an opening of new thinking and possibilities that you hadn't previously seen. As it's done for me and thousands of others, this shift will make a profound impact in all areas of your life.

Your <u>thoughts</u> determine your reality by guiding your <u>actions</u>.

What are your <u>thoughts</u> right now? *I doubt this stuff could work.*
   Or ...*I wonder how it could help me?*

What is your <u>action</u>? *Toss the book.*
   Or...*Turn the page.*

Either way...now is a turning point for you.

PART I:
Unleash Your Hidden Power

Chapter 1:
The Beginning—Start Here

"Genius is mainly an affair of energy..."
— Matthew Arnold

Everything in the universe is made of energy. This book. The soundtracks on the enclosed CD. The light falling on these words. The very thoughts bombarding your mind as you read these words. The air you breathe.

Energy inside of you. Energy outside of you. The sun is the source of the energy on the outside. **Your brain controls the energy on the inside**.

Plants, animals and humans have thrived because they were able to transform the sun's energy to meet their survival needs. But we humans desire much more from life than just survival.

We want to be richer, sexier, smarter. We want happier, fuller and more rewarding lives, and ultimately, to understand our place in the universe. The key to satisfying our human desires is controlling the power of our brains. And it all has to do with energy and how we direct it. Let me explain.

Your life is a dynamic balance of energy exchange between your inner and outer worlds. Your thoughts are the energy of your brain. And it's through your thoughts that you direct that energy— influencing your emotions and mood, and your reality by the actions and choices you make. In doing so, your outer world is (or becomes) a perfect reflection of your inner world.

Perhaps one of the great untold discoveries of this century is the knowledge of how to manipulate this energy. To orchestrate the energies of consciousness. To expand brain power and improve psychological well-being. Ways to harmonize the brain's left and right hemispheres to maximize cognitive functioning and mental performance. Methods for accessing the unconscious (or inner mind as its been called) to transform negative beliefs and self-sabotaging behaviors. And most important of all, the ability to achieve higher states of consciousness and unleash the true potential of a human being.

A key element to achieving all this is having the ability to redirect your brain's energy—shifting your mind state into optimal patterns where you become more receptive to new learning, creative insights and psychological rescripting.

How can you do this? The best way for me to answer this question is to introduce you to a technology that's existed for thousands of years, whose purpose is to manipulate the "energies" of the brain. A technology that is considered by some to be a religious practice and others just a tool for mind expansion. It has been used to heal the sick, enable super-human feats, and achieve enlightenment. I'm talking about **meditation**.

MEDITATION: A NEW MENTAL STATE

Over the last 30 years, a great deal of scientific research has been conducted on meditation practices. In the late 1950s, scientists discovered that deep states of meditation actually cause certain physiological responses in the body that are not the same as those observed while sleeping or simply relaxing. These include: a decrease in oxygen consumption, a reduction in carbon dioxide elimination, a reduction in heart rate, respiratory rate, blood pressure, and blood cortisone levels. In addition, there are changes in the patterns of the brain's electrical activity. EEG (or electroencephalograph) analysis indicates an increase in the intensity of slow Alpha waves and occasional Theta wave activity.

Researchers in the 1970s began to describe meditation as "an alert, hypometabolic state constituting a fourth major state of consciousness." In the 1980's, meditation was fast becoming a popular method used for spiritual awakening. For many people in the 1990's, the primary motivation for learning to meditate has been the well documented health benefits. Many stress-related illnesses can be completely cured within a few weeks of regular practice. Anxiety, stress, tension, and aggressiveness all seem to decrease while, at the same time, there is an increase in self-control and improvement in general health and energy. But perhaps even more startling is that, with much practice, one can learn how to program their physiological responses to head off stress before it has a chance to affect the nervous system.

Besides the obvious health benefits, what has meditation got to do with achieving higher states of consciousness and increased mental awareness? Well, something else is going on besides just deep relaxation and stress reduction. Something truly profound.

ZEN MONKS & FIRE-WALKING YOGIS

Experienced meditators, such as yogis and mystics, spend a majority of their life learning to control certain physiological responses. After years of practice, they develop an ability to tap into the unconscious portions of their minds and unleash creative and mental powers that cannot be accessed in their normal waking state. We've all heard and read about the firewalking yogis who can walk across a bed of burning coals at temperatures that should have reduced their feet to smoldering stumps; yet at the end of their walk, they suffer not so much as a blister. Most of these mind over body feats are ignored by Western science because the very idea of such mental powers simply does not fit into our belief structure, and is therefore rejected.

For those new to meditation, it is very difficult to grasp the concept that our so-called "normal" waking state is neither the highest, nor the most effective state of which the human mind is capable. In fact, there are other states of much greater awareness where one is able to enter into for brief periods of time, and then return—enriched and enlivened. How is this possible?

THE SECRET PATH

It's widely known by science that only a small part of our total mental activity takes place in the conscious part of the mind. Science has no idea what really goes on in the vast portion of the unconscious. This is unknown territory. The unconscious mind is continuously processing ideas, images, and sensory data and doing things about which we know very little.

What we do know, however, is that those who do make direct contact with their unconscious mind through meditation, find incredible personal insight and are able to remove self-limiting blocks that prevent them from achieving their goals and finding happiness in life.

A wonderful passage from Paul Bruton's book *The Secret Path* describes the experience this way, "Once we push the gate of the mind slightly ajar and let the light stream in, the meaning of life becomes silently revealed to us. The gate may be open for one minute or for one hour, but in that period we discover the secret, and neither weary time nor bitter woe can tear that priceless knowledge away from us."

Part I

Unleash Your Hidden Power

———

12

For those who are able to look through the gate into their own being, an amazing truth is revealed: a capacity for infinite wisdom and happiness is available to them. This is why people spend years studying meditation practices. The Eastern mystic seeks, through meditation, to empty his mind so that higher knowledge can be revealed to him. To reach into these higher states of consciousness; to access deep mystical truths; and unlock the mysteries of the Universe. **To unfold a state of enlightened awareness.** These are the goals of meditation.

The difficulty however with traditional mediation practices is that it can take many years to train your brain to redirect its energy into optimal patterns.

Now, what if I told you there is a way to achieve higher states of consciousness, without being an expert in meditation? A way to drive the brain into an altered state—automatically, at the push of a button? If you're skeptical, I understand. But that is precisely what you can look forward to with regular use of the *Super Intelligence* soundtrack included with this book.

Instead of spending many years in meditation training, learning the correct physiological responses required to induce this deep state of meditative awareness, the *Brain Supercharger* technology incorporated into your *Super Intelligence* soundtrack can help you get there almost effortlessly.

Listen: I wouldn't ask you to make this leap of faith without using it yourself and basing your answers on personal experience. That's why I've included *Super Intelligence* on the CD enclosed with this book. So you can experiment with it—and experience it firsthand.

All you have to do is set aside 28 minutes each day. Find a quiet place where you can be alone undisturbed, and using stereo headphones plug yourself into this special soundtrack. During each session, the *Super Intelligence* soundtrack will drive your brain into an altered state of consciousness by coaxing your brainwaves to match the electrical frequencies necessary for deep meditative awareness. Unlike a mystic or a yogi, you don't have to spend years sitting in a cave, staring at a candle or chanting a mantra to start realizing the benefits of this deep, meditational state.

As you use the *Super Intelligence* soundtrack you'll begin to experience a shift in the energies of your brain. As you go deep into the meditational experience, after only a few weeks or months of regular use, you'll reach new levels of mental awareness, and feel a greater sense of well-being and centeredness. Many people report that they undergo a transformation, which opens them up to the experience of higher states of consciousness. They have reported highly transcendental states where deep intuitive knowledge and personal truths were revealed to them. It is often impossible for an individual to express their experience in words because these deep insights and truths transcend the senses or even ordinary reason. They are transformational events that dramatically alter their life from that moment forward.

Chapter 1

*The Beginning—
Start Here*

13

So, how does the *Super Intelligence* soundtrack open up your mind to these higher states of consciousness? How can it be used to achieve deep meditative awareness? What does all this mean in the context of everyday living? These questions will be answered in the following chapters. But first, it's important for you to understand what the different mind states are, and learn exactly how the *Brain Supercharger* technology incorporated into your *Super Intelligence* soundtrack works to evoke a specific mind state. Then, I'll describe the profound affect this experience can have on your life.

THE SECRET LIFE OF BRAINWAVES

Let's say right now that you're able to hook yourself up to an electroencephalograph (or EEG machine). Electrodes would be attached to your scalp and routed through the EEG machine. The electrodes would detect weak electrical currents generated by your brain. The currents would be amplified and displayed on a meter as frequency patterns.

For example, as you are reading this page your brain is concentrating on the words and their meaning. Because of this mental activity, it is likely the dominant brainwave frequency pattern displayed on the EEG machine would read Beta. If you were to close your eyes and roll them up slightly toward your forehead and imagine yourself laying on a tropical beach enjoying the sounds of ocean surf, almost immediately your dominant brainwave frequency pattern would shift down into the "Alpha" level.

"Beta," "Alpha," "Theta," and "Delta" are really just descriptive tags for different frequency patterns generated by your brain. Measured in cycles per second these frequency patterns represent specific mind states. For example, when we say you are in an "Alpha-Theta Mind State," it means that the brainwave activity being measured is dominant in the Alpha-Theta range (a frequency rate anywhere in the 8 to 13 cycles per second range).

While scientists do not know specifically how these waves of energy affect the world outside, they are beginning to understand how they affect the world inside. And even though it is still a crude way of measuring a very complex mind/brain system, it does provide us with a labeling mechanism for describing a range of mental states.

The four brainwave patterns generally associated with specific states of consciousness are: "Beta," "Alpha," "Theta," and "Delta."

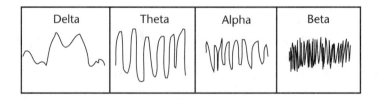

Delta	Theta	Alpha	Beta

"Beta," the alert state, is measured as a frequency in the 13 to 30 cycles per second range. It's associated with active thinking, speaking, and solving concrete problems. The strength of the "Beta" frequency is increased by anxiety or focused mental activity.

"Alpha" is actually the most prominent frequency pattern in the entire realm of brainwave activity. Rolling between 8 and 13 cycles per second, most people can produce Alpha activity by simply closing their eyes. It's a relaxed and calm state, but generally not associated with inwardly direct attention, relaxed awareness, or strong feelings of well being.

"Theta" is below the "Alpha" range, measuring 4 to 7 cycles per second. This frequency is dominant while in the dream state. It's associated with creativity and access to the unconscious mind, as well as deep meditation.

"Delta" is the fourth mind state and it's primarily associated with deep sleep. The brainwave patterns are very slow, measuring from 1/2 to 4 cycles per second. There is now some evidence to suggest that "Delta" is prominent during the onset of psychic phenomena and extra-sensory awareness.

What does this have to do with supercharging your brain?

JOIN THE ALPHA-THETA FRATERNITY

A number of studies have focused on the relationship between the dominant brainwave frequencies of experienced meditators and altered states of consciousness. When in a deep meditative state, Zen monks and yogis experience a higher or *ultra* state of consciousness.

By using EEG machines, researchers have been able to measure their brainwave frequencies during this altered mind state. The findings revealed that while in Alpha-Theta states, yogis were able to perform incredible feats such as walking across burning hot beds of coals without feeling pain, or even receiving the slightest blister. It is in this mind state that brain chemistry appears to be altered and the left and right hemispheres of the brain become synchronized.

These Zen monks, yogis, and others who are experienced meditators, have learned to alter their mind state through years of training and discipline. They are able to shift their internal state at will, driving their brains into altered states of consciousness, slowing down their dominant brainwaves and synchronizing the left and right hemispheres. This deliberate switching-off of external stimuli appears to alter the content of their awareness, suspending normal reality, and shifting focus and attention inward.

Dr. Tomio Hirai, one of Japan's leading neurophysiologists, discovered a connection between meditation and brainwave frequency patterns by correlating brainwave patterns with certain stages of meditation. Dr. Hirai writes; "Meditation is not merely a state between mental stability and sleep but a condition in which the mind operates at the optimum. In this condition, the person is relaxed but ready to accept and respond positively to any stimulus that may reach him."

The work of Dr. Hirari and other researchers now confirms that brainwave frequency patterns correspond to certain states of consciousness. This suggests that individuals capable of altering their brainwave patterns can have significant control over other mental and physiological functions. As Elmer and Alyce Green of the famous Menninger Institute first reported in the 70's; "...simply causing your brain to generate Theta activity for a few minutes each day seems to have enormous benefits, including boosting the immune system, enhancing creativity, and triggering "integrative experiences leading to feelings of psychological well-being."

Many years ago while I was studying meditation and altered mind states, the idea of altering brainwave frequencies raised an intriguing question: What if there was a technology that could stimulate the brain to produce specific energy patterns? Essentially driving it into a mind state such as the Alpha-Theta wave trance of a Zen Monk or yogi. How would I do it? Would I use pulses of electricity, light, or sound, played in specific combinations to coax the brain to follow a desired frequency pattern? And if I did, what would happen? How would this "brain stimulation" affect my inner world?

This was a big question and an important one. Because if this concept was valid, it meant that I could manipulate the energy patterns of my mind at the push of a button. Such a technology would have profound implications. This question was also the catalyst for my quest that led to the development of the *Brain Supercharger* technology.

In the next chapter, we'll explore how our brains work and how the *Super Intelligence* soundtrack can help unlock the mysteries of our inner world.

Chapter 2:
Your Genius Potential

"The really valuable thing is intuition.
Through meditation I found answers
before I asked the question. Imagination
is more important than knowledge."
— Albert Einstein

A genius is thought to be someone with a high IQ; able to solve complex problems with logic and reasoning. An inventor or business leader with a vision or insight. A scientist who makes a breakthrough discovery. An artist who composes or plays brilliant music. This is how we typically define genius. A measure of extraordinary mental output or creative activity.

Now, allow me to reframe the concept of genius. Instead of being measured by activity or output, let's consider genius from the perspective of potential. Science says we use only 10% of our brain's power. What then is the other 90% for? Is it our latent potential waiting to be unleashed? And if it were possible to tap into even a small percentage of this potential what greatness could we uncover?

Scientific studies have shown that, while the number of brain cells an individual has is a factor in intelligence, far more important is the way in which our brain cells are stimulated and the resulting pathways they form. Let me explain.

Contrary to popular belief, our brains don't soak up information like sponges. Instead, the human brain contains a large complex network of interconnections that enables energy to flow where it is needed. Like a vast cross-country telecommunications network in miniature, this energy contains primitive survival instructions— necessary for physical body functioning—as well as thoughts and ideas.

Your ability to think is dependent upon how well your brain is connected. In other words, the more connections your brain has, the greater the capacity for processing, storing, and recalling information. An examination of sections of Einstein's brain in the early 1980s showed what neuroanatomist Marian Diamond expected—an increased number of glia cells—the connective tissue or glue that binds the network of connections. So how can we increase the neuro pathways in our brains and improve the network of connections?

THE INFANT BRAIN: A MODEL OF UNLIMITED POTENTIAL

You were born a genius. Your brain was teaming with trillions and trillions of neurons capable of receiving and sending electrical impulses. These electrical impulses created the mental circuits between neurons, branch-like structures called dendrites and axons— that transmitted electrical signals from one neuron to another. Each impulse transferred tiny bits of information signaling growth, learning, memory, and life.

Some of these neurons were pre-designated as circuits that regulate the autonomic functions of heartbeat, breathing, and body temperature. Still, trillions more held raw energy, waiting to be transformed by your experiences to release their potential; which, in turn, would release the potential in you.

What is most fascinating about the infant brain is that if it does not begin to use these trillions of neurons, connecting dendrites and forging new pathways routing the brains information highway, it automatically starts to trim them. In other words, the brain removes what is not used. A kind of pruning takes place. So it really is true that "if you don't use it, you lose it."

This is why it is so easy to teach foreign languages to children. Their brains literally have more language learning circuitry available to them, waiting to be wired up. A child's brain accepts the new input and, almost effortlessly, etches out new learning pathways. Some researchers are so excited by this idea they are experimenting with teaching babies complex subjects like calculus and geography at only a few months old, before they've even learned how to speak. They believe the infant brain is capable of absorbing any new input—no matter how complex—even though the language circuitry has not been fully wired to communicate.

When you were an infant, your caregivers engaged your intellect using language, and encouraged you to interact with your environment. All that baby talk and playtime exposure to visual images, blocks, music, beads, etc., was critical in the structuring and developing of your neural pathways. Each new experience lit up your brain like a Christmas tree in Rockefeller Center. The arc from deep darkness to blinding brightness occurred in a microsecond and happened again and again and again—every time you were presented with a new experience.

When these neurons of raw energy were stimulated through an experience, they become integrated into your brain's circuitry by connecting to other neurons. This happened at such an astonishing rate of speed, as you grew from infant, to child, to adult, the number of connections in your brain grew larger than the number of galaxies in the known universe—over 100 trillion connections.

It is these connections—not the number of neurons themselves—that determines your brain power. Even though your brain reached 90 percent of its total size on your sixth birthday, it continues to "grow" as the number of connections between neurons increases with each new experience. To accommodate a growing brain in a skull that can't keep pace, the surface of the brain literally folds, or wrinkles, into itself creating the well-known grooved and rumpled neocortex look. (Commonly referred to as "gray matter.")

Does this mean that if your brain was not sufficiently stimulated as an infant, your wiring would be fixed thus limiting your intellectual capacity later in life? The answer is no. In fact, studies have shown that it is possible for the brain to expand its neuro pathways at almost any time in its life. This increasingly accepted theory by neuroscientists means that life-long learning can open up new worlds of opportunity and achievement.

What's important to understand is that our brain's network of connections increases with each new experience. In other words, scientists now have the empirical evidence to say without a doubt what many intuitively knew all along—that the brain literally expands the more we use it.

The point is—experience stimulates intelligence. But what kind of intelligence, and how can we access it?

THE SPLIT BRAIN THEORY

In 1983, Roger Sperry of the California Institute of Technology won the Nobel Prize for his discovery that, "...the two distinctive hemispheres of the brain (the left and the right) have specialized functions. Linking these two hemispheres is a complex network of nerve fibers called the corpus callosum."

Your left brain is your logical, analytical, verbal brain. It rationalizes and processes such things as language, mathematics, and sequential steps with explicit detail. It understands the concrete and prefers goal-oriented thinking. In contrast, your right brain has the ability to deal with conceptual thought and symbols, along with visual impressions, color recognition, spatial patterns, music and movement, and such abstracts as the emotions of love, loyalty, and beauty. It is the nonverbal, holistic, playful part of you that is both spontaneous and intuitive.

When going to see a movie, it is your left brain that deals with the plot sequence and the information in the dialogue of the characters. It's your right brain that hears the stirring music and feels the passion for the characters.

Another example of the specificity of left and right hemisphere functioning, is what happens when you meet someone for the first time. Your right brain takes in all the elements you are seeing, hearing, and feeling and synthesizes the pattern into a whole so that, in the future, you will recognize the person immediately. The right brain also processes emotional elements; such as noticing if the person you're meeting looks distracted, seems tired, or is happy. The left brain records more tangible data—height, weight, and name. It literally scans each part of that person to "build up" a "logical" picture of him or her for your mind to decipher, store and recognize.

It is because of the nature of the right brain that you can recognize a person after not having seen him or her for 20 years or more. When you think about it, that is a remarkable ability. Everything about the person has changed due to the aging process— the weight, the color and style of the hair, the wrinkles and lines and folds under the chin. Yet something about the face will be familiar— even if you can't recall their name. That "something familiar" is a patterning element that the right brain puts together into the whole memory of the person or experience being retrieved.

It's the same patterning element that lets you find your way to a place you've only visited once. While you couldn't begin to describe the directions in words to someone else, you would somehow be able to find it as you drove along. This is the power of your right brain working for you—infinitely intuitive, but hopelessly mute. The challenge is to find a voice for its deep knowing. The voice is in the left brain. The secret is finding a way to pass the knowledge from the right brain to the left brain through the corpus callosum. That is the promise of whole brain thinking.

THE RIGHT START

When you entered kindergarten as a child, you were basically using your right brain. You finger-painted, created games, and sang. As you got older, more and more attention was given to the left brain activities of reading, writing and arithmetic. Historically, western civilization has tended to stress the values and functions of the left brain—analysis, logic, discipline, and attention to detail.

Today, however, the trend is to put more emphasis on right brain activities. The reason is simple: performance in both academic and business settings dramatically increases as the abilities of the right brain are stimulated along with those of the left brain.

Schools, which have increased the proportion of art, music and physical education classes (right brain courses) to that of analytical classes (left brain courses) have found that all levels of scholastic performance have improved. Businesses, too, are waking up to the fact that the combination of a global competitive market and an overload of information demands less reliance on traditional business skills (statistics and linear models of production) and more emphasis on intuition, creative solutions, communication and interpersonal skills.

THE ADVANTAGE OF WHOLE BRAIN THINKING

Whenever there are two of anything in the body, one is usually dominant over the other due to innate tendencies as well as influences by your family and society. Just as you are naturally right—or left-handed, you also have a dominant eye, foot, kidney, etc. Therefore, most people are either dominantly left-brained or right-brained.

Geniuses, however, are whole-brained thinkers. They experience, in their everyday waking life, an ideal state in which the two hemispheres of the brain work in harmony together, allowing the brain to shift easily and quickly from one side to the other depending on the nature of the task.

In *Handbook of States of Consciousness*, Patricia Carrington of Princeton University writes, "Man's highest achievements require the complementary workings of thought processes from both sides of the brain. Intuition and hunches must be shaped through logical, disciplined thinking for a work of art, and the most rigorous scientific and philosophic reasoning requires the enriching leaven of hunch and inspiration. We need a harmony, a coming together of our two 'selves' into one mind."

In this cooperative state, the mind is purposefully focused and highly productive. Physically, you feel relaxed and mentally, your mind is open. Stress melts away and you are unaware of the passing of time. You are completely absorbed and aware; you are **in the moment**. While the experience is slightly different for each person, the characteristics that accompany this mind state range from intense mental clarity and heightened awareness to lucid dreaming, a lessening of anxiety to disappearance of chronic pain, increased creativity and flashes of insight, to peak experiences.

Two examples of these exceptional whole brain thinkers are Einstein and Leonardo da Vinci. While Einstein is well known for his left-brain scientific accomplishments, he credited his imagination and intuition (right brain specialties) for the insight that led to his achievements. Einstein appeared to live in a semipermanent Alpha state. Even while solving complex mathematical problems he was able to maintain high amplitude Alpha waves (a brainwave pattern normally associated with relaxation and meditation). He would often take naps and daydream to unleash this ability. He was daydreaming on a hill one day when he imagined riding on beams of light to the far reaches of the universe. When finding himself returned "illogically" to the sun, he gained the insight that the universe was curved, which was contrary to what he had been taught. Working "backwards" from this insight, he developed the Theory of Relativity

Part I

Unleash Your Hidden Power

22

using numbers, equations, and words (the specialties of the left brain) to prove what his daydreaming mind had envisioned.

The Mona Lisa is perhaps the most well-known painting of all time but its creator, Leonardo da Vinci, actually spent very little of his time painting. His personal notebook, called the Codex Leicester, is filled with scientific notes and drawings on his experiments with hydraulics and his observations about the relationship of the moon to the earth. Microsoft chairman Bill Gates (who purchased the Codex for $30.8 million at an auction at Christi's) writes this of da Vinci: "Leonardo pursued knowledge with unrelenting energy. His scientific 'notebooks' are awe inspiring not simply as repositories of his remarkable ideas but as records of a great mind at work. In the pages of the Codex Leicester, he frames important questions, tests concepts, confronts challenges, and strives for answers...His writings demonstrate that creativity drives discovery and that art and science—often seen as opposites can in fact inform and influence each other."

Leonardo's bold ideas 500 years ago became some of the transforming technologies of the 20th century—the parachute, the helicopter, and underwater diving apparatus. These were all original ideas of the Renaissance master.

An accomplished man in art, sculpture, physiology, architecture, mechanics, anatomy, physics, invention, meteorology, geology, engineering and aviation, da Vinci could also play many stringed instruments. His genius came not from his achievements in one area, but rather from his ability to transfer the knowledge he learned in one field through a creative application into another.

UNLEASHING YOUR GENIUS POTENTIAL

Unleashing your genius potential and becoming a whole brain thinker is one of the goals of this book. The ability to draw from both hemispheres of your brain, and tap into an inner universe of intelligence that is not only synergistic and therefore greater than the sum of its parts, but a force beyond measuring. Again, it's not about being better at test taking or knowing more facts so you can impress your friends. It's about connecting and stimulating your brain in ways that can result in new patterns of thinking. To feed your brain with "experiences" that can develop its "weaker" side. And to be able to open a doorway into the inner mind to unleash your deeper intuitive powers.

Once you've strengthened and stimulated these areas of your potential with the appropriate exercises, you can improve all areas of your mental performance. As well as tap into a new power, that can unfold new levels of insight and wisdom that will transform every element of your being.

THE POWER OF EMOTION

Part I

Unleash Your Hidden Power

24

When profound, historical events, like the death of President John F. Kennedy, or the explosion of the Challenger Space Shuttle take place, most people remember exactly where they were and what they were doing when they learned of the event. The same is true for profound, personal events as well. Let me explain.

Everyone, at some point in their lives, has experienced falling in love. For some, it was a first boyfriend or girlfriend. For others, it was a high school or college sweetheart. And still others fell in love later in life. Whenever it happened, the experience of being in love is indelibly etched into your memory. Think about it.

The first time you held hands. Your first kiss. Or a walk in the park. When you knew in your heart that the person you were with at that moment was the only other person in the universe. Can you remember how powerful your feelings were? Your heart was pounding and your head was spinning. Can you remember in vivid detail your surroundings? The scent of orange blossom on a summer night. An ocean breeze. Such memories of love are so powerful they last a lifetime.

So what's going on? Why are these memories so strong and how can they evoke such powerful feelings? The answer is: emotion. Emotion is the key to linking experience to memory. When your experience is linked to emotion, a bio-chemical chain reaction occurs in your brain locking the memory in place.

What if you could use this experience/emotion/memory process in a controlled way? In other words, what if a technology could be developed that utilized our innate memory linking abilities, and tapped into left/right brain activity, resulting in whole brain functioning—awakening our genius potential?

Neuroscientists have recently discovered that certain areas of the brain most involved with learning and receiving new information are those areas where endorphins, the body's natural opiates, are generated. Scientists have even mapped what they call "reward pathways" and found them to be connected to specific learning centers. The idea is that when we receive new information, and suddenly there is an emotional connection—the light bulb in the brain goes off and you get the "Aha experience"—and, at that moment, the brain rewards the body with a surge of endorphins and other pleasure producing chemicals.

Now imagine living the "Aha experience" 100% of the time. Endorphins pumping through your brain and your entire being is on fire with the intense feeling of aliveness—all the time! I don't have to imagine it—I know what it feels like. And you can too. In the next chapter I'll share my discovery of the *Brain Supercharger* technology and how it has changed my life forever—and how it can change yours.

Chapter 2

Your Genius Potential

25

Chapter 3:
The Brain Supercharger Discovery

"99% of the world is asleep. The 1%
that is awake remains in a constant
state of amazement."
— Meg Ryan to Tom Hanks
in the movie "Joe vs the Volcano."

Since that fateful day in 1987, the *Brain Supercharger* technology has enhanced my well-being and launched me into incredible new levels of awareness. It has also enabled me to experiment with altered states of consciousness, unleashing the deep intuition and creative insights of my higher mind. I want to share those experiences with you now. Not just talk about it—but give you the technology so you can experience it yourself—firsthand.

Enclosed with this book is a CD with a unique experimental soundtrack incorporating the *Brain Supercharger* technology. A soundtrack that can drive your brain into an altered state of consciousness through special sound engineering processes. A synthesis of Eastern philosophy and Western high technology, the *Brain Supercharger* technology is a powerful tool for transformation and unleashing whole brain thinking. What's it all about? How does it work? And how can you use this remarkable tool to further your own personal growth?

ALTERED BRAIN STATES: IS IT THE SECRET BEHIND "SUPERHUMAN" FEATS?

Biofeedback researchers have found that people who enter the "Theta state" expand their states of consciousness, acquire super-receptivity to new information, and demonstrate a greater ability to "rescript" material on a subconscious level. Even more astonishing are the findings of a study on a group of chronic alcoholics at a University in Colorado. After 13 weeks, the group that learned to generate Theta and Alpha brainwaves, showed a far greater recovery rate, and a complete transformation of personality. There is a remarkable body of evidence to support the claim that teaching people to enter into altered states on a regular basis can dramatically improve their mental functioning, emotional stability, and heighten intuition and perceptual ability.

It has also been researched and demonstrated that most artists, musicians, and athletes are prolific producers of Alpha-Theta brainwave patterns. Creativity and strong Alpha-Theta activity appear to be linked. Studies done at the University of Colorado Medical Center found that when people were trained to achieve and maintain "Theta" brainwaves using biofeedback techniques, not only did they learn at an accelerated rate and show remarkable increases in creativity, but many emotional and attitude problems were solved at the same time, along with the health-related benefits of stress reduction.

Hundreds of these studies over the last 30 years have confirmed that meditation leads to heightened mental awareness, improved IQ, memory, and creativity. The health benefits of stress reduction and strengthened immune functions are also well documented. So why aren't more people doing it? Most forms of meditation require years of concentrated practice to advance into these higher states of awareness. In addition, many in the West feel uncomfortable with such practices; finding them strange or in conflict with their religious beliefs.

An easier and effective alternative began twenty to thirty years ago, as researchers developed biofeedback equipment which allowed people to train themselves to maintain this brainwave rhythm and evoke specific mental states. Biofeedback equipment however, is expensive, difficult to operate, and most people wouldn't know how or where to access it, let alone use it on a daily basis.

What is required is a technology that can stimulate desirable mind states without a great deal of effort or cost. To allow anyone to experience and access these altered states of consciousness without the use of drugs, expensive machinery or having to sit in a cave and chant for 30 years. This idea was the driving force behind my quest. The result was the *Brain Supercharger* technology.

PUSH-BUTTON MEDITATION

I spent years pursuing this idea. A simple, effective technology that could unleash the potential of the mind. As I stated, one of my goals was to find a specific (non-drug) process that could drive the brain into an optimal state of expanded awareness. It had to be inexpensive, easy to use and accessible to anyone. The discovery I stumbled across was to have a profound impact on my life and the lives of thousands. Here it is:

> **Certain sounds using the right frequency combinations and harmonic effects could alter consciousness and drive the brain into an altered state similar to that achieved by experienced meditators.**

The idea that sound could shift mood and stimulate certain psychological and physiological responses in the brain is not a new idea. In fact, it's a very old one. Ancient cultures with their shamanic rituals up through the modern masters of music have used sound to heal, affect mood, and induce trance states. The brain seems to automatically follow the "beat" of the drums, and speeds up or slows down to keep pace with the music. Why? Why are certain music and sound patterns so powerful in affecting mood and altering brain chemistry?

My goal was to take this idea as far as possible. Not to create elevator music that resulted in pleasant relaxation, but to discover what causes the "effect" and be able to manipulate and enhance it a thousandfold. I wanted to develop a specific technology that could stimulate optimal states at the push of a button, accelerate the process of personal transformation, and allow a listener to experience transcendental states without any prior practice. I went into this project with a total Beginner's Mind (see **Zen**), and an enthusiasm that I could make it happen.

What I discovered was not only the *Brain Supercharger* technology for unfolding these mind states and accessing higher forms of consciousness, but also a philosophy for living that profoundly shaped the rest of my life. I must confess most of these insights are not original. Even though at the time they were revealed to my "beginner's mind" I felt as though I was the only one who had ever experienced them. Many others have peeked behind the curtains of the universe, and within an instant their lives too were transformed forever. This is what's in store for you if you choose to walk this path.

HOW CAN SOUND FREQUENCIES ALTER MIND STATES?

When I started my quest to develop this technology, I really knew very little about sound design, the recording business, or the effects of music on the mind. Certain experiences opened doorways which led to the answers I needed. Looking back on it a decade later, it was as if some magical force or unseen hands were pulling at me, forcing me to take certain paths so I might experience things that would eventually lead me to where I am today (see **Synchronicity**).

For example, in the late 70's I was shopping with my wife and daughter. We were in one of those large warehouse stores with skylights and enormous ceiling fans. It was a beautiful sunny day, and the sunlight shone brightly through the skylights reflecting off the blades of the ceiling fan which created an almost disco-like light show throughout the warehouse. As I passed through the path of the flickering beam, I experienced a sudden and extremely powerful emotional response.

It was uncanny but the sunlight strobing across my face seemed to pull at me. I felt a tingling sensation on my neck and arms, and my feet felt heavy. I was compelled to just stand there while this very strong light source flickered across my face and body. I closed my eyes and could feel the strobe effect even through my closed eyelids. A red pulsing (from the blood in the eyelid) created phenomenal kaleidoscope-like effects. It was hypnotic to say the least. I remember thinking, "Can a person's mind state be altered through flashing lights at the right frequency? Is this anything like brainwashing?" I knew the experience meant something, but I had no idea what it meant at the time[1]. It was only years later that I learned flicker stimulation produces extraordinary responses in the brain. Light sends a coded message across all areas of the brain, not just the visual cortex. Brain cells it turns out are very sensitive to light and are structured to act like light transducers. Light pulsed in the Alpha-

---

[1] Less than 7 years after this experience I founded a company that evolved into the world's largest manufacture of light-sound machines (approx. $40 million per year) that included a patented self-learning technology incorporating light-sound processes.

Theta ranges (4-8 cycles per second), creates a stimulation of memory and creativity.

I'm sure I looked pretty weird standing in the middle of that store, eyes closed, with bright sunlight flashing across my face, but something powerful was going on and I wanted to experience it. I was calm and relaxed and somehow drawn into an altered state by the frequency of this strobing light. I stood for almost a half hour, completely lost in the moment, only to catch up with my family who were already in the checkout line. I never shared this experience with anyone. I did however mentally log it as something I felt would come up for me again in the future.

IS LIFE A SONG?

A few years later, I was reading a book about Shamanism and Aboriginal music with its use of drums, chanting and flickering campfire lights which were used in rituals to stimulate mystical trance states. I began to think about this idea of sacred sounds. Certain musical forms that could evoke mystical experiences. About that same time, I came across an article about a doctor involved in genetic cancer research who was studying the structure of DNA and thought it looked an awful lot like the structure of music. The doctor wondered if he could play DNA code as if it were a piece of music. He was a trained pianist and just for the fun of it he took a piece of DNA (using code from a virus I believe) and converted it into musical notes. When he played it on the piano it sounded like Chopin. It had the form and structure of a finely composed concerto.

I was quite excited by this idea, and immediately called the doctor at the research center. I wanted to know more. I especially wanted to know what it all meant. We agreed to meet over lunch. As we finished our lunch conversation, I realized he didn't have a clue. In fact he agreed to meet with me because he thought I might know the answer. I didn't. What the doctor discovered was that the structure of a DNA molecule appears to have a similar organizational quality as music, and when converted into actual musical notes and played on a piano it sounds, not like random key strokes as you might expect, but has a musical form like a Master had composed it. God's great symphony? Perhaps life really is a song.

The doctor provided me with a few of his Chopin-like DNA

symphonies, and, every now and then, I play them and contemplate the great mystery of the universe. This idea has never led to anything specific regarding DNA music, but at the time I remember feeling this incident was important and those unseen hands were compelling me onward.

EXPERIMENTING WITH FLOTATION TANKS

Coincidentally around this time I was experimenting with floatation tanks, and having some pretty wild experiences. I was inspired by John Lilly and the movie *"Altered States,"* which was loosely based on Lilly's work with LSD, psychotropic drugs and sensory deprivation. My personal experiences in the tank (without the use of drugs) were quite profound to say the least, and were very unlike friends of mine who found the experience too "weird" or "boring."

For those of you who don't know anything about floating, you strip naked and climb into a sealed chamber about the size of tent. The chamber is filled with a water and salt mixture to make the floater completely buoyant. Also the water is heated to match your skin temperature of 98 degrees, so you can't even sense you are in water. When you climb into the tank and close the hatch, you are sensory deprived. You're in total darkness, and cut off from all visual stimuli. Your eyes never adjust to the darkness so you can't tell if your eyes are even open or shut. The extreme buoyancy of the salt water simulates a zero gravity environment. Your body floats without any effort or movement. You're wearing wax earplugs to not only keep out the water, but prevent sounds from leaking in.

After an hour or two of floating in this extreme sensory deprivation your brain goes crazy. Think about it. You're constantly bombarded by stimuli your entire life. Your brain is always processing something, including constant input from your senses and continuous adjusting for the forces of gravity. Now take all of that away. No gravity. No visual stimuli. No sound. No sense of feel. Totally alone with your thoughts. Timelessness. Nothingness (see **Void**).

Everyone's interpretation of their personal floating experiences are different. But the initial feelings I suspect are probably very similar. You go nuts. Your mind screams out for attention and stimulus. Freaked out by the nothingness, your mind begins its relentless chattering. Self talk, self evaluation and analyzing every little feeling and sensation. What you did last week. The last movie you saw. Where you left your car keys. How you're going to make your next mortgage payment. Your mind is desperate, looking for something to do.

Over time, as your attention becomes further driven inward, you shift into a new pattern of awareness. You forget where you're at, who you are, or that you're even floating. You begin to experience a new reality outside your normal waking or sleeping state. Your ego melts and you experience a new form of consciousness, witnessing yourself as you become the experience. You feel this expansiveness and connectedness like nothing you can describe in words. Similar to a deep meditation, it feels a lot like dreaming only you are wide awake. Perhaps more awake than you've ever been in your life.

The first time I went in, I did a three hour session that felt like only 5 minutes had passed. I'm serious. And I was totally blown away by it. I had a transcendental experience that may have lasted for only a moment, but in that moment I saw the universe with incredible clarity unlike anything I'd ever experienced up to that point in my life. You'd think I would emerge from such a powerful experience with a new seriousness about life but it was just the opposite. Everything seemed uniquely funny. I could not stop laughing. All I can remember thinking is how absurd everything seemed. The cosmos had a kind of sitcom reality to it and I remember laughing harder than I ever had before.

As I climbed out of the tank, I could hardly walk, I certainly couldn't drive for several hours. As I waited for my "ordinary" consciousness to return, I noticed an extreme sensory acuity. I could see and hear amazing details way off in the distance. And everything gave off a radiating glow of energy. I suppose I was reacting to the release of endorphins in my brain. The world seemed physically so much more alive and colorful. The sky appeared bluer than I had ever remembered it. And the grass **was** actually greener. I watched the ebb and flow of street traffic and it seemed like a surreal cartoon. Everyone rushing to get somewhere in an unconscious robotic sort of way. As I stood observing the world outside and taking in as much sensory experience of my "new reality" as possible, I wondered what it would be like if everyone could feel this good. What an empowering idea. I wanted more.

Chapter 3

The Brain Supercharger Discovery

33

Of course there were other ways to get "it." After all, this was the 80's. Alpha mind training groups and hypnosis classes were quite popular. EST and other seminars were at their peak. I went to several of these and picked up some training tapes and programs. Most were of good intention but had very limited practical value or were poorly produced. Some of the tapes would claim to induce an Alpha mind state by listening to white noise or the clicking sounds of a metronome (a timing device used by piano teachers) synced to an Alpha frequency (8 cycles per second). I'm sure these tapes and trainings worked for some students. They were just of such poor quality, I couldn't stick with them for very long. All along I kept asking myself can a person's mind state be altered through light and sound frequencies? And if so what would be the optimum way to accomplish it?

A few weeks after my float session, I was at the recording studio taping a sales training program. Talking with the studio engineer about my float experiences and my research into sacred sounds and "Alpha" training, we discussed the idea of designing a special soundtrack that could alter consciousness. Using state-of-the-art equipment, we began experimenting with different sound effects and sound engineering processes. Based on prior research, and plenty of trial and error, we stumbled onto a powerful combination. The proprietary technique we discovered is still considered a trade secret so I can't discuss the specifics except to say that it involves a matrix of sound frequencies, phased in such a way that the brain is compelled to follow it. Acting as Guinea pig, the effects on me were nothing less than stunning. Similar to my flotation tank experience, except I didn't need to get wet.

Initially I didn't know where I was going with my discovery but the direction felt right. And I decided to totally let go and follow my intuition (see **Intuition**). The result was an audio mix of sounds and environmental effects that had a powerful, compelling, and almost instant effect on the listener. Experimenting with different frequency matrices and harmonics, these soundtracks have now been tweaked and developed into different flavors, that will deliver a revelatory altered states experience to anyone using them. They **will** take a listener's brain into a state of deep meditative awareness at the push of a button. I began selling them, and my company quickly became the largest of its kind in the world.

OVER 500,000 *BRAIN SUPERCHARGERS* SOLD

I started selling *Brain Supercharger* tapes in 1988. The response was immediate and overwhelming. Since then, more than 500,000 copies of recordings utilizing this technology have been distributed throughout the world, and I've received literally thousands of letters of support. Most users were grateful for the stress reduction in their hectic lives. Several were suicidal and the regular use of the soundtracks totally turned around their depression. Many discovered their true mission in life, shifting careers and redirecting their lives toward greater fulfillment. Others launched their consciousness and had bonifide mystical experiences. As for me, I was thrilled by all the interest, even though I knew we were only scratching the surface of what was possible.

People came to visit me from all over the world. I was invited to speak and do seminars. I never thought of myself a guru. In fact I've intentionally avoided all publicity and never accepted any of the speaking engagements offered to me. I consider myself a tool maker. Nothing more. I had no answers for anyone. In fact, I was struggling to discover them for myself. Part of my joy in all this was the fact that I had a business/hobby that allowed me to pursue these ideas. I was just another seeker on the path like most of my customers.

I say "most" because I did have several customers that didn't fit the seeker mold. And you might be surprised when I tell you who they were. I don't mean movie stars or famous people of which we had plenty. Instead I mean people like the CIA, Lawerence Livermore National Laboratory and Air Force Intelligence. What would these folks want with a meditation tape? I asked a Director of Lawerence Livermore who called me personally in 1989 to ask questions and order several of my soundtracks. (Lawerence Livermore National Laboratory is a multi-billion dollar government research group whose projects include the Hydrogen Bomb and the "Star Wars" program.) He said, "We are looking for tools to help our scientists relax." I told him I was glad I could be of help. Later that year I received a visit from an Air Force Intelligence officer who also wanted to "talk" about the technology. I even heard from the CIA[2] who purchased several *Brain Supercharger* programs. Perhaps they too were interested in stress reduction for their personnel. Or—maybe it was something more. We'll explore the something more...next.

Chapter 3

The Brain Supercharger Discovery

35

---

[2] I enclosed a copy of the CIA purchase order in the appendix.

Chapter 4:
Mindscripting—A Technology For Programming Your Inner Mind

"Something we were withholding made us weak
until we found it was ourselves."
— Robert Frost

If the *Brain Supercharger* technology was just a tool for expanding consciousness and experiencing higher mind states it would be awesome enough, but there's something else going on here. Something with even deeper, more profound implications.

Many psychologists and neurologists now believe that while we are sleeping, our brains use the "Theta state" for psychological and physiological programming to heal our minds and bodies. They have discovered that when we sleep at night, we go through several 90 minute sleep cycles with several minutes of REM (rapid eye movement) activity at the top of each cycle. REM sleep is associated with dreaming and it is during this REM phase that we produce strong "Theta" brainwave activity. Why? And, maybe more importantly, why do we dream anyway? It is believed that dreaming is our brain's way of processing our daily experiences. Through imagery and symbols, dreaming is a tool used by our unconscious to make sense out of our personal reality (see **Dream Workshop**).

What I've discovered, is that by training my brain to enter into this "Theta" mind state on a frequent basis, interesting things happen. It opens a window into the unconscious mind, paving the way for positive changes to occur. And because I'm giving my brain more opportunities for psychological processing the benefits are far greater than just a pleasant listening experience. I allow positive thoughts and imagery to enter my inner world. Stress and tension melt away and I feel energized. I also seem to need less sleep. Why?

The *Brain Supercharger* technology gives my brain a concentrated dose (28 minutes) of extra "Theta" level activity each day. This activity feeds the brain with additional dream processing time, so I no longer need a full 8 hours of sleep. I've received dozens of letters from people claiming they could get by on as little as 3 or 4 hours a night so long as they were "Supercharging" on a regular basis. No studies were ever done to confirm this, but it warrants further investigation. Imagine having a tool that enables you to compress your sleep mode, adding an extra 3-5 hours to your day. As it is, we sleep fully one third of our lives, and, if it were possible to reduce this by any significant amount it would be an incredible benefit.

I've also received many letters from people who used their *Brain Superchargers* to reduce the effects of jet lag. One person told me that on a flight from LA to New York, an hour or so before landing, he would plug in, and disappear into the Alpha-Theta zone for 28 minutes. Upon landing instead of being wiped out by the trip, he reported feeling as if he had just awakened from a full nights sleep. Even more remarkable was his claim that it seemed to reset his biological clock, making jet lag less of a problem.

The point I'm trying to make is that something powerful is happening with the unconscious mind and the altered states experience. Somehow a window opens, providing an opportunity to do some amazing things that simply cannot be done in a "normal" conscious waking state.

I'm going to reveal what I believe is going on, and how you can use this technology not only to access your unconscious—but also to literally rewire it. That's right. The ability to reprogram your beliefs, erase negative self-sabotaging behavior and transform how you see yourself and the world. In my experience, when you can do this, you can accomplish almost anything.

NOT ONLY A NEW MIND STATE, BUT A NEW REALITY

Our experiences form our internal images of "self." These inner self-images of success or failure radiate outward into the world and affect the way we are judged and treated by others. Stored on the unconscious level, these internal images of "self" can be either good for us or barriers to our growth.

WHY IS CHANGE SO DIFFICULT?

The reason change is so difficult is that years of defeating self-talk, fear, and negative reinforcing experiences have created a mindscript in the unconscious of failure and limitation. Your inner images have become your outer reality.

For example, if you see yourself as a poor public speaker your unconscious mindscript will cause you to stutter, stammer, or become nervous during your speech. Likewise, if you see yourself as a great performer with a natural ability for public speaking, you probably would have no trouble speaking in front of an audience.

Reason: Your unconscious mindscript keeps you acting in a manner that is consistent with your internal images and beliefs.

The fact is we really have **two** minds. A conscious and unconscious or "inner mind" as it's sometimes called. Your unconscious or inner mind is the true source of your attitudes and behaviors. It acts like a computerized auto-pilot directing your actions and behavior according to a set of scripts that have been programmed into it since early childhood. Based upon this scripting, it automatically steers the direction of your life to match your internal images of reality.

THE UNCONSCIOUS RECORDS AND STORES OUR EXPERIENCES

Through repetition, your experiences generate learned automatic patterns of behavior—such as tying your shoes, driving a car, or riding a bicycle. All of these activities begin on a conscious level initially, but through repetition they become scripted into the unconscious resulting in habitual behavior patterns.

Your internal mindscripts control the direction your unconscious autopilot takes, so if your internal programming is negative or self-defeating, your outer experiences will end up mirroring this inner reality. On a conscious level, you may want to change the direction of your life but your unconscious is in the driver's seat. You end up as a passenger going along for the ride often wondering how you ever ended up where you are!

The key to creating lasting and permanent change is having the ability to reprogram your internal mindscripts. You need to give your unconscious autopilot a new roadmap and rescript your self-limiting beliefs, so you direct your life onto a new, positive course. This is not an easy thing to do. Years of self-reinforcing experiences have established a mindscript encrusted with negative thinking and self-defeating emotions.

DIRECT ACCESS TO YOUR UNCONSCIOUS

The reason why the *Brain Supercharger* technology is so effective in changing personal behavior and modifying self-image is that the affirmations (positive experiences) are directed toward the unconscious, while you are in a state of peak receptivity for psychological programming.

The conscious mind will reject any statements which are in conflict with what it knows to be true, but the unconscious doesn't know the difference between a truth or a lie. Unlike your conscious mind, the unconscious can be tricked into believing a new reality.

The most important fact you need to know about the unconscious is this:

> **The unconscious mind doesn't know the difference
> between real and imagined experiences!**

Most self-improvement techniques are designed to work only with the conscious mind. You listen to motivational speakers who get you pumped up for a day or two. Or you read self-improvement books that contain great principles and ideas only to forget them a few weeks later. Perhaps you repeat positive affirmations on a conscious level, and instead of a quick fix, you just feel silly! The problem isn't that these things can't work. It's just that they require an immense amount of effort and repetition to penetrate the conscious mind and rescript years of negative programming that already exists in your unconscious. The problem with all these methods is they don't directly address the true source of your behaviors. So when you tell your conscious mind, "I am wealthy," or "I am thin," it knows you are lying.

One woman I know, who was trying to lose weight with conscious affirmations said, "I have affirmed that I am thin until I am worn out. I knew that when I was telling myself those statements that it was obviously not true." Her statements were rejected by the conscious mind and the very opposite of what she outwardly affirmed was manifest. She actually gained weight! The unconscious mind will take your fears and limiting beliefs and, in its own way, bring about the obstacles, delays, and limitations into your life to fit your internal image of reality. That's why if your outer reality isn't working, you need to work on your inner reality. **Your outer world is or becomes a reflection of your inner world.** It's just that simple.

What's required then is a technology that can bypass the conscious mind and address the unconscious directly. In effect, opening a window into your inner mind so you can implant positive programming. Through repetition and real life experiences that begin to mirror this new internal reality, it becomes self-reinforcing and self-perpetuating. Once locked in, your mindscript is modified permanently. The unconscious then acts in accordance with its new programming and brings about changes in your everyday experiences to match this new reality.

THREE DISCOVERIES INCORPORATED INTO THE *BRAIN SUPERCHARGER* TECHNOLOGY

How can the *Brain Supercharger* technology do this? It is an effective tool for rescripting negative self-defeating beliefs because of three unique discoveries incorporated into the soundtracks.

1. **The ability to facilitate whole-brain synchrony entirely through sound. This represents a major breakthrough in safe, inexpensive, and effective psychotechnology. By applying the use of certain musical harmonics and sound frequencies, mood can be shifted, "right brain" awareness activated, and whole brain synchrony promoted. It is also believed that people who enter this mind state have a greater ability to "rescript" material on an unconscious level.**

Chapter 4

Mindscripting

2. The use of affirmations to direct positive programming to the unconscious which helps in rescripting negative self-defeating beliefs. (The *Brain Supercharger* technology incorporates a set of powerful mindscripting affirmations at or near the threshold of conscious perception. These affirmations succeed because they do not produce a mental conflict with your critical conscious mind which questions and rejects change. This mindscripting technique is intended to bypass the conscious mind and be picked up by the unconscious only. By bombarding the unconscious with new internal images and experiences you are literally re-writing your internal mindscript. Your unconscious auto-pilot then directs your behavior and outward experiences to re-align and match these new inward images of reality.

3. Holographic 3-D sound design delivers spatial effects into a listener's mind, engineered in such a way that you "feel" the sounds moving around inside your head. In addition to providing an interesting aural environment, it is designed to further distract the conscious mind and increase the effectiveness of the mindscripting process.

TRANSFORMING A LOSER MIND-SET INTO A WINNING ONE

Let's say you need some help losing weight, quitting smoking, or you want to transform a loser mind-set into a winning one. Using this technology, you can plug your brain into a specific version of the *Brain Supercharger* soundtracks that have mindscripting affirmations embedded within the audio matrix dealing with these subjects.

The soundtrack unfolds its unique audio matrix transporting you from an alert Beta conscious state to a deeply relaxed Alpha-Theta mind state. When asked to describe the experience, sometimes the best description is simply "**mind awake–body asleep.**" Because when you are in this dreamy mind awake–body asleep state, you open a window into your inner mind (unconscious) and become more receptive to suggestion. The soundtrack delivers positive suggestions using affirmations. These affirmations are delivered at or near the threshold of conscious awareness. Since you are addressing the unconscious directly and bypassing the critical conscious mind, you have a greater opportunity to allow these suggestions to penetrate and affect real change in attitudes and beliefs.

The theory of mindscripting is simple:

> **Induce a relaxed suggestible mind state, similar to deep meditation, open a channel into the inner mind, and send carefully crafted affirmations—positive statements that describe a reality you wish to create for yourself.**

Now I must add a caveat here. I consider *Brain Supercharger* technology to be experimental. Although I, and thousands of others, have used and benefited from the technology, I don't want you to believe that it is some sort of panacea—a "magic pill" that will solve all of your problems. It is designed to be used as part of your personal development program. Results will vary because people are psychologically complex. Everyone's emotional makeup and belief systems are self-reinforcing and self-fulfilling due to environment and a multitude of other variables. Each one of us is subject to a great many influences in our lives. Attitudes and beliefs generated from a very early age have been scripted into a set of patterns that are difficult to change all at once. The *Brain Supercharger* technology should be considered just another valuable resource in your personal arsenal of self-help approaches that can make a difference in your life.

But how can you introduce a new set of beliefs and "experiences" into your inner mind when your old scripts are still in control of your life? All that you see around you...your relationships with others...the job you have...the home you live in...the way your very existence is organized, has everything to do with the way your inner mind has been programmed. Any permanent changes you want to make in your life, must address this underlying programming.

Since a new script will initially be in conflict with your old scripts, it is likely to cause some disturbance. You may feel agitated and disenchanted with yourself. A small percentage (about 5% of *Brain Supercharger* users) experience this to such a high degree that they literally can't stand listening to the soundtrack. I've heard from some who have in the middle of the program ripped the headphones off their head and thrown them against the wall. This after listening

Chapter 4

Mindscripting

43

to it 20 or 30 times with no problems at all. Why the sudden dramatic reaction? It's because of this internal conflict. The human psyche is protecting its old scripts. Some never can get past this stage in their development and discontinue the program. They would rather remain in their comfort zone and so they quickly revert back to old patterns of thinking and behavior. They may not be happy with the direction their life is going, but the idea of change is just too threatening.

It is important that you understand it will take repetition and reinforcement to break these old patterns of thinking to realize the kind of results you want. When I first started this project, I understood how resistant human beings are to change, and I was skeptical that these techniques could make any significant lasting impact. Experimenting on myself I realized the shifts were subtle, but quite profound as I measured the changes over time. The key word here is **time**. It takes time for the internal changes to take effect, redirect and focus the energy that shapes your external reality. Because it is subtle and cumulative, the best way to measure this progress is to keep a journal. By writing a daily record of your thoughts and feelings, which in and of itself is valuable (see **Journaling**), you can go back weeks or months later and identify those subtle changes in your perceptions and feelings and see how the process is affecting specific issues you are dealing with. This is a powerful tool because it affirms your progress and gives you tangible evidence that is self-reinforcing.

It's easy to forget what you had for dinner last night, so it's not unusual to not notice subtle shifts in your thinking and feelings over weeks or months. I used to offer the following explanation to my friends and clients who were "Supercharging" and would ask me about this. Here is what I would say: "I can't tell you how different I feel between today and yesterday, but I can tell you how different I feel between today and six months ago. It's a lot like exercise. You go to the gym and workout and may feel a little improvement each day, but it's the cumulative effect after months of regular exercise that deliver the before and after results. This process is similar except that you are working on a psychological level, which is even harder to quantify."

I invited feedback from people who were "Supercharging" regularly and one of the most commonly reported benefits was the overall decrease in feelings of stress and anxiety. Irritants and stressors like standing in line at the bank or maneuvering through rush hour traffic that used to set them off, just didn't seem to matter much any more. They became calmer and more centered, and life in general seemed to be more blissful. Some noticed this change almost immediately, for others it took several months.

MASTER STRESS

Here are reprints from two letters I received from *Brain Supercharger* users that demonstrate this effect (more of these are included in Part III).

Letter #1

Dear Dane,
When my husband and I heard you on "The Radio Show" on CBC radio, we knew that it was something very special. We had used meditation and relaxation techniques in the past and both felt the enormous untapped potential which exists in the mind and soul. What you have offered is a most effective tool for reaching this potential.

Six weeks ago, we received your "Stress Management" tape; the changes in us have been joyously profound. While actually using the tape, I've experienced mental processes similar to dreams during which I've been able to face negative occurrences of the past (both recent and long buried ones, unsuccessfully buried in my subconscious mind) and simply examine them objectively and thus resolve them.

Just this ability alone has helped me eliminate so much unnecessary emotional baggage—it's been like untying several uncomfortable knots. I've been able to finally get in touch with the strong, serene person I'd always hoped was within me.

We are so happy with your product that we have ordered two more as gifts.
Thank you for developing the technology to make this wonderful experience available. I have two wishes—that everyone have the opportunity to use your tapes and that you achieve all the success you so very richly deserve.

Sincerely,
M. C.
P.S. My husband has told me that, while listening to the tape, I'm usually smiling. Thanks!

———————————

Letter #2

Dear Sirs:
Recently I purchased two kits from your company. They are the "Mastering Stress" and "Winning Self Image" tapes. I have listened to them faithfully every day for a little over a month, and the results as far as one of them is concerned, have exceeded my expectations. I am aware that I have to work at gaining the benefits I expect. The tapes are not magic and won't do it by themselves. However, I feel these tapes are worth more than their weight in gold! I cannot recall the last time I purchased something and knew that I had received more than my money's worth!!

The kit "Mastering Stress" has paid for itself many times over. I work at a job that creates tension in me and I feel the need to smoke whenever this occurs. After listening to "Mastering Stress" for as long as I have, it paid off in a way that I never imagined in my wildest dreams! I no longer feel the urge to smoke! I feel calm and relaxed, and I know my work has improved in that I complete it faster. My temper is much more improved and I do not tend to snap at someone when asked a question, as I was wont to do, several times when I was under a lot of tension. I know beyond a shadow of a doubt that I would have had to go to a non-smoking class, or be hypnotized, or something similar. But with the "Mastering Stress" tape helping me relax I do not feel the urgency to smoke to calm down, as I did before.

Another thing that occurs when I am tense is I have trouble sleeping. My job works from 11:45 PM to 7:45 AM and I really have trouble sleeping during the day, what with noisy neighbors, lawn mowers, saws, etc., but the thorns in my paw are children and dogs. I know there is nothing I can do to hush them up and I really do not want to because kids and dogs are naturally kids and dogs, but I do need to get my rest. With these tapes however, I can be very tired and still work without problems. I could not get more than 2 hours sleep before going to work tonight, and yet listening to "Mastering Stress" for an hour or two and dozing for an hour helped tremendously. I don't feel full of energy but I do feel refreshed and capable of doing my job with no problems. The best thing about this tape however is that when I get very little sleep I tend to get headaches, especially if tension is created. "Mastering Stress" gets rid of my headaches. I am sure there would be plenty of people who would say that my headaches and tension, etc., were psychosomatic. I am here to say they are wrong! My stomach feeling like a balloon blown up to bursting point and headaches so bad they cause tears to run down my face, (and that is definitely a first for me!!) are not psychosomatic! I am here to testify that these tapes are fantastic as far as I'm concerned. My stomach feels relaxed 99% of the time and when it doesn't I simply listen to my booster tape and the tension drains away. My headaches either totally disappear or they are so mild that no aspirin or tapes are needed.

But the greatest benefit of all as far as I'm concerned is my quitting smoking! I do not feel the urge to smoke when around someone who does, and best of all I do not feel the urge to berate someone who does smoke as so many reformed smokers I have encountered do!! I smoked since I was about 22 years old. I am now 37 and I have inhaled cigarette smoke all these years, so I feel quite a feeling of accomplishment and gratefulness to you for helping me quit this expensive habit.

Sincerely,
C. B.

THOUGHTS ARE THINGS

Perhaps the most important subtle effect of "Supercharging" is how it assists in ridding your mind of negative thinking, which is probably the most destructive force in your life. Imagine if you could remove all negative thinking from your being. Then, add willful purpose or intent toward a goal. It could be anything. Changing careers or starting a business. Finding a new relationship. Writing a screenplay. Even healing disease. When you can create an environment totally free of doubt and negative thinking and you have strong intent to accomplish a goal, the objective of which you can clearly see in your mind, the forces of the universe automatically align to this new energy and attract the circumstances that mirror that reality. It's a law of the universe.

However, if your vision is ambiguous, or there is self-doubt or internal conflict, this weakens the intention, and the result is weakened to a like degree.

As James Allen said in *As a Man Thinketh*; "A man's mind may be likened to a garden, which may be intelligently cultivated or allowed to run wild; but whether cultivated or neglected, it must, and will bring forth. If no useful seeds are put into it, then an abundance of useless weed-seeds will fall therein, and will continue to produce their kind. Just as a gardener cultivates his plot, keeping it free from weeds, and growing the flowers and fruits which he requires so may a man tend the garden of his mind, weeding out all the wrong, useless and impure thoughts, and cultivating toward perfection the flowers and fruits of right, useful and pure thoughts. By pursuing this process, a man sooner or later discovers that he is the master gardener of his soul, the director of his life. He also reveals, within himself, the flaws of thought, and understands, with ever-increasing accuracy, how the thought-forces and mind elements operate in the shaping of character, circumstances, and destiny."

Thoughts are mental things that tend to become material things. Just as the vibration of a particular atom attracts it to another atom which is aligned to its vibrations, so do the vibrations of our thoughts exert an urge and attraction upon us, and others in harmony with our vibrations. In other words the energy of your thoughts has a magnetic quality that attracts circumstances in the external world, which are mirrored by what is going on in your internal world.

James Allen continues; "The soul attracts that which it secretly harbors; that which it loves, and also that which it fears; it reaches the height of its cherished aspirations; it falls to the level of its unchastened desires and circumstances are the means by which the soul receives it own. Every thought-seed sown or allowed to fall into the mind, and to take root there, produces its own, blossoming sooner or later into act, and bearing its own fruit of opportunity and circumstance. Good thoughts bear good fruit, bad thoughts bad fruit. The outer world of circumstances shapes itself to the inner world of thought, and both pleasant and unpleasant external conditions are factors which make for the ultimate good of the individual. As the reaper of his own harvest, man learns both of suffering and bliss."

The power of thought can influence reality. Impossible you say! How do you know? Intense negative thinking guarantees you can't make it happen. The idea that our thoughts can influence reality has been discussed and written about for centuries, and yet some still dismiss it as being simple-minded. But wait a minute. Assume you were capable of removing all negative thinking from your life. No fear, guilt, anxiety, hostility. None of it. Then replace it with pure intention. With a force of mind so potent in its single-minded intensity and non-ambiguous goal-seeking; it makes realization a certainty. If you could train your mind in such a way, you could achieve miracles. I really believe this. This should be one of your

Chapter 4

Mindscripting

▬▬▬

47

goals as you use the tools and technology presented here. The elimination of negative thinking, replaced with positive focused intention. Even if you're not able to be positive 100% of the time, think of the wonderful benefits while working toward this goal: And what could possibly be the downside? Think about it.

BREAKING OLD PATTERNS

You have a powerful new tool for creating positive change in your life. A technology for communicating with your unconscious, and rescripting old patterns of negative thinking and self-sabotaging beliefs. Just doing any of the "Supercharger" programs (including the *Super Intelligence* soundtrack packaged with this book) on a consistent basis will begin to transform your life. Add to that the power of your own intention and desire to make a conscious effort to eliminate negative thinking and you have an incredible force of mind.

As we've discussed, breaking old patterns of negative thinking and self-destructive behavior can be very difficult when you are only addressing the problem on a conscious level. With the *Brain Supercharger* technology, you are establishing new mindscripts, laying a foundation of positive emotions and new attitudes about "self" which is the energy your mind uses to transform behavior.

When you record a pattern of new experiences onto your unconscious (whether through actual experience or "mindscripting" techniques), the connections which are formed in your brain create a new layer of circuitry that direct behavior. This new "neuro" pattern becomes reactivated or replayed each time you encounter similar triggering thoughts and experiences. It's why "success breeds success."

Thoughts occur in less than a microsecond, too short to be consciously aware of but long enough to create emotions, thus giving life and energy to your actions and behavior. These feelings and actions then reinforce each other in a positive self-expectancy cycle. Because your brain now believes what you are telling it, you find yourself feeling differently about almost everything.

FEELING GOOD

The relationship between the world and how you feel is not caused by the actual events you are experiencing but by your interpretation of the events. It's our perceptions (the way we think) that determine our mood. According to eminent psychiatrist, Dr. David Burns in his book *Feeling Good: The New Mood Therapy*; "Your emotions result entirely from the way you look at things. It is an obvious neurological fact that before you can experience an event, you must process it with your mind and give it meaning. You must *understand* what is happening to you before you can *feel* it." He goes on to say that feelings are created by thoughts not actual events. As you experience events either positive, negative or neutral, your brain interprets your experiences and then creates thoughts that judge and categorize the event. It is these thoughts that generate your feelings.

This is an important idea, because it means that if we can manipulate our thoughts, we can manipulate our moods. "Feeling good" has nothing to do with your external reality. It is your internal dialogues and negative thinking that shifts your mood. And mood plays a powerful role in your actions and behaviors. It is the stimulant, or energy, behind it all. So another benefit of this technology is that it not only offers a powerful tool for accessing and programming the unconscious mind, but also it can act as a therapy for addressing mood problems and, ultimately, your experience of the world.

Chapter 4

Mindscripting

49

GLAD TO BE ALIVE

Back in 1989, I was shooting a *Brain Supercharger* TV infomercial and, as you may know, every good infomercial has its share of customer testimonials. For me, finding positive testimonials was easy. I just dipped into my "Supercharger" letter file and pulled out a dozen or so customers who lived within a 50 mile radius of our office. I picked up the phone and called. They were all eager to participate and, without any compensation, they provided glowing testimonials for our 30 minute TV show and all were very generous and loving.

A lot of them talked about their careers, their self-confidence boost, and how success was so much more attainable since they started "Supercharging." One of these customers, however, was different. Her name is Helen. I especially remember Helen, even though her testimonial was not the hard-edged sound clip you want to use in a TV commercial. She didn't talk about success, career or money. For her, it was the way the *Brain Supercharger* made her feel. With a glow and smile that accented her external and inner beauty she exclaimed, "I'm just glad to be alive."

"Just glad to be alive." I knew exactly what she meant because I felt the same way. At the time I was "Supercharging" quite a bit, and it made me feel like I was on fire with aliveness. It was all I could do to contain my excitement and bliss wanting to share these feelings with everyone. The reason I'm telling you this is because even though I can talk about the practical aspects of mindscripting, of being able to change unwanted behavior, rescript bad habits, or transform a loser mind-set; there is a more profound and less reported side benefit to all this. Plugging into the soundtrack makes you feel good! Perhaps it's a change in brain chemistry. A shift in endorphin or serotonin levels. Maybe it's just the reprogramming of negative thinking which allows you to see the world differently. Whatever it is, it doesn't really matter. It's about **experiencing** it, not analyzing it.

You want to feel good? To be in a blissful state of existence, "just glad to be alive?" Then become a fellow "Mind Warrior" and "Supercharge" your brain on a regular basis. After all feeling good and experiencing aliveness is the point of living. It is what **everyone** is seeking.

Chapter 5:
"Plugging-In" to Super Intelligence

"Man alone is the architect of his destiny.
The greatest revolution in our generation is that
human beings, by changing the inner attitudes of
their minds, can change the outer aspects of their lives."
— 1902, William James,
American Psychologist

It's called *Super Intelligence*, the first experimental soundtrack on the CD enclosed with this book. Incorporating the *Brain Supercharger* technology, it includes mindscripting affirmations specific to creativity, intuition, learning, and intelligence. Through regular use of this tool, it will be possible for you to evoke an Alpha-Theta mind state and hold your brain there long enough to experience deep relaxation. When you do this, it's possible to enjoy the benefits of whole brain synchrony. A state of consciousness achieved when the EEG patterns of both hemispheres are simultaneously equal in amplitude and frequency.

To what purpose? What is the ultimate goal of this? The objective is transcendence—the transformation of your being. This is an entirely new level of experience, that is beyond your thinking or intellect. You could call it a state of super consciousness or super intelligence—the evolution of man into superman. That is the purpose. The training of the human mind to evolve consciousness to a godlike quality of enlightened awareness.

This does not mean you are going to have a mystical experience the first time you plug into *Super Intelligence*. What it *does* mean is that you have a powerful transformational tool with which to experiment. It's an opportunity to experience the technology first hand and explore altered mind states associated with deep meditation and higher consciousness. I think you'll be impressed by the possibilities it will open up for you.

ZAP STRESS, BOOST BRAINPOWER, & EXPAND CONSCIOUSNESS

For you, the first time you listen may result in a pleasant, relaxing experience. Or it could be something much more. It depends on a number of factors including your level of personal development. As you use this tool frequently, you should notice a cumulative effect that is subtle but profound. A primary benefit most everyone experiences (from only a short period of regular use) is a decline in stress level. Stress prevents you from functioning at your optimum so any reduction of stress can allow you to approach your daily life with less effort and greater joy in everything you do.

For many people, there is a deeper experience I have been alluding to, which may occur after only a few weeks or months of regular use. It might happen all at once in sudden flash, or develop over time through a series of minor sparks of insight. This is a peak experience or moment of enlightened awareness I was talking about earlier. Accessing a higher state of consciousness and releasing your genius potential, which is what this program is all about. And it's why the soundtrack on your CD is titled *Super Intelligence*. It's not the kind of intelligence you measure on IQ tests. No. It's more of a cosmic intelligence or "super" consciousness. Accessing a potential that is possible only through direct experience.

What is it? Lets take a few minutes and try and put into words something that transcends words. Enlightenment simply means that one is privileged to see and hear what's been there all along but which others fail to perceive. It's like being able to suddenly see in the dark. The experience is not reserved for the deeply spiritual or the genius mind. It can happen to anyone willing to explore their inner potential. In this state your mind begins disappearing into the experience. You sense an overwhelming blissful sense of oneness and connectedness to all things. People describe it as feeling more "centered" and having a greater sense of "aliveness" and "focus" as they engage in their daily activities. This is the ecstasy of awareness.

As your consciousness evolves into this new awareness you'll see everything in your life as distinctly as before but with a new mind that perceives the universe in a completely different way. As I've said and many others before me have as well, it is impossible to describe, and can really only be experienced to be understood. And when experienced—even for a moment—it's so profound it can instantly transform you forever. That is the true intent and purpose of the *Brain Supercharger* technology. To help you experience those states of consciousness, and return to life renewed, enlivened with a greater sense of meaning and purpose.

EVERY AGE HAS ITS ENLIGHTENED CULTURE

Many of history's creative geniuses have had enlightened experiences. Their sudden transformation of consciousness was the seed for many breakthrough inventions and literary ideas that left a permanent mark on the world.

These include authors, inventors and creative thinkers such as Emerson, D.H. Lawrence, Kipling and more. Wordsworth spoke of his trance-like states that he entered to stimulate his creative thinking. Mozart walked alone at night to hear the whole of his composition revealed to him in a flash of a dream. Poinecarrie, too, used the semi-hypnotic state of the morning or evening to stimulate visions of mathematical breakthroughs.

Einstein took naps during his working day to develop new theories. Wagner would force himself to stay awake late into the night until his mind was in the semi-hypnotic trance to come up with new musical themes. Bore, the physicist, dreamed of a planetary system as the model for the atomic structure which led eventually to a Nobel prize, while he was in the state of hypnotic trance. The laboratory procedure for the development of insulin came from a dream state, as did thousands of other famous inventions and discoveries.

But these breakthrough experiences are not limited to geniuses or visionaries or artists or inventors. With this technology, you can slip your mind into its most receptive state for stimulating these peak experiences. Simply listening to *Super Intelligence* on a regular basis induces that special mental mode which is optimum for liberating the higher wisdom and intuition of the creative genius within us all.

BECOMING ONE WITH THE SOUND

As you listen, the frequency matrix in the recording takes you from a conscious "Beta" state into a deeper more relaxed "Alpha-

Theta" state until you mentally disappear into the sound. The objective you are working toward is that the observing mind (your ego) and the sounds that you're contemplating actually fuse into one. The powerful audio matrix forces the mind to follow the soundwaves and your brain becomes so deeply absorbed by the "beat" that you become oblivious to your surroundings. Driven inward, the brain is fed with a powerful flow of psychic energy that provides that flash of illumination and intense awareness.

As the experience unfolds, you are forced to go through various stages of deeper relaxation and altered consciousness, quite unlike sleep or your normal waking state. You feel the pleasant bodily sensations of floating and experience vivid awareness of your breathing and your heartbeat. Lucid mental images increase and there is sometimes an alteration between internal and external awareness. As you go deeper, you may feel a detached calmness which becomes extremely satisfying. You may feel intuitive insights and see old concepts in new ways, especially in the relationship of opposites.

Entering these mind states on a frequent basis has been known to provoke a shift into a higher level of consciousness. This is often not without some emotional disturbance preceding the shift. Early on in the development of the *Brain Supercharger* technology, I discovered one of the side effects was a tendency for the listener to experience cathartic events prior to a shift in awareness. Just as is the case with certain meditation practices, the process can surface repressed emotions, unresolved feelings of anger, fear, guilt, or grief. This is not only common, but an important part of the personal growth process. To reach a higher level of consciousness requires breaking old patterns and unresolved feelings that are blocking your path. It's like disturbing the muddy bottom of a pond. It may look clear on the surface until you stir up the muck underneath. Just surfacing these emotional blocks and negative feelings is often all that is required to breakthrough to the next level of awareness. A powerful way to address the cathartic process is through journaling which is addressed in greater detail in Part II (see **Journaling**).

The point is this is a powerful mind tool, with profound personal growth potential. You are literally shaking up the organization of your brain. Touching trillions of neurons and dendric connections to reprogram existing connections in novel interactions. Old patterns and ways of thinking are being provoked into a newly coalesced whole. To evolve your mind/brain into a higher order. Like turning a kaleidoscope, the shift can be sudden and a whole new picture emerges. You're reinventing the organization of your mind.

TRANSFORMATION: UNLEASHING A NEW VISION

At some point everyone has had a flash of insight, fallen in love, suddenly understood the punch line of a joke, or all at once learned how to drive a stick shift on a car. What scientists believe precedes this jump in perception is a transition in your brain where, all at once, a new pattern of connections emerge between the neurons to fire new thoughts of energy through your mind. This felt shift is the appearance of new knowing.

But what's it like to experience a transformation of consciousness so profound a paradigm shift occurs that reveals a totally new vision of reality? As Fyodor Dostoevski says of it reported by Marilyn Ferguson in *The Aquarian Conspiracy*; "I have seen the truth. It is not as though I had invented it with my mind. I have *seen it*, seen it, and the living image of it has filled my soul forever...In one day, one hour, everything could be arranged at once! *The chief thing is to love!*"

The transformation has historically been described as an *awakening*, an awareness of personal reality that is all encompassing. "To see the universe in a grain of sand." To free the mind from its attachments to cultural patterns and conditionings. Once the "social trance" is broken you come alive, born again into a new skin that perceives the universe in an entirely new way.

As one man in his forties put it, "I've spent my life in a cage, chasing a buck, raising a family, doing things I thought were important but struggling to find happiness...pursuing goals society judged as important. I woke up one morning and realized it was all bullshit. Now I'm outside the cage and it feels wonderful."

Once freed from the self-imposed "cage," life becomes more fluid and exciting. Uncertainty is welcome because there is no fear or anxiety about the future. You allow it to happen in the firm belief that the universe will support you, and the future will unfold in an appropriate way. The letting go of your attachments and addictions shakes up and restructures the core elements that make up your life. Your focus shifts from outcomes to processes. The journey **is** the

Chapter 5

"Plugging-In" to Super Intelligence

55

destination. Each day is a voyage of new learning and fulfilling experiences. It's about seeking self-knowledge—not gain.

And with this new vision you return your spirit to a kind of childhood innocence, where all your senses are sharpened and open to the experience of just *being*. The world seems new again, and the sheer thrill and joy of just *being* fills you up, like the ecstasy you experienced as child playing in the sandbox, or going on your first merry-go-round ride.

Part I

*Unleash Your
Hidden Power*

━━━━

56

Along with your new vision comes a greater authenticity about your life, that is immediately sensed and irresistibly attractive to others. The facades and false masks are removed. You are able to express yourself in an open way without fear of what someone might think. Your soul rises and reveals itself. And since this is who you really are (the genuine source of your being), you never have to explain yourself. It takes a lot less effort to live this way. Once you commit your life to this genuine quality a kind of mystical force aligns itself to your energy. As Buckminster Fuller[3] was quoted, "The minute you begin to do what you want to do, it's really a different kind of life."

As Ouspensky said, "Man is asleep; for compared to what we are capable of, our normal waking state is more like sleepwalking." When awakened you become aware of your potential and can see that potential in everyone and everything. For me, this was the seed of my personal breakthrough and became the focal point around which I chose to organize my life. What I wanted to do was develop the technology and tools to access this potential and awaken others to the "experience." This path not only felt right for me, but things fell into place as if it were meant to be.

When you are in alignment with your true purpose, unseen hands seem to surround and guide you. Life really does take on a mystical quality. Strange coincidences occur with regularity. Events and people appear in your life just when you need them. Carl Jung calls this phenomenon Synchronicity (see **Synchronicity**). He defined it as "the simultaneous occurrence of two meaningful but not

---

[3] Buckminster Fuller was the Earth's "friendly genius." Best known as the inventor of the Geodesic Dome he consciously chose to make his life a working experiment focusing on the creation of artifacts that supported man and nature.

casually connected events." It's because your mental state is now in perfect alignment with your activities that you are connecting with a higher energy force. It's like owning a TV set but not being able to turn it on. If it's not plugged-in, you can't receive the broadcast.

When your mind is "plugged-in" to the energy grid of the universe and "tuned" into the right frequency you are opening a channel. An entirely new level of possibilities open up to you. As William James describes it; "Mystical states seem to those who experience them to be states of knowledge. They are insights into the depths of truth unplumbed by the discursive intellect." It becomes the source of deeper meaning for one's life. Edgar Mitchell, the astronaut who founded The Institute of Noetic Sciences to study states of consciousness said; "I feel almost as if I'm operating under orders...Just when I think all is lost, I put my foot down over an abyss—and something comes up to hit it, just in time."

Frankly, with words I am barely able to touch on describing the transformational experience or what it means. Language fails. It is a dimension that transcends intellectual thought. We just don't have the lexicon to describe what must be felt directly. It must be **experienced** to be understood.

"To a frog with its simple eye, the world is a dim array of greys and blacks," notes Michael Murphy in *The Future of the Body*, "Are we like frogs in our limited sensorium, apprehending just part of the universe we inhabit? Are we as a species now awakening to the reality of multidimensional worlds in which matter undergoes subtle reorganizations in some sort of hyperspace? Is visionary experience analogous to the first breathings of early amphibians? Are we ourselves coming ashore to a 'larger earth'?"

As you experiment with altered states of consciousness, the success of your personal growth will depend on how well you learn to **let go**. This may be the most difficult thing for you. Not to chase it, but allow the experience to chase you. To just be, and flow into it. When it happens, you'll recognize it, so there is no need to take a position or hold onto anything. As you become the experience, even the experience itself disappears, and all your problems with it.

But will it happen to you? Carlos Casteneda in *Journey To Ixtlan* writes; "All of us, whether or not we are warriors, have a cubic centimeter of chance that pops out in front of our eyes from time to

Chapter 5

"Plugging-In" to Super Intelligence

━━━

57

time. The difference between an average man and a warrior is awareness of this, and one of the tasks is to be alert, deliberately waiting, so that when the cubic centimeter pops out he has the necessary speed, the prowess, to pick it up."

Maybe this is your cubic centimeter of chance.

YOUR DAILY 28 MINUTE VACATION

Unlike meditation practices and biofeedback equipment, the *Super Intelligence* soundtrack is easy to use as a mind tool to enter into and experiment with these altered states. Because it meditates you, there is no need for any special training. You simply find a place and a time when you can be alone and undisturbed for at least thirty minutes every day. People with busy schedules find that the morning or late evening is best. However, if you do choose late evening, recognize that it may interfere with your normal sleep cycle. Several users have reported a need for less sleep. Therefore know that it may keep you awake for several hours if you use it before bedtime.

You'll also need a quality CD player with stereo headphones. After putting on your headphones, lay your body down flat so that your spine is completely straight. Adjust the volume control so that it is at a pleasant listening level. Cue up the *Super Intelligence* track and push play. Close your eyes and let the soundtrack meditate you. Don't think about anything or try to judge the session—this will only create endless internal dialogs to separate you from the experience. Just let it happen. Continue to relax and not focus your thoughts on anything in particular. By letting go of any expectations you'll eventually disappear into the sounds. All of your thoughts and feelings then become a part of the meditation as you move through them.

If memories or unpleasant thoughts do surface, just let them pass; don't hold onto any thought in particular or even think about what it is that you're doing. Let it unfold and flow, as you become the experience. Some people may find that these sessions become boring. They feel as if nothing is happening and they become disenchanted with the investment in the time they are spending with this. Know that this is the way in which the old you is holding on and preventing you from experiencing transformation. Suspend any judgments about what you are doing for at least 30 days. Be open to whatever experiences unfold in your sessions. Don't become fixated on a particular point of view of how to evaluate your experience. The less you expect and the less you judge, the further you can progress.

For many this "letting go" can be very difficult, especially left brain dominant types who tend to be more analytical. If this is your tendency, give yourself permission to let go completely with this project. See what happens. Embrace the experience without thinking about it or judging it. Just do it. What you're seeking is a transformation of your being far beyond that which any specific experience can give you. Perhaps the best point of view is one held by the Zen Monk, "Expect nothing, but be ready for everything."

As you begin "Supercharging," you may have some questions about your experiences. In Part III I've included a Q & A section that may be of some assistance. In addition there are reprints of letters I received from users of this technology which may give you some additional insights and understanding about what it all means.

In the next chapter I'm going to shift the focus away from the *Brain Supercharger* technology to a discussion of music and the mind and introduce you to the concepts behind the second soundtrack tool on your CD called *Mozart Brain Boost*.

Chapter 5

"Plugging-In" to Super Intelligence

59

Chapter 6:
The Powers of Music and the Mind

"Music is well said to be the speech of angels;
in fact, nothing among the utterances allowed
to man is felt to be so divine. It brings us
near to the infinite."
— Thomas Carlyle

The other day while I was driving in heavy traffic, a song came over the radio that instantly took me back to another time and place. It was a love song that my high school sweetheart and I would dance to. The moment I heard that song, strong emotions welled up inside of me and I remembered, with amazing clarity, a wonderful experience that happened many years ago. After a few minutes of this blissful reverie, I realized that the stress and aggravation I had been feeling for the last forty-five minutes were gone. Only the sweet feelings I felt long ago remained.

Almost everyone has had a similar experience: you hear a piece of music and instantly a vivid memory is recalled. So vivid in fact that sometimes you can even remember the temperature of the day, the smell of fresh cut grass, or even the feel of a mountain stream rushing over your feet. So what's going on? How can music have such a profound affect on us, and even more importantly, what potential does the "power of music" hold for enhancing the quality of our lives?

In this chapter, we'll seek answers to these questions by: examining the "music healing rituals" of ancient cultures; learn how today, scientists are validating the use of music in medicine; and discover why music is being accepted more and more as a key factor in accelerating the learning process and even increasing IQ.

THE POWER OF MUSIC TO HEAL

Today's science is simply confirming what the ancients knew long ago. From the medicine men of the Native Americans to the mystics of India and shamans of the Amazon rainforests, music has been used for thousands of years to promote healing.

Ancient healers used musical sounds through prayer and exorcism to enlist the divine help of great spirits to heal and protect. In Navajo cultures in the American Southwest, healing rituals known as "singings" are still performed today.

USING MUSIC TO HEAL AND COMMUNE WITH THE GODS

During the Navajo "singing" ceremonies, a medicine man supervises members of the tribe as they create a religious sand painting of a spiritual deity. The "patient" then sits in the middle of the sand painting as the medicine man pours sand over the sufferer while both chanting and music are performed to invite the spirits to cleanse and heal the patient. The Navajo believe that this ritual creates a channel through which the mortal human can commune with the divine gods. It is their medium to higher consciousness.

The world's first physician, Aesclepius of ancient Greece, used music to heal the citizens of their advanced civilization. Early cultures in the far East also promoted healing using melodic sounds in specific musical patterns.

In America, Edwin Atlee began experimenting with the healing properties of music as early as 1804. His report, *An Inaugural Essay on the Influence of Music in the Cure of Disease*, supported the theory that music "has a powerful influence upon the mind, and consequently on the body." Yet it wasn't until the 1870's that this theory was put to use in an innovative way. During those years, the New York Musicians Guild, along with the Ninth Regiment Band and a well-known pianist of the time, John Nelson Pattison, performed a therapeutic series of concerts at Blackwell's Island, New York's facility for the insane.

In 1890, Utica State hospital then took the lead by holding live musical performances for their patients. However, it took another nine years before any controlled studies were done to authenticate the therapeutic effects of music. Conducted by neurologist James

Corning, his report *The Use of Musical Vibrations Before and During Sleep* stated that participants listening to the music of Wagner and other Romantic composers showed a decline in morbid thoughts.

The American Medical Association first began treating music as therapy in 1914 when it published in its professional journal a report by Dr. Evan O'Neill Kane who used a phonograph for "calming and distracting" patients during surgery. The idea of using music as therapy gained more ground in the years following World War II, when it was used as a treatment to lessen the fatigue that continued to hamper the soldiers long after they had returned to their homes and families.

During the ensuing 50 years, music therapy became more widely accepted as western scientific study began validating the healing effects of music—effects which had been experienced by people from all cultures around the world for hundreds of years. The focus on music therapy was no longer a question of whether or not it worked, but rather how did it work? That answer is still being pursued today.

MUSIC PREVENTS DISEASE

Recent studies in immunology have shed some light on the healing properties of music. One such study conducted at Michigan State University in 1993, focused on the effect music had on the chemical components of the blood. Here's how it worked:

There were two groups of participants. During a 15 minute period one group rested while they read magazines. The second group rested while they listened to music of their choice—Ravel, Mozart, light jazz or New Age.

While there was no change in the blood composition of the group reading magazines, those listening to music showed an increase in the level of proteins called interleukin-1. These are the proteins associated with blood and platelet production, lymphocyte stimulation, and the action of protecting the cells against AIDS, cancer and a whole host of diseases. All of these processes require large amounts of oxygen. And as this controlled test proved, the increase in oxygen was a result of listening to the music.

While the ability to deliver oxygen into the bloodstream is one possible explanation for the healing properties of music, there is still much more to be learned. One way to begin to unravel this great mystery is to understand how music enters the body via the brain.

HOW MUSIC ENTERS THE BRAIN

How does music enter the brain? The fact is that no one really knows for sure. However, current neurological research suggests that a combination of three processes interprets the music as it passes into the brain.

From the book *Healing Imagery and Music*, author Carol A. Bush summarizes these processes as follows:

1. **Music moves from the ear to the center of the brain and the limbic system, which governs the emotional responses of pain and pleasure as well as such involuntary processes as body temperature and blood pressure.**

2. **Music can excite peptides, agents in the brain that release endorphins which produce a "natural high" and also serve as a natural deterrent to the experience of pain.**

3. **Music may activate a flow of stored memory across the corpus collosum. As a result, the recall of associational memories is greatly enhanced by music.**

While the first two processes appear to support the theory that music contains intrinsic healing properties, the third process addresses the theory that "music is a key factor in accelerating the learning process."

THE POWER OF MUSIC TO ENHANCE LEARNING

Around the same time that the Greek physician Aesclepius was using music for healing, one of his contemporaries, Pythagoras, was using music on his students to eliminate blocks to learning—fear, worry and anger. He found that by playing the music during his geometry lessons (out of which came the discovery of the well-known Pythagorean theory), his students simply absorbed the material more easily and with better retention. This was in the circa 530 BC. It was the birth of using music to enhance and accelerate the learning process. Incredibly, it would be another 2400 years before this discovery would be brought to the world's attention. But instead of making news in the classroom, it debuted in a study on the effects of music on growing plants.

PLANTS GROW FASTER WITH MUSIC

In the 1960s, Dorothy Retallack, a graduate student at Temple Beull College in Denver, wanted to know how music would affect growing plants. She built five small identical greenhouses. All were the same size and received the same lighting, water and soil. In each she planted corn, squash, marigold, zinnias and petunias.

For several months she piped in a different type of music to each greenhouse: Bach, Indian classical music, loud rock, and country-western. The fifth greenhouse received no music at all. The plants that thrived the most were the ones which received either Bach or Indian music, in fact—the vines even grew to reach out in the direction the music was coming from. While the plants exposed to rock and roll fared the worst, the country-western music had no effect at all.

These findings created quite a stir among the scientific and educational communities. However, because the "participants" in this study were merely plants, the bigger question was: would music have a positive effect on people?

MUSIC ACCELERATES LEARNING

Around the same time that Dorothy Retallack was experimenting with her plants in the United States, a Bulgarian scientist was using music to teach foreign languages at an accelerated rate. Dr. Georgi Lozanov (as reported in his book *Suggestology*), discovered that when music was integrated with the teaching of foreign words, students were able to increase their ability to learn by as much as 300 percent. Students who learned no more than 30 words during a study session without music, were able to increase their vocabulary to 100 words in a single session with music.

This amazing discovery was kept secret for many years by the Bulgarian government because of its potential use as a training technology, and Dr. Lozanov wasn't able to share his work until he left the country in the 1970's. Since then, the technology of Accelerated Learning has gained world-wide recognition and is being used more and more in classrooms and self-learning environments. Can certain forms of music actually make people smarter?

MOZART MAKES YOU SMARTER

Without question, Mozart was a musical genius. By the age of five, he was composing minuets and other pieces which, even in his early years, showed an amazing grasp of the musical form. Although he died at the age of 35 (as his friends and family gathered around him singing selections from his unfinished Requiem) he had already composed vast collections of operas, litanies, and cantatas as well as orchestral works plus chamber music and keyboard music.

The sheer beauty, perfection and profundity of his music has astonished and delighted people throughout the past 200 years. And now, it appears, it has the power to make us smarter as well.

In the early 1990s a research team at the University of California in Irvine tested the effects of Mozart music on college students and children. After listening to ten minutes of Mozart's Sonata for Two Pianos in D Major, scores for the 36 students were eight to nine points higher on the spatial part of the Stanford-Binet intelligence test.

In a follow-up study, 16 abstract figures (resembling origami shapes) were projected on an overhead screen for one minute each to three different groups of students. The exercise tested the ability of students to predict the unfolded shape. Each group had a different sound environment—either a Mozart sonata, mixed sounds (music by Philip Glass, a dance piece, plus an audio-taped story) or silence. Over the five-day testing period the group listening to the Mozart music experienced the highest increase in scores—62% compared to the 14% for the silent environment and 11% for the mixed sounds.

As an explanation for the superior tests results for those listening to Mozart, the researchers concluded that the music of Mozart helped to organize the firing patterns of neurons in the cerebral cortex, especially strengthening creative right brain processes associated with spatial-temporal reasoning. In other words, listening to Mozart's music exercises your brain. It improves your ability to concentrate and opens up your channels to intuitive leaps of the imagination.

ANOTHER DIMENSION OF TIME AND SPACE

The Irvine research with the origami shapes showed that the music of Mozart improved the brain's ability to conceptualize space. It also affects the way we perceive space around us. Here's how:

The space in between the notes of music played at a slow pace is greater than the space between the notes of fast music. It has been shown that playing slow music in a hectic environment (rush hour traffic, busy offices, airports and hospitals) promotes a more open, and spacious feeling. Slow music also seems to make the passage of time slow down and promotes a relaxed atmosphere.

Muzak, a multi-million dollar corporation, creates music programs for specific environments to achieve behavioral results: worker productivity in offices, consumer spending in stores, stress reduction in a doctor's office, etc.

Just as music played during exercise classes improves the stamina of the participants, music played during academic classes helps the brain focus for longer periods of time and retain information more efficiently.

So what is it about Mozart's music that can create these results? Is it the tempo or rhythm? What about structure, melody, harmony, and instrumentation? Or is it a combination of all of the above? And what about the music Lozanov used to accelerate the learning process? Are there characteristics common to both Mozart and Lozanov's Accelerated Learning music? If so, what are those characteristics and how can we identify them?

First, we need to understand some simple basics of music.

MUSIC THEORY 101

It is not important that you learn the complexities of music theory. However, knowing the basics of music will help you understand and identify certain kinds of music that can have a profound impact on your health, mental functioning, and ultimate happiness.

All music contains four primary ingredients:

1. **tempo**–measures the amount of time (rate) it takes to play a rhythm pattern.
2. **rhythm**–a pattern represented by beats that are played at a specified rate.
3. **melody**–a series of pitches, represented by musical notes, that are played one after the other, at a rate specified by the tempo.
4. **harmony**–groups of pitches (notes) played simultaneously that enhance the melody.

Each ingredient can be expressed in a myriad of unique ways, and can be appreciated on its own. However, it is when they are combined in certain ways with all the ingredients interacting to express passion and joy that the magical effects occur.

LOZANOV'S ACCELERATED LEARNING MUSIC

Lozanov discovered that music caused his students to absorb and retain information quickly and easily—a process he called "accelerated learning." The characteristics of this Accelerated Music are found in many pieces of music written in the baroque, classical, and romantic periods.

The tempo of this music falls in a range between 40 and 60 beats per minute, with a simple rhythm pattern of approximately one beat per second. Often called a largo rhythm, this tempo/rhythm combination is similar to the beating of the human heart. The healthy heart at rest beats between 60 and 80 beats per minute. However, the heartbeat of people listening to a largo rhythm will actually slow down to follow the music. This "following response" literally means being in sync with the music.

As your body relaxes to the rhythm of the music, your mind becomes alert in a simple form of relaxation—without telling a muscle to relax, without concentrating on a meditation mantra, without focusing on your breathing. As the music plays, your mind simply opens up as with meditation.

What's going on here is a kind of "sonic massage" that eliminates the stress of hard mental work. The music helps redirect the focus of attention inward instead of outward to produce a reverie state. And in this state, Lozanov discovered his students were more relaxed, and amazingly, actually able to learn more in less time.

Another characteristic of Lozanov's Accelerated Learning music is the melody and harmony of the music is written in a "major" mode. Remember that melody is "a series of pitches that are played one after the other," and harmony is "groups of pitches played simultaneously that enhance the melody." A piece of music written in a "major" mode means that the pitches, represented by musical notes, relate to one another in a way that causes the music to sound a certain way. In a major mode, the music sounds positive or happy, while a minor mode sounds serious, somber, or even sad.

Composers have found that the way in which you build melody and harmony affects the emotional tone of the music. Each note is a vibration. And the vibration acts upon our bodies and minds in either a happy or sad nature.

In her book *Sound as a Tool for Transformation*, author Vicki Dodd writes, "Sound reaches down to the cellular level. It is most likely that sound patterns are really the dance of molecules and atoms."

Again, we are drawn back to the overall effect that Lozanov sought to create with music, which was to unlock the abilities of his students by eliminating fear, worry and anger. This in turn, opened up a new space in the mind (previously occupied by negative feelings) into which learning could "pour in" without any obstructions.

Through the affective powers of music, a deeper dimension of awareness is achieved. It stimulates positive emotions and drives attention and focus inward. Like a rainbow of vibrational feelings, these emotions (previously neutered by fear and worry) build a bridge into higher awareness—with all the suddenness of a rainbow whose pure colors of light arch effortlessly into the heavens against the threatening darkness of a thundering summer sky.

USE THE POWER OF LISTENING TO BECOME MORE THAN YOU ARE

One of the reasons great singers, speakers, and actors have such an effect on their audiences is because people are listening so deeply to them. When we are focused on listening to that which moves us emotionally, breathing becomes deeper, muscles relax, and endorphins flow into the bloodstream to produce contentment and serenity.

Music enhances the experience. George Gershwin said, "Music sets up certain vibrations which unquestionably results in a physical reaction. Eventually the proper vibration for every person will be found and utilized."

Everything in our universe is in a state of vibration. Music is vibrating sounds. It affects the heartbeat, pulse rate, and blood pressure. By placing a cup of water next to a speaker, you can see the vibrations of the music move across the water. Considering that our bodies are over 90% water, it is not hard to imagine the effects of music on our delicate cells, tissues, and organs.

ALL MATTER VIBRATES

Musical notes and colors vibrate at specific cycles per second. A below middle C vibrates at 213 cycles per second, which is similar to the vibrational level of the color red-orange and the metal copper. B below C vibrates at 240 cycles per second, which relates to the color yellow and the mineral zinc. According to Chemistry expert, Dr. Donald Hatch Andres, in speaking to this commonness in vibration levels said, "we are finding that the universe is composed not of matter but of music."

When a note or chord is struck, it vibrates. This vibration forms patterns and creates energy fields of resonance and movement in the surrounding environment. These energies enter our bodies and alter our breath, pulse, blood pressure, muscle tension, and skin temperature. These energies also affect the rhythms of our brain.

THE SCIENCE OF CYMATICS

The ability of music to shape matter was first discovered by Ernst Chladni, a German acoustical physicist and amateur musician in the 1800's. By placing sand on a metal plate and then drawing a violin bow vertically along the edge of the plate, Chladni showed that the musical tone moved the particles into mandala shapes.

A hundred years later this discovery grew into a science called "cymatics", or the study of waves (from the Greek kyma, "wave"). Using twentieth century technology, Swiss scientist Hans Jenny recorded, through photographs and film, the effects of single tones and harmonies on matter such as moss powders, iron filings, and liquids.

His film, *Cymatics* clearly proves the power of sound to form shapes and "vibrational sculpture." While sustained sounds at low frequencies produce simple mandalas in the matter, louder sounds show eruptions in the matter with movements that are eerily similar to the formation of mountains and the breaking of waves along the shore. All of these shapes and forms created by sound are found in other natural and organic structures, including the cells and tissues of our bodies.

A modern composer, Murray Schafer, expands on this idea by writing in his book *Tuning the World*, "...music is the search for the harmonizing influence of sounds in the world around us. We must try once again, to find the secret of that harmony."

So it seems that listening to music can make you more than you are. Perhaps it has to do with its ability to organize and align the energy patterns emanating from you. As one composer put it; "just like an appliance, you can't compose music until you're charged with an electrical current." Music **is** an energy that charges our souls. It acts as a trigger mechanism to release our emotions and turn us "on" to the world.

So how can you benefit from this idea...to create and to learn? How is it possible to access the power of music to trigger your potential?

A GIFT FROM THE UNIVERSE: *MOZART BRAIN BOOST*

On your CD is a second experimental soundtrack. An accelerated learning tool called *Mozart Brain Boost*™. It uses a composition by Mozart that was validated in scientific research conducted in the University of California, Irvine study. I selected Mozart's Sonata for Two Pianos, not only because it was validated in scientific research conducted at UC Irvine, but because of its key musical characteristics for learning as identified by Lozanov's research: largo rhythm, melody and harmony in a major mode, and the use of stringed instruments (including the piano).

In addition we added several additional elements into the mix to enhance its effect. First, I didn't just license a piece of music and slap it onto a CD. To insure the intention of the performance I invited my composer friend, Rob Hopping to not only record the Mozart piece but to make it more effective. I've worked with Rob for more than 10 years now on similar mind development projects, and know of his reputation for musical perfection. He has significant experience in designing accelerated learning programs and creating soundtracks that affect the mind and body in positive ways. After analyzing the Mozart piece and breaking it down into its primary musical components, Rob enhanced the composition by adding violins, violas, and cellos. These stringed instruments are known to stimulate learning and memory and their addition to the Two Pianos Sonata is dramatic. He recorded all of the instruments using state-of-the-art digital technology adding into the mix a number of special effects, developed at our Mind Lab. These effects include an environmental bed and special mindscripting affirmations specific to learning and memory. The result is more than just a beautiful piece of music.

This soundtrack is designed to provide an optimum learning environment when played while learning new information. Use it to study, memorize facts and figures, stimulate creativity, and increase focus and concentration. In addition to the positive learning effects, I think you'll discover *Mozart Brain Boost* to be an outstanding listening experience. As the music plays, your heart will beat more slowly, your blood pressure should drop and your brain slow into an Alpha pattern as you relax and flow into a state of whole brain synchrony.

But can it improve learning? Perhaps the best validation is the test of personal experience. Create your own private Mind Lab at home. Play it while you read or study. See how it affects your thinking. As your mind and body flow in sync with the music you'll intuitively understand what the mystics and mathematicians have felt throughout the ages—that this music has an uncanny ability to involve us emotionally. When this happens, we feel expanded somehow and become more than we presently are. And it is through our emotions that we connect better with what we are learning.

A number of recent studies suggest that molecular and electro-physiological changes take place in the brain's neurons when you learn to associate a stimulus (such as the *Mozart Brain Boost* soundtrack) with a previously unrelated response (learning behavior).

In other words, there is literally a physical change in the makeup of your brain caused by the music and this, in turn, becomes linked with learning. It is believed this has to do with the way in which we hear pitch.

Pitch is not given to the mind directly, but rather is reconstructed by the brain. When a note is sounded (for example, middle C on a piano), a complex set of oscillations of air is transmitted to the ear. The auditory receptors in the inner ear break down musical sounds into their frequencies which are then forwarded separately into the auditory system.

The brain, then, reconstructs the perception of pitch from this frequency information. This can be demonstrated by a scientific experiment that deletes one or more frequencies. Yet, when this is done, the brain still perceives the missing frequency.

Music, then, is a learned pattern. Even in the absence of sound, it can reconstruct an entire sequence from memory. So much so that even recalling the *Mozart Brain Boost* soundtrack can trigger the

Chapter 6

The Powers of Music and the Mind

▰▰▰▰

73

memory of the learning material. This is a little known but important concept with profound implications. It means that the brain has somehow become mapped by the musical patterns with a particular activity, feeling or thoughts. The music triggers this mental map and forces the brain into action[4].

Science is still at a loss to explain the neurological basis for the accelerated learning effects of music which gives us all the more room to investigate on our own. You are now a part of that grand experiment.

Listen. Listen deeply. Flow into that musical space. Let your emotions respond as the music dares you to become more than you are by becoming one with the universe...if only for a moment in time. Just as your mind can use the power of music to recreate a forgotten memory from a senior prom in an instant, it can recreate this moment in time for an eternity. That is what super brain power is all about.

Part I

*Unleash Your
Hidden Power*

74

---

[4] This is a very potent idea with far reaching implications. Although still in the experimental phase I am working on several applications incorporating this technique.

Chapter 7:
The Way Of A Mind Warrior

"The greatest human quest is to
know what one must do in order
to become a human being."
— Immanuel Kant

As the new millennium unfolds, it presents incredible challenges and opportunities. Science will unlock the genetic code, and all disease will be curable. Computers will connect everyone everywhere providing instant access to everything. Free energy will be perfected. People will travel the world in minutes. We will colonize space—journey to Mars and other planets. These things are within our reach now.

Yet the mastery of genetics, atomics and space travel are only side trips when compared to the main human journey. Science and technology have become the gods of Western society—the external world and its physical rewards the primary focus of our attention. In the next millennium this will shift, and I predict so will the direction of the human adventure. The biggest and most important discoveries, will come not from the external world but from the journey within ourselves.

Advances in science and technology will be marvelous and far reaching but not as profound as the realizations that lie dormant, hidden within us all. My bold predictions for the new millennium are: mental telepathy, clairvoyance, psychic healing, remote viewing and other extra sensory perception (ESP) abilities will not only be accepted and commonplace, but taught and developed in schools. Devices will be invented that will amplify our psychic powers. We will use the frequencies of sound and light to heal our mind and body and manipulate matter. Brain research will advance to a completely new level and reveal far reaching secrets about the true nature of our minds. And my boldest of all predictions:

The "Mind Warriors" who pursue the development of their inner potential will evolve consciousness at an ever accelerated

rate; increasing their mind power and leading the human race to a new era of enlightened awareness. The third millennium will become the millennium of mind.

THE BEGINNING IS NEAR

Mind is the true undiscovered country. The evolution of the human brain was completed some fifty thousand years ago and although its physical architecture has remained virtually the same, its untapped potential lays dormant waiting to be awakened. Once we unlock its secrets the destiny of mankind will be forever changed. Let me take a moment and give you a glimpse of what I think that is and your important role in this.

The human brain is made up of three brains; a brain stem often called the reptilian brain which deals with involuntary responses. Surrounding this is the limbic system or mid-brain as it's sometimes called, involved with expression and emotional experience. The outer part is the neocortex used for thinking, which as humans developed, grew and expanded at an phenomenal rate unprecedented in evolutionary history.

The three brains within a brain are all linked and perform in a synergistic way. The current scientific view on how the brain functions is through hierarchically organized and interconnected neural networks. This is essentially the bio-computer model. Some scientists however, believe much more is going on than the mere storage and retrieval functions of a sophisticated computer. We now know that memory is distributed over the whole cortex in much the same way a hologram functions[5]. Brainwaves, as we've discussed, also play a significant role as they relate to states of consciousness, and especially altered states. The exploration of these states through meditation, biofeedback and other modalities seems to bring about an extraordinary acceleration in psychological information processing, as well psychic phenomena, and peak experiences. These brainwave states also seem to shift one's personal space-time experience. Why, and how?

---

[5] The holographic brain model states that memory is not stored in one place, but rather acts like a hologram where each part contains a complete record of the whole image produced by means of an interference pattern.

Mystics talk of the altered states experience as the "eternal moment," a sense of "timelessness." As D.T. Suzuki said in *Essence of Buddhism*; "In this spiritual world there are no time divisions as the past, present, and future; for they have contracted themselves into a single moment of the present where life quivers in its true sense...The past and future are both rolled up in this present moment of illumination, and this present moment is not something standing still with all its contents, for it ceaselessly moves on."

These kinds of statements by mystics are very difficult to understand for those who have not had such an experience. Let me present you with a theoretical model for what may be going on inside the brain, which I believe science is on the precipice of discovering, and will be the opening of a new era in mind development.

YOUR BRAIN IS REALLY A SPACE-TIME MACHINE

It is now well established that in certain altered states experiences (especially prolonged meditations), there is profound shift in brainwave rhythms associated with peak experiences—those moments of illumination where the experience plugs you into the "eternal moment" and connects you with the universe. What is not really understood is how this process works and what it means. Here is one hypothesis.

The brain and its internal substructures give off magnetic fields of energy. Although these energy fields are very subtle, it is possible with sophisticated equipment to detect and measure them. One of these instruments is called a SQUID. It is a helmet sensor device that maps the brain's energy, specifically tuned to detect magnetic fields in the ultra low frequency (ULF) range. Using a computer, these energy fields can be mapped and plotted on a graph. One scientist reported hooking himself up to a SQUID helmet sensor while in an altered states experience. Focusing this sensitive instrument on the mid-brain region (where the Thalamus-Pituitary-Pineal glands reside) the geometry of this magnetic field when plotted on a three dimensional graph had the same shape and appearance of an Einstein-Rosen space-time bridge.

What's an Einstein-Rosen space-time bridge? It's a wormhole. A funny sausage shaped structure that is able to tunnel its way through space-time. (A cosmic wormhole is a gravitational field that warps

Chapter 7

The Way of a Mind Warrior

77

time-space—connecting two parallel universes or distant parts of the same universe. It derived its name for the shortcut a worm takes by boring through an apple, rather than crawling across it.) I'll admit, a cosmic space-time bridge formed within our brains (even one that is only a few centimeters long), is a pretty far out idea. But if it turns out to be accurate it answers a lot of questions and provides a biophysical basis for mystical states, and psychic phenomena.

The human brain emits energy fields that resemble structures and processes found in the cosmos. If this model is a correct representation of what is going on inside our heads it could be speculated that such a system would also act in much the same way as a universe. In other words the brain isn't just a hierarchy of neural networks processing and storing sensory input. It may also function as a biological space-time energy transducer. A mini-universe within the universe. The implications are literally astronomical.

The ancient Chinese always believed this was the case; that "the Tao (the universe) was in our head." According to Fritjof Capra in *The Tao of Physics*, "The Eastern sages, too, talk about an extension of their experience of the world in higher states of consciousness, and they affirm that these states involve a radically different experience of space time. They emphasize not only that they go beyond ordinary three-dimensional space in meditation, but also—and even more forcefully—that the ordinary awareness of time is transcended. Instead of a linear succession of instants, they experience—so they say—an infinite, timeless, and yet dynamic present."

He goes on to state in the words of Louis de Brogile; "In space-time, everything which for each of us constitutes the past, the present, and the future is given en bloc...Each observer, as his time passes, discovers, so to speak, new slices of space-time which appear to him as successive aspects of the material world, though in reality the ensemble of events constituting space-time exist prior to his knowledge of them."

Meditation, according to the mystics, allows us to transcend the space-time experience and enter into a fourth dimension where space and time are integrated into a whole, where all events are interconnected. Space-time becomes unified in a four-dimensional continuum, where there is no "before" or "after," and so there can be no cause and effect relationships. It is only in our lower dimension of reality that we experience a temporal sequence of events, moving through time in a linear succession of cause and effect moments. Perhaps a mechanism in our mind-brain entraps us into this denser reality construct, in much the same way as physical forces in the universe operate to entrap and enclose space. Through meditation and altered states experiences we are somehow able to manipulate our consciousness and shift this energy field escaping the world of cause and effect.

THE ENLIGHTENED MIND

The secret of enlightened human beings, such as Jesus or Budda, was their ability to manipulate the energy of consciousness and co-exist in both realms. A mind that is less evolved has simply not learned *The Way* to use its consciousness to turn off the reality distortion field that surrounds them creating the three dimensional experience of time and space.

Chapter 7

The Way of a Mind Warrior

79

The idea that we live an "illusion" has been a central thesis of mystics and sages long before the so-called New Age movement picked up the banner. But illusion is a wrong term because it implies that your experiences aren't real. Life really is happening to you—it is not an illusion. However your experiences of cause and effect events are real only within this entrapped three dimensional reality construct. Perhaps a better way of understanding this idea is to see your reality not so much as an illusion, but rather a distortion. A space-time reality distortion.

As long as you remain within the energy grid of your space-time distortion you will experience time as you do now, and the succession of cause and effect events that define your reality. Learning how to transcend this reality construct is the objective. To evolve and co-exist in both dimensions as Jesus and Budda were able to do. The only way to do that is by manipulating the energy of your mind. Consciousness is the connecting bridge between these universes.

THE "FIFTH" FORCE

A major quest of science (physics in particular) has been to find a unified field theory. A force that connects the primary four forces of the universe (gravity, magnetism, weak nuclear force, and strong nuclear force). It is the Holy Grail of physics. To find the "fifth" force in the universe, the theory that connects all the other forces to explain how the universe operates. To understand precisely why the same particle can exist simultaneously in two different places at the same time. Or even stranger are the questions dealing with how the mind is able to influence the outcome of quantum events.

Einstein spent most of his later life unsuccessfully searching for the unified field theory. Physicists have many partial theories that take into account some of the strange ways the universe seems to operate, however they are still unable to discover the ultimate theory of the universe. Perhaps it's because the answer lies outside the boundaries of science. Beyond what mathematics can quantify. The "fifth" force may be consciousness itself. The universe is mind. And the mind is a universe.

As Marylin Ferguson explains it in *The Aquarian Conspiracy*, "In a nutshell, the holographic supertheory says that *our brains mathematically construct "hard" reality by interpreting frequencies from a dimension transcending time and space. The brain is a hologram, interpreting a holographic universe.* We are indeed participants in reality, observers who affect what we observe. In this framework, psychic phenomena are only by-products of the simultaneous-everywhere matrix. Individual brains are bits of the greater hologram. They have access under certain circumstances to all the information in the total cybernetic system. Synchronicity—the web of coincidence that seems to have some higher purpose or connectedness—also fits in with the holographic model. Such meaningful coincidences derive from the purposeful, patterned, organizing nature of the matrix."

WHY PRAYER & VISUALIZATION REALLY DO WORK

This model may explain why images visualized in prayer or through transcendental mind states can influence reality, and affect what we visualize. Perhaps the brain's space-time bridge opens a channel, where the vision transcends your distortion reality construct. The vibrational patterns of the image established in the mind interact within the matrix of energy patterns in the universe. This vision creates a kind of "interference pattern," that becomes aligned and converges within the universe's web of probability patterns. As science has come to learn, the mind interacts with matter at its most primary level, where in the quantum world inside atoms, matter exists only in terms of probabilities. In this quantum world, it seems consciousness really does play a role in creation and the way the universe gets experienced. The sixteenth century philosophers who believed the human mind was divine and contained all the secrets of heaven may have been very close to a universal truth.

How do you access and turn on or off the space-time machine inside your head? Certain altered states experiences such as the deep meditative trance states we've been talking about, reorganize the energy fields in your brain, opening your own personal wormhole into the universe as it were. Once you've opened this window you are now in contact with a new realm of possibilities. A boundless, timeless, ever changing universe of probabilities where the past, present and future do not exist. You are tapped into the infinite, the source of everything. Where all that has ever happened or will happen occupy the same space. William Blake, an English poet who experienced such visions as a child, went on to produce a body of work to describe it. He wrote:

> *To see the world in a grain of sand*
> *And a heaven in a wild flower*
> *Hold infinity in the palm of your hand*
> *And eternity in an hour.*

THE PATH OF A HUMAN BEING

During the early 80's while I was floating, meditating and experimenting with altered states experiences I was actively seeking answers to life's big questions. To me the ultimate question was, "What is the purpose of the universe?" It became my own private Koan (see **Zen**). To me, finding a suitable answer to this question was the key to it all. I would meditate for hours and days at a time on this question. There were moments when I felt I could almost grasp it, and then I would forget everything the next day. To me this was the big philosophical question. I believed that if I could know the answer that it would open a door of understanding and everything would fall into place. For several years while I was experimenting with psychotechnologies, floating, reading and doing seminars to improve my mind, this question was my focus.

"What is the purpose of the universe?" kept rolling over and over in my head. One summer evening in July I was out for a walk in the park, and came across a little league game in progress. It was a perfect evening, the sun was just setting, and the smell of freshly cut grass floated along a gentle breeze. The kid at bat had just connected with the pitch and hit a long pop fly out into middle field. He then began running the bases while his supporters cheered him on. As he rounded third base the pitcher scooped up the ball from an outfield pass and tossed it to the catcher who tagged him out as he slid into home. At that very moment I heard a voice inside my head say, "...**the purpose of the universe is to BE!**" It was a sudden flash of insight. This was it. The big answer I was searching for. But it wasn't what I expected. The vision that flowed into my mind seemed too simple to be right. It took me some time afterward to assimilate and understand its greater meaning.

Part I

*Unleash Your
Hidden Power*

▬▬▬

82

My metaphor for the way the universe operated became the baseball game I was watching. A field with agreed to dimensions and rules, and players who interact with each other. You have witnesses (parents) who cheer and coach the players. At the end of the game everyone leaves the field and they come back in the future to play it out all over again. Each game is totally unique with its own nuances and outcomes, although the process for playing it is the same. The game has no real purpose other than the joyful experience of playing it. In my vision I saw the universe playing out a similar scenario. The key players, matter and energy acting in this fluid and ever changing interplay of creation and destruction.

Consciousness is not only a spectator in the stands witnessing the game unfold, but is also a coach and referee, imposing rules, manipulating events, and influencing the outcome. Matter, energy, and consciousness all dynamically interwoven, interacting and influencing each other to create a matrix of existence, the purpose of which is to simply exist and play the game. Existence becomes its own purpose. The result of the experience of "being."

For me this idea was a flash point. The perfect solution. It was a high point in my life. I wanted an answer and it found me. A conceptual map to frame it all in. This was my beginning. Over the next six months I fleshed out my metaphor, and began keeping a journal, jotting down notes and fleeting thoughts so I would be certain not to lose it. Although they are personal, to make my next point I'll share some of my notes with you...

"... If I were God, the best universe I could imagine would be one in which existence is filled with infinite possibilities. I would design a matrix where everything that could exist, did exist—does exist, for the purpose of experiencing "being." This matrix would be an open system with a creative dynamic that combines energy and matter in an ever increasingly complex array of forms. Where all potentials exists at once. Where every permutation of existence could be played out. The point of this universe is to "experience" existence and creation in all its forms."

———————

"Matter is not solid. The structure of atoms are like miniature solar systems made up of mostly empty space. If an atom were the size of the Houston Astrodome, its nucleus would be smaller than a grain of sand. The electrons whirling around the edges of the dome would be the size of dust particles. <u>Matter is mostly empty space</u>. If I were God and wanted to "experience" existence and creation the place I would want to be is at the center of it all. The empty space that occupies matter—inside an atom, all atoms <u>everywhere</u>. What if God is the empty space that fills most of the universe?"

———————

"Life is everywhere on Earth. Every possible place it can exist it does. Why? A lichen grows in Antarctica in a place where it is impossible for life to be. It's 80 degrees below zero and so dry it hasn't rained for a thousand years. Yet it manages to cling to the underside of rocks drawing moisture and its life from the rocks. New species are discovered at the bottom of the ocean where no plant life should exist because there is no sunlight for photosynthesis. Yet tube like plants do exist miles down at the bottom of the ocean in total darkness surviving by sucking energy from subterranean volcanic vents. To ask the question does life exist elsewhere in the universe is little like asking the question; "Is there gambling in Las Vegas?"

———————

"There are an infinite number of permutations possible within infinite levels of existence. Planet Earth, is just one of the baseball games going on in space-time. As the game of the universe gets played out via the creation matrix, the game on Planet Earth evolves. Life gets added to the matrix. It is self organizing and adds many new combinations, layers, nuances and

Chapter 7

The Way of a Mind Warrior

83

flavors to existence. Existence is good. Life eventually becomes aware of itself. This is good. It adds to the consciousness stuff of the universe."

THE OMEGA POINT

The stuff of the universe has a creative tendency to organize itself and develop into greater and greater levels of complexity. Why? **To add to the consciousness stuff of the universe.** That's why.

According to Jesuit priest, scientist, and author, Pierre Teilhard de Chardin's[6] "law of complexity-consciousness" states that this complexity is accompanied by a corresponding rise in consciousness. Teilhard writes, "The living world is constituted by consciousness clothed in flesh and bone." His idea was this, as living organisms increase the diversity and complexity of their nervous connections—it gives birth to new consciousness.

Evolution is creative, driving toward greater complexity and consciousness. Teilhard describes it as a crystallization of energy: "A glow rippled outward from the first spark of conscious reflection. The point of ignition grows larger. The fire spreads in ever-widening circles...till the whole planet is covered with incandescence."

Teilhard's major thesis was that the mind goes through an evolutionary process of development until it reaches a level he called the "Omega Point"—**the discovery of its own evolution**. At this point the entire human species has the potential to become enlightened all at once. This occurs when the "collective soul" of humanity achieves a critical mass of awareness. Consciousness rises to an evolutionary point, when we all go "on-line" so to speak, and we self-evolve into a new enlightened species.

Which leads me to the point of all this, and why I told you my personal story. *Consciousness!* That is the prize. The reason for the universe to play the game. To **evolve** and **experience** itself. The resulting increase in consciousness is like a process of fusion. You end up with more than you started with. Consciousness is the food of God. The point of playing out the game of existence. To *"Be"* and

---

[6] Author of "The Phenomenon of Man," and many other works, Teilhard's books were once repressed, because they went against the teachings of the church.

experience *"Being"* becomes its own purpose. It is the milk of existence. To evolve into new forms and "experience" it. To create and destroy and "experience" it, and so on and so on, as the game of the universe continually expands and evolves. Matter and energy *AND* consciousness interconnected in the web of existence, for its own ultimate purpose—*"Being."*

This realization was the turning point in my life. That idea that just being "alive" was the point of it all. Existence is its own reward. That within our own eternal inner universe the "experiencing" of aliveness brings you closer to the source of your being which is the same as the *"Source"* in the universe. The experience of which, not only makes you more than you are—it makes the universe more of what it is. Wow, what a rush!

I spoke earlier of an important role you have in all this, which I'd like to address with you now. I'm sure you've heard of or read reports of near death experiences. People who clinically die yet are brought back to life. For them the experience is a transformation. When they return to life they are literally *born again*, and go about the business of living with a different perspective. They recognize the sacredness and importance of life, yet are totally unafraid of death and dying. They are more centered and energized about living. Relationships, love and the joy of real moments become their focus. They are more connected with the "experience" of being alive. Careers, money, and ego fulfillment activities become much less important. It's about "being" alive (see **Near Death Experience**). And that is the point.

It doesn't matter what you do for a living. What matters is that you **live**. That you add your drop of "existence" to the consciousness stuff of the universe. That is the underlying mission for all of Planet Earth and its occupants. And there is something more. As humans evolve into more complex, higher consciousness beings, we will awaken from our sleep. Teilhard's "Omega Point" will be reached when enough self-realized human brains go "on-line" and critical mass is achieved. Our "collective soul" achieving consciousness fusion, and unfolding our destiny—an enlightened race of beings. Who will lead the way?

Chapter 7

The Way of a Mind Warrior

85

A PARADIGM SHIFT FOR YOU

We are an oscillating field of energy, operating within larger fields of energy. Our brains respond well to the rhythm of sounds, pulsations of light, and the frequency of colors. By understanding how to manipulate the energy within our brains we can transcend to a higher level of consciousness, and ultimately evolve the consciousness of the entire planet.

On this higher plane, you are able to tap into new sources of knowledge that were previously beyond your reach and discover your true self, your authentic soul—your essence. This shift can happen suddenly, even though it may take time to work up to it. It all may seem new to you—yet strangely familiar with a knowing confidence that it was part of you all along.

This new knowing is a paradigm shift that gives you a new way of thinking about old problems and old situations. Or perhaps it will create a restless feeling that the comfortable, yet mundane lifestyle you're living, suddenly won't do anymore.

A paradigm reveals a framework of thought, or a reality, that was always present but never understood. A paradigm shift occurred when the flat world was discovered to be round, and when the sun (rather than the Earth) was discovered to be the central body in our solar system. These paradigm shifts illustrate a major tenet of their acceptance: one cannot embrace the new paradigm without letting go of the old. You don't figure it out step-by-step, rather it is suddenly seen all at once. This is a change that "finds you," occurring in both the mind and the heart.

More than 200 years ago, Sir Isaac Newton portrayed the universe and everything in it as operating on the same principles as a mechanical clock which could be broken down into its elements to understand the inner workings. Now science is showing this not to be true. In fact, the whole is greater than the sum of the parts. Even more surprising is that these wholes are related to an even larger whole through intricate relationships that are constantly in flux. It is these relationships that determine the structure (and your experience) of the universe.

PROCESS IS THE LANGUAGE OF THE UNIVERSE

Process is everything. Quantum physics is showing us that solid objects aren't really solid, they are patterns of energy. What was once labeled as a fear is no longer seen as a block in the mind but a process of habit that can be modified. Same too with a cancerous tumor—it is a process of a growing malignancy that can be stopped and reverted. We only need to learn how. Rather than seeing the object, the fear, or the tumor as fixed elements, each is recreating itself every moment and thus has the potential for being changed, reordered, transformed.

The nature of the mind is process. Like a dance of neurons branching out and connecting through dendrites, firing synapses like fireworks across an inner sky that ride on brainwaves rippling through the left and right brain. We are not here for survival. We are here for transcendence. When the brain's waves are synchronized into patterns and frequencies that model desired states of consciousness, you have the ability to provoke your brain into a higher order and evolve your consciousness.

Chapter 7

*The Way of a
Mind Warrior*

▬▬▬

PROCESSES TO PROVOKE YOUR BRAIN TO A HIGHER LEVEL

In Part I you learned about the *Brain Supercharger* technology and how sound and music can be used as tools for change and transcendence. With its intricate harmonics and musical overlays, it gently slows both sides of the brain into an "Alpha-Theta" synchronicity to integrate and unfold you into whole brain awareness. This is the optimal state for learning and rescripting your unconscious. It is a process. Trust the process and your personal growth. Suspend your judgments to allow you to approach uncertainty with confidence. Remember to think mystery—not mastery. Think progress—not perfection. Go for a direction—not a destination. Allow "it" to find you.

In Part II you'll be introduced to a wealth of other tools that will help nudge you in this direction. Here you'll go through a creativity workshop and learn a four-step process for jump-starting your brain into higher efficiency. It demands constant experimentation and with that comes flexibility and the tendency to transform. As you do, you will use your right brain to connect you to your dreams (both waking and night) in your search for new patterns and insights that can be the seeds of your breakthroughs.

You'll learn to trust your intuition to take you further and faster than analytical thinking alone allows. You'll explore how to still your left brain and call on the "Void" to create a mental space for accessing new ideas. You'll discover how to look for "Synchronicity" and rely on it as an instrument of the universe to guide you in the absence of concrete evidence, that you are on the right path. You'll learn how to use "Meditation" to still your mind, to experience a new dimension of being where time has no hold over you.

DIRECT EXPERIENCE IS YOUR TEACHER

The purpose of these tools and the many others you'll be exploring in Part II is to shift the energy within your mind to achieve a higher order of being. Each is designed for direct experience since only that which is felt can change you. The transformation process is more to be **experienced** than studied.

This book and CD is offered as an agent of change. Like a teacher who can't impose learning, it can't impose change but rather helps you discover your own power within to bring about change. By applying this knowledge, you'll discover connections and cultivate an openness to new (perhaps strange) possibilities. Through these tools, you'll gain an amazing ability to detect patterns and tendencies, which can give you the superhuman skill of creating an accurate picture from minimal information. You will soon discover, through direct experience, the immense capabilities of your mind while functioning in an altered state of consciousness. In these peak experiences, you are connecting with all that is divine in the universe in the goal of becoming more than you are. This (the transformation of your consciousness) is beyond the limits of language. You can't explain it, because it must be experienced to be understood. Words simply cannot describe it.

Although evolution can be a slow process with its many reversals and setbacks, as we approach "The Omega Point" and increase our consciousness energy, adding it to the collective soul of humanity, the Earth "gets a new skin," as Teilhard would say. You are an important part of this grand plan—the great human adventure. It is the way of a "Mind Warrior."

PART II:
Mind Development Tools and Workshops to Transform Your Inner Universe

Introduction To Part II

"You have the power in the present moment
to change limiting beliefs and consciously plant
the seeds for the future of your choosing. As you
change your mind, you change your experience."
— Serge Kahili King

The first flight of Wilbur and Orville Wright at Kitty Hawk in 1903 lasted only 12 seconds. But the fact that it happened at all was significant. Once the possibility of flight was a reality, the ability to fly further and higher was just a matter of fine-tuning the process.

This story serves as an analogy to your mind development. We are all capable of reinventing ourselves, of transcending our present conditions. Once this possibility is established, unfolding your potential is just a fine-tuning of the process.

In Part I, I introduced you to a powerful new technology that uses sound frequencies to shift the energy in your brain and access your hidden potential. In Part II you'll discover additional tools and techniques to transform that energy to achieve whole brain thinking, stimulate your creative and intuitive abilities, and awaken more of your inner genius. Any one of these ideas may be an opening point— giving you a glimpse of your true potential. Your collective use of them can be a turning point in your life.

DIRECTING THE ENERGY IN YOUR BRAIN

Most people in the West are products of a "left-brained" educational system, which emphasizes logical, analytical, and verbal skills. Whole brain thinking requires you to tap into the gifts of your emotional, nonverbal, right brain. Its specialties include conceptual thought and symbolism, recognition of spatial patterns and the whole, plus music, movement and intuitiveness. The tools and techniques in this section are designed to access and unleash your right brain potential to lead you to the experience of whole brain thinking. As you perform these exercises pay attention to the shift that is going on in your head—from left brain to right brain functioning. Your goal will be to discover how to call forth its creative and intuitive powers on demand.

The intent of these exercises and workshops is to give you evidence through "direct experience" not concept, of that energy shift taking place in your brain and give you a means for repeating it whenever you wish. Some of these ideas may seem overly simplistic. They are intentionally so. The point is to move you through experience, instead of bogging you down in the theory and philosophy behind them. I've included a bibliography at the end of the book for further reading, and I encourage you to pursue this knowledge more deeply if you so desire.

HOW TO USE THIS SECTION

These workshops and exercises are not arranged in any particular order. You can begin with the ones that appeal to you most. Or, if you wish, you can take them one by one in the order that they appear. The first of these is the **Creativity Workshop** which is the most extensive of the workshops because it incorporates many of the other mind tools presented in this section. While their value is in their collective use, you can begin to benefit by using just a few of these ideas on a regular basis.

Just a comment about these tools and workshops. Some of these ideas may initially seem silly to your intellectual left brain. This is because the left brain is the home of your critic, your censor—the one who protects you from change. Again as I've said, these tools and their exercises are meant to be **experienced**. It is through action, not cerebral activity, that will open up more of your right brain. If it doesn't click into place for you the first time you read it, continue on. As you move through the other tools you will come upon many related ideas, connections, examples, similar applications and illustrative stories. Each tool is meant as an exercise and experiment designed for direct experience to move you into a new perspective. Each is a little discovery for you.

REINVENTING YOURSELF THROUGH YOUR SPECIAL ENERGY

We are all born into this life with the innate power to give our gifts to the world and in doing so create fulfillment for ourselves. What is your special gift? It exists in the form of a potential that was imprinted on millions of neurons in your brain on the day you were born. You still carry it. It is an energy waiting to be born into existence. Only through self-discovery will you unleash your gifts into the world.

The work you do on yourself is important, and the rewards are great. You can transcend old self-limiting mindscripts and negative conditions. You can let go of dirt-poor expectations and the "me against the world" beliefs. Once you do you will come to see that you live in an abundant, open and creative universe. One that will support your core values, and your authentic being.

There is a way for you to bridge the scientific and spiritual traditions of the ages in a practical way to improve your relationships, creativity, happiness and physical being. All you have to do is peel away the layers of fear, judgment and opinion that obscure the radiance and wisdom that are your own true nature, your authentic self.

The tools you are about to experience will show you how to cultivate the inner you, which is who you really are. To nudge you forward in your personal development. To awaken something in you, and illuminate a new vision of yourself and your role in the universe. This new vision will show you that you are far smarter than you imagine. Far richer too. When you turn on this power you automatically open yourself up to greater abundance, and opportunity. You sense the enormous potential of your mind, and not only make connections with your brain, you make connections with the universe.

Make this a joyful experiment. One without fear, without guilt, and without judgment. Become that child again as you let yourself go, and melt into the experience. Learn to be alive, and enjoy the moment.

I believe that once we open ourselves to our present experiences we realize that "right now" is it. We have the opportunity **RIGHT NOW** for happiness. We are no longer preoccupied with the past, or fearful of the future. The present will lead us there no matter what we do. By making the present moment vibrant and alive, we are fulfilling our most important function in the universe. And that is to "*BE.*"

Creativity Workshop:
A Toolkit For Personal Breakthroughs

"It is not the subconscious or unconscious,
but the supraconscious energies that are the
real source of all great human creations,
discoveries and inventions."
— Pitirim A. Sorokin

Regardless of your age or occupation, the ability to practice "everyday creativity" is a necessary life skill in today's constantly changing society. Students need new ways to process the overload of information. Employees need effective ways for applying old skills to new jobs in a changing marketplace. Government and businesses need better ideas for running larger programs on smaller budgets. And families need innovative ways to balance the increasing demands of work and home life while enjoying a comfortable lifestyle.

Each person has the potential and the requirement to be creative. As Carl Rogers says, "The action of the child inventing a new game with his playmates; Einstein formulating a theory of relativity; the housewife devising a new sauce recipe; a young author writing his first novel; all of these are; in terms of our definition, creative, and there is no attempt to list them in some order of more or less creative."

Creativity is nothing more than the ability to generate and implement new solutions to problems and challenges. While Western society tends to assign this idea to certain professions (such as artists, musicians, architects, actors and the like), creativity is an innate human ability. And just as with other abilities, our creativity skills become more proficient the more they are utilized.

As with the development of other skills, it takes determination and persistence to achieve a higher level of creativity. The benefits however are well worth the effort. Creative individuals are able to face uncertainty with confidence and are not afraid of a future filled with risk. They forge ahead with a calm sense of knowing in the absence of concrete evidence, while those around them wait for step-by-step instructions—sometimes into destruction.

Just as their spontaneous nature leads them to unplanned and lucrative opportunities, their flexible mind lets them connect one seemingly unrelated idea to another to lead to discovery, or use the knowledge gained in one area to spawn insight in an unrelated field. Through this ability to transfer knowledge, creative people see not one solution but many. Since they are always open to options, it seems the world is always open to them.

But how does a creative person do this? And what, really, is creativity?

CREATIVITY IS A PROCESS

The premise of this workshop is that creativity is a gift we all possess, rather than a gift that belongs only to gifted individuals. You owe much, if not everything, to your creativity. It is the innate energy that allows you to be a unique individual in a world of increasing conformity.

The way to develop your creativity is to first separate the creativity process from the creative product. All too often, we judge creativity by the end result, which is more indicative of time spent in training to master techniques for drawing, computer programming, singing and the like. The more immediate way to build creativity is to focus on the process that leads you to the product. The tools and techniques in this workshop will show you how to enjoy the journey, not just the destination. Secondly, we will look at the blocks to creativity that our Western society has historically encouraged us to believe.

After separating the process from the product, and diffusing the blocks that are holding you back from the full expression of your creativity, we'll examine the four stages of the creative process. Here we'll build on your learning of the specialties of the left and right hemispheres and experience the left to right brain shift which, in effect, "jump-starts" your brain into the creative process. As you continue to practice these exercises, you'll strengthen the neural pathways that lead to a creative mind-set. Just as a well traveled path through the woods is easier to follow than a seldom used trail, this continual forging into your brain's creative pathway will give you the ability to access this mind-set quickly, easily, and naturally in your everyday thinking.

By using a specific process, (along with a set of creativity tools) you'll be able to train your brain to operate in an enriched creative and problem solving mode. The process itself can be so empowering it will feel as if you've awakened from a deep sleep. In this powerful mode, you'll never see problems as problems again but as opportunities for testing your creative abilities.

PLACING THE VALUE ON PROCESS, NOT PRODUCT

The ability to unleash your creativity begins when you are able to distinguish the creative process from the creative product. This releases you from the judgment of the critic in your left brain who censors your every action and puts limits and restrictions on your right brain.

In their book, *Life, Paint and Passion,* authors Michell Cassou and Stewart Cubley write that too often "the product of the creative action is put forth, subtly or not so subtly, as the final fruit of the creative experience." As they point out, this wrongly allows the "creativity to be equated with results and therefore must be justified by explanation, analysis, critical evaluation, and superimposed meaning."

Instead of placing the emphasis on the end result of the creative endeavor, the importance lies with the process. Again from their book, Cassou and Cubley write, "It is the basic tenet of this book that the creative process is enough. It is not only enough, it is the doorway into a direct experience of the essential life force which is at the root of the urge to create art. It is the process itself—in the creative energy it releases, in the new perceptions it brings, and in the deepened connection with oneself it fosters." While they were specifically speaking about painting, this open-minded attitude applies to all works of creativity.

The challenge is to let go of your expectations for the product or result which you are creating. An effective way to get around the critic in you is to model the traits of those who display creativity. They are open to and unafraid of new thoughts and ideas. More importantly, they define these new thoughts and ideas not by the praise or criticism of others but by what *they* feel within. To do so requires a trust in your inner nature.

Joseph Chilton Pearce has said "To live a creative life, we must lose our fear of being wrong." The creative attitude is one of progress, not perfection. It delights in mystery, not mastery. Let the words of Einstein guide you, "The most beautiful thing we can experience is the mysterious." By cultivating this attitude, life becomes filled with awe. And the creative blocks you may feel inside can be redirected into opportunities.

REDIRECTING THE ENERGY IN YOUR CREATIVE BLOCKS

A creative block is a feeling of being powerless, of mentally being tongue-tied, of being bound up with ropes that restrict your thinking. The benefit of these mental blocks is that they are filled with tremendous energy. The secret is to learn how to channel this energy to your advantage.

Creative blocks fall into two categories—those inside and those outside of you. The creative blocks inside of you came from your parents, friends, family, and teachers whose well-meaning but stifling comments made you abandon your creativity in the past.

A small child might say, "Daddy, the moon looks like a face. Is there a man up there?" The father, being an adult conditioned by the left brain world would reply "Don't be silly." After hearing that type of response hundreds of times, you become more likely to reject fantasy and analogy as appropriate strategies for gaining knowledge.

Another scenario played out again and again is the lack of encouragement given to teenagers in pursuit of the arts. A talented student who wins praise by his art teachers is told by his parents that "Art is fine for a hobby, but you don't want to be a starving artist. You need to find a real career." Faced with the fear of not being able to support himself with his artistic abilities, the student abandons his talent and pursues a more logical left-brain path.

All of us are creative when we are children. We befriend imaginary people, we invent our own games, enjoy make-believe tea parties, role play with make-believe wars and doctor visits. At one time or another, we've all been told to "behave like other children," as if our soaring imaginations were getting in the way or causing a problem.

Once a child enters school, the creative output is changed. As a student, a child learns to not vocalize fantasies but rather to internalize the imagining process. This is, of course, only natural. Internal fantasy become images in a child's mind, external fantasy becomes play. It should be noted, however, that children with strong internal fantasies are found to have longer attention spans and to move from subject to subject with more flexibility.

Educator Neil Postman once said that "children enter school as question marks and leave as periods." In time, rules about grammar, about math, about spelling—all appealing to the left brain, that part of the brain that rationalizes and deals with analytical ideas— become the norm. Rules even begin to structure playtime, as children engage in competition and are taught player's positions, the meaning of a foul, and become focused on the product (the score) instead of the process (the joy of the game). A conditioning effect occurs that makes the score (the product) the most important thing, instead of the joy of doing it (the process).

As a child gets older, conformity along with left-brain orientation wins higher praise in school activities than creativity. The rule oriented subjects—reading, writing, and arithmetic—are emphasized as the important subjects to learn. Creativity is reinforced out of a person, by stressing uniformity, predictability, and orderliness.

We live in an age of tremendous mass communication. Television shows produced in New York and Los Angeles establish a level of conformity for everyday life. Magazine ads sell an entire nation on what we need to buy to become models of perfection. Suburban sprawl from coast to coast creates clones of shopping centers rolled out like seeded peat moss mats from instant garden cans. Every city looks the same. Everybody wears the same clothes. Every brain is fed the same information written or spoken on a generic level to win appeal by the masses in order to be a success in the marketplace.

This is not to say that technology is bad. In fact, the irony is that creative individuals are those who created technology in the first place—the architects who designed the malls, the actors and producers of the television shows, the writers and publishers of the magazines, the entrepreneurs and marketing minds who developed the products sold in the malls, magazines and broadcast media.

The point is that the creative mind must be able to rise above its social conditioning. To live a creative life means letting go of pre-existing ideas, thinking outside the norm, breaking down the structure and seeing a new vision rise out of the pieces. As Picasso said, "Every act of creation is first of all an act of destruction." To create means to be a little lost. But that is the essential nature of the process. A requirement of creative discovery is to not know the outcome. If you are always sure of where you are going, you'll never be surprised by what you find. To create is to hold hands with mystery and explore uncharted waters.

It is akin to the way you feel when you are stirred by a song, frightened by a movie, or moved by a book. These emotions occurred because you were open to the experience and approached your encounter without expectations. In your involvement with the song, movie, or book, you are performing a creative act. It is triggering something in your brain that didn't previously exist. This is what you are seeking. An open mind that silences your internal critic (the left brain) and allows you to step over the blocks of negative comments from the past, so you can see a world of options and possibilities.

USING A "CREATIVITY WELLNESS" PROGRAM

The way to become more creative is to make creativity a natural part of your everyday thinking. Like a daily diet to nourish your creativity, you need to follow a set of basics that will develop your creative impulse on an on-going basis. There are easy tools you can use to accomplish this. These tools are not specific to a particular project you are working on. They act as a creativity wellness program to prevent creativity blocks when you are facing a challenging task.

This wellness program lays the groundwork, or sets the stage, for the four steps that you will pass through in the creative process whether you want to solve a specific problem, invent a new product, stimulate your imagination or simply generate new ideas easily and quickly.

This laying of groundwork focuses on your right brain. The idea is to set your right brain free and keep it active by continually exercising it and feeding it with the type of experience it needs to develop. The four primary ways of accomplishing this are through affirmations, visualization, mindfulness and dreams. We'll explore each of these tools on the following pages.

Some teachers of creativity refer to this laying the groundwork as "composting," or "mulching"—the gathering of ideas, hunting for opinions, canvassing your everyday environment for creative fodder just as you would compost the soil in your garden to fertilize it for future planting. It is also during this stage that you reprogram your blocks to creativity and release yourself from self-imposed limits.

> **Key Point:** There is a very simple but profound truth connected to your creative capabilities: **If you believe you are creative—you are.** It's your own attitudes and beliefs more than any other factor that act as mental blocks restricting your creative flow. We end up "seeing" only what we expect to see.

In order to transform your creative blocks into building blocks and maximize your creativity, you must first restructure your belief system by reprogramming your unconscious idea processor to see yourself as being creative. This allows your inner mind, which already has the necessary wisdom and insight, to make the creative breakthroughs for you. The tool for accomplishing this is affirmation.

TOOL ONE: AFFIRMATIONS THAT DISSOLVE THE BLOCKS TO CREATIVITY

Affirmations are strong, positive statements or thoughts that something already is. In this case a helpful affirmation is "I am creative!" By repeating this statement to yourself over a period of time, you are implanting new, more flexible unconscious beliefs in place of old beliefs that may limit your potential to be creative. The power of positive affirmation plants a seed which redirects the mind toward your stated goal.

Our behavior tends to be shaped far more by our unconscious beliefs than by those beliefs of which we are consciously aware. It is because of these belief systems more than anything else—the belief, for example, that an "A" in math is better than an "A" in painting— that in our everyday experience, we see what we expect to see.

Our belief systems create our attitudes and these attitudes, in turn, become the mental blocks that prevent us from being as creative as we could be. Yet part of the problem is that we have unconscious defenses against changing our belief systems. This is why, if we encounter knowledge that would alter our belief system, our internal censor treats the knowledge as a threat—ignoring or resisting it.

The key is to silence the critic long enough to have the affirmations become effective. The *Super Intelligence* soundtrack on your CD contains affirmations related to creativity. Using the mindscripting technology (covered in Chapter 4) they are designed to bypass the critical conscious mind and imprint a new belief system into your subconscious. Your subconscious then acts in accordance with these instructions to make it so.

While the affirmations on the *Super Intelligence* soundtrack work below your conscious level of perception, you can use these same affirmations to work on a conscious level through the left brain. They are provided for you below. Silently thinking them, speaking them out loud, or writing them down a few minutes each day will help reprogram your belief system and open up your powers of creativity.

Here are the Creativity affirmations:

I now remove all limitations I have placed on myself
I am a creative person
I have remarkable insight and bursts of creative energy
Many new ideas come to me
My mind is connected with the intelligent universe
I am wise
I am relaxed and creative
I discover new ways to do things
Ideas flow from my creative mind
My mind is free
I can tap my full creative power whenever I wish
I am wisdom and energy
I trust my intuition
I profit from my creative ideas
I see things differently
I like to explore new ideas
My mind is focused and I pick up on ideas quickly
I write my ideas down
Everything I do stimulates my creativity

Creativity surges through my mind and body like electricity
I solve problems easily with my creative powers
I look for unique ways to solve problems
I have fully developed my intuitive powers
I see things from a creative perspective
I visualize easily
I see the big picture and how things are connected
My mind works like magic
I feel like a creative genius
I am a creative genius
I feel my creative energy flowing through me like electricity
New ideas come so easily to me
My creative mind can solve any problem
I have the answers
My mind is open
I am one with the universe

Here are the Accelerated Learning and Memory affirmations:

I learn quickly
I have instant recall of everything I read
All knowledge is available to me
I am wisdom
I am an advanced learner
I am learning faster each day
I like to learn new things
My IQ goes up
I am intelligent and wise
I learn faster each day
I like to read
I am articulate and knowledgeable
I read faster and remember more
I am a student of life
Learning new things comes easily for me
I discover
I am a quick study
I am relaxed and calm
I am wisdom and learning
I remember everything
When I learn new information I focus my attention
I learn faster than others because I'm focused
My memory improves daily
People around me are amazed at my ability to learn so quickly
I accelerate my learning
I can do it
I read faster and remember more
I remember everything I see
New concepts come easily for me
I see how things connect
I have an excellent memory
My reading comprehension goes up
I have instant recall
My memory improves
The more I read the quicker I learn
I am an unlimited person
My mind serves me well

Creativity Workshop

——

103

TOOL 2: VISUALIZATION—PICTURE THE POSSIBILITIES

Now that you have a mechanism for developing a creative mind-set, you are ready to use the tool of visualization to conjure up images and visions in your mind's eye. Vision is the dominant means of perceiving the world around us. When you can learn how to imagine, or see images in your mind's eye, you will have taken a major step toward becoming more creative.

A large portion of the right brain is devoted to image processing. Scientists believe that these images impose a certain structure on the way information is encoded and organized in our brain. When we think about something, an idea, a place or a person, our brain assembles bits and pieces of imagery we have experienced in our lives, and puts them together to create a perceptual vision in the mind's eye. This is the work of our creative imagination (see **Imagination**) which actually creates new images and experiences that have never occurred, out of this vast imagery data bank.

What's so amazing about this process is that these images created by our imagination (**and manufactured only in the mind's eye**) cause the brain to react as if it is a real thing. The brain secretes hormones, and stores these "make-believe" visualizations as if they really exist. Imagery is the language of the unconscious.

Try a quick experiment. Close your eyes and imagine holding a red delicious apple in your hand. Feel the smooth texture. Examine the colors. Look at the ends. See the stem? Now toss it up and down in your hand three times. Bring it up to your mouth and take a bite out of it. Hear the crunch as you bite down. Do you feel the juice explode in your mouth? Now taste it, as you chew and swallow. Do you feel the saliva building up in your mouth?

Were you able to imagine the apple in your hand? Did you see it clearly? Experience the way it felt in your hand? Any odor? How about when you took a bite out of it? Could you taste it? Do you feel a slight increase of saliva in your mouth right now?

Imagining something to be true though vivid detailed imagery, the mind accepts that imagined outcome as a reality. The significance of this concept is that it means you are able to transmit messages deep into the unconscious, and also bring inspirations from deep within to the surface of awareness by creating mental images.

This is **Visualization**. It is the process of creating a strong mental image, and sending it to the unconscious, so it can act upon it. The key idea here is that the stronger the signal you send the unconscious—in the form of intense inner resolve and fixed purpose—the higher a priority it will assign to a problem, preparing the way for creative breakthroughs.

The following example shows how you would use visualization to make a creative breakthrough.

FROM BANKRUPTCY TO MILLIONAIRE

Imagine you have just purchased a jeans manufacturer near the point of bankruptcy with the resolve to turn the business around. You are desperate for creative ideas to make this business a success. After analyzing the problem, you conclude that it is primarily a marketing issue. No one knows about these well-designed jeans. The challenge is to create a successful marketing campaign that will differentiate your jeans from the well-known brands.

The first step is to engage your unconscious idea processor by visualizing your jeans line as if it were already a tremendous success. Visualize people racing through the aisles and fighting over the stacks of your jeans as they try to buy them. Your vivid image is sending the message that consumers just can't get enough of your new line of jeans. You see hundreds of people waiting in the check-out line with armloads full of your jeans. You overhear the sales associates talking about the incredible madness that has seized consumers over your jeans. Your only problem now is finding manufacturers that can keep up with the demand!

Notice how in our example, the visualization contained vivid imagery loaded with emotion. This is the one of the secrets of the technique (see **Visualization**). Once you are able to do that, you turn the problem over to your subconscious to find the answers for you and make your visualization a reality. As you burn those positive, emotion-filled images into your brain for several days, simply ask your mind to supply you with the answers to bring about the desired reality. It may take hours, days, or weeks. But soon (and probably when you least expect it) an idea will pop into your head that will give you the creative inspiration for solving the problem.

Visualization sounds almost too simple to work. But that's because the mechanism that makes it work is invisible. It is occurring on a deep level within your being. The key to making it a success is not an understanding of this deeper process, it is simply the ability to establish strong mental imagery in the mind's eye and energize it with positive emotion. That's all that is required.

As you become more accomplished at visualizing, you'll be able to easily reprogram your mind to make creative connections. To help you get started on developing your ability to create mental imagery, read the following text which describes a journey. As you read, visualize by deeply imagining what you're reading. Try to picture everything described in detail, and include your other senses as well. Feel, smell, touch, hear...and enjoy!

You step barefoot from the hot, black pavement to the warm, fine, powdery sand. You sink into the smooth tan mounds with each step, watching the sand shift with your weight. You feel it slide pleasantly between your toes, and bury the tops of your feet. Every time you lift your foot, it feels heavy, and a spray of sand follows behind. The sand feels warm and inviting against the soft soles of your feet as they sink down, taking you towards the water.

You stand for a moment, deciding where to sit. You look around. Straight ahead is the water, about 50 feet away. It's a beautiful deep blue-green, with the sun dancing off it. The waves are rolling in, not violently, but methodically, peacefully.

The waves crash with a spray of white foam as the water hits the beach, and then slowly return to the sea. You watch the waves do this several times...rolling...then one crashes, and subsides, just as another crashes, and subsides, and another crashes, and subsides, always with another to take its place.

You sit down and shift your weight until the sand molds to your body and supports you into a comfortable position. You take a deep breath, close your eyes, and feel the sun on your face. You can smell the salt air on the warm breeze. It reminds you of another time you visited the beach, and smelled that same salt air. You hear the crashing of the waves and the surging of the foam as the small bubbles pop and retreat. You hear a sea gull flying overhead. You open your eyes, but have to squint and quickly raise your hand to shade the sun from them to see it. You close your eyes again, and drink in the warm sun along with the peaceful relaxed feeling.

Did you feel the sand on your feet? Could you see and hear the waves crashing? Did you smell the salt air? Did you feel the warm breeze? Did you imagine in color? Were your images vivid?

If you were having difficulty "seeing" this exercise, you are not alone. Many people do not find it easy. Now ask yourself one more question—did you see the waves as 50 feet away, or as merely straight ahead in a vivid blue-green? If you said "Yes, precisely 50 feet away." then you are most likely left-brain dominant, or very analytical, and able to judge distances and logical elements very well. On the other hand, if you said "Yes, ahead in a vivid blue-green, with little sparkles reflecting off the water, reminding me of..." then you are more likely right brain dominant, or visual and emotional.

The person who can see the water as exactly 50 feet away will experience greater difficulty with visualization exercises because of the way their brain operates. If this is you, know that left-brain dominants can become mixed brain dominants by developing their right side with tools such as this. You'll have more opportunities to practice this in the upcoming exercises.

TOOL 3: PRACTICING MINDFULNESS TO AWAKEN YOUR RIGHT BRAIN

Affirmations and visualization are tools that you apply directly to a creative challenge. Unlike the next tool of mindfulness, they have specific goals—to rescript your mental attitude on creativity and to boost your mental eye's ability to focus on specific images. Mindfulness takes you in a different direction.

As a tool, mindfulness inundates the mind with sensory input and asks you to consciously focus on things entirely separate from the creative challenge at hand. This intense focus "elsewhere" stimulates the brain to make creative connections, forcing it to see things differently. The following example details this process and the beneficial effect it has on creativity.

Imagine you are writing a novel. Each afternoon you go for a walk to take a break from your daily routine and to give yourself some exercise. Normally, when you go for a walk you are thinking about your novel, what you're going to eat for dinner, how to settle a difference you had with your spouse, and other issues in your life. Your brain is so preoccupied with thinking, that as you walk, you are not paying attention to the rhythm of your walking or the sights, smells, and sounds around you. Instead, your mind is busy tending to the ideas and conversations inside your head.

A mindfulness exercise encourages you to consciously focus on the external stimuli in your environment through the use of your senses. This forces the logical left brain to not think, while it allows the sensory right brain to see, feel, hear, smell, and taste all that is going on around you, as described in the following passage.

Walking down the path, you hear the leaves crunch under your feet and imagine them to be nature's tapestry covering the ground with a brilliant vibrancy. You hear birds singing in the tree you just passed. How many—2, or is it 3? What is the song like? Do they sound happy?

Off to your left you hear scurrying and you look to see a gray squirrel climbing on the side of walnut tree. His cheeks are heavy with nuts. You look closer and see the incredible texture of the bark on the tree, and the craggy looking branches suddenly seem like hundreds of witches' fingers. Moss hangs from several branches, and you reach out and touch it. It's soft. You tear off a piece and bring it to your nose. It smells musty, but not unpleasant. You drop the piece of moss, and watch it fall to the ground. It lands next to a caterpillar, a multi-colored tube of fuzz.

Suddenly the wind comes up and the rustling of the branches is so loud it sounds like the crashing of waves on the beach. You pause in your walk and, raising your head to watch the branches swaying overhead, you smell the air, just as a dog sniffs the wind. Standing motionless and quiet you hear the rhythm of your heartbeat playing against the roar of the wind. Although you've walked this path a thousand times before, you've never experienced the awe you're feeling this moment. And as you enjoy the experience of participating in the beauty of nature through your senses, you feel one with your surroundings and the world.

Mindfulness is one of those exercises that is deceptively simple, but profoundly powerful. The first few times you do it you might feel nothing. Then one day you learn to see it all, with a new set of eyes, and suddenly the universe opens up and reveals its magic. This has been my experience. I have had profound meditations that opened me up to new levels of thinking—which led to creative breakthroughs, just by paying attention and "soaking up" the sensory pleasures of my immediate world around me.

Creativity Workshop

Sometimes I would imagine myself as a tree or an ant, and launch my consciousness into these "other" worlds. My experiences at times could become so intense I would lose myself completely in the moment, to where "I" no longer existed. The resulting realizations were of an amazing planet—incredibly detailed, rich and beautiful beyond anything I can say or comprehend in words. When these experiences occurred I felt an intense gratitude for being alive and being privileged to experience such "aliveness." All this life is going on around us, all the time, and we are for the most part asleep—oblivious to it. The rewards of letting it in, even for a few moments is a genuine bliss that opens the gates of your mind.

109

The benefit to your creativity is that you are refocusing your brain to see things differently. You are consciously directing your mental energy to see what is already there, but from a new perspective. This can be very liberating. Not only does it provide inspiration, but it also opens the mind by direct experience through the sensory brain. Getting back to our earlier example, our writer will return to his novel with a renewed freshness stimulated by the sensory stimuli found in the patterns of nature. And too, by giving his logical brain some downtime, he will feel rejuvenated and better able to express his thoughts in a richer way.

Practice the mindfulness exercise several times a week by taking a walk or going jogging. Instead of thinking about things other than your walk, focus intently on all that is going on around you. Pay attention to the sounds, sights, smells and textures in your environment. Practice moving your head from side to side so you can take it all in. Look off in the distance and then up close. Pick things up, examine their texture. Smell the air, the dirt. Look up at the sky.

Fill your mind with sensory input. When you do, the magic and mystery will open up your mind and spill over into your creativity.

TOOL 4: USING *SUPER INTELLIGENCE* TO CAPITALIZE ON YOUR NIGHTLY DREAMS

When we dream, we are in direct communication with our unconscious. Many cultures throughout history have called on the power of their dreams to deliver prophetic information of the future. Even in our rational Western culture, dreams are viewed as a valuable source of new ideas and direction as confirmed by inventors and scientists who received illuminations and breakthroughs during their sleep.

Dreams lead us to these insights through a process of free association that is very hard to reach in the waking mind. That is why dreams are so hard to describe—they make no sense to the logical mind because they are not restrained or governed by the forms of reality. They make use of intuitive links, unthinkable connections, and fantastic visions that our waking minds simply cannot detect.

The first step to benefiting from dreams is to remember them. If you're a person who has difficulty remembering dreams, you'll find your *Super Intelligence* soundtrack can help you access and recall them much more easily. The information processing state you enter into with *Super Intelligence* is very similar to dreaming. In addition, it contains affirmations that program your subconscious to release your visions upon awakening. Simply listen to this soundtrack before you fall asleep and experiment with it as a dream incubator.

In addition to helping you recall your dreams, this soundtrack can enable you to direct your dreams to help you solve a specific task or problem you are facing. As you listen to the soundtrack, lightly focus on the challenge confronting you. Instruct your dreams to deliver options that will solve this challenge. Then upon wakening, journal the messages, images, people, and content of your dream.

Many inventors keep a notepad by their bedside to capture inspiration that springs from them upon wakening. Learning how to capture and interpret these messages is a fascinating process that offers incredible insights into your unconscious. For a more complete explanation, please go to the **Dream Workshop**.

THE FOUR STAGES OF THE CREATIVITY PROCESS

As you use the right brain tools of affirmation, visualization, mindfulness and your dreams, you are laying the groundwork in your unconscious to open your creativity channel. These tools are very simple yet have a magical effect on expanding your creativity by provoking your brain into seeing more options and possibilities. In this mind-state, you are able to make creative connections and intuitive breakthroughs that can lead to something totally new.

It takes a new mind to see a new world. Through your creativity training you are giving birth to a new mind. It is not an intellectual process. Your mind must learn to shift the energy from left to right brain awareness. You do this through direct experience—the direct knowing of your right brain. You may have heard the saying, "Before you can become a success at (fill in the blank) it has to go from your head to your heart." Well the way into your heart is through the right brain. It is your sensory brain, your emotional brain, the one that learns by direct experience, by direct knowing.

Creativity Workshop

111

There are four stages in the creativity process. Rather than learn these as linear logical steps that you take to arrive at an idea, it is more effective if you also assume the "role" and characteristics you are portraying as you pass through each one.

Through the following pages, you will come to know these stages as you came to learn about the seasons of the year as a child. You will gather leaves in the fall (**stage 1**), sit by the fire in the winter (**stage 2**), burst into the warm sun in the spring (**stage 3**), and enjoy the fruit of the plants in the summer (**stage 4**).

Through this process, you will associate each stage with an activity instead of a label as the end result. You will also assume the character of the creative person in each stage through role playing—Info-seeker (gathering in fall—stage 1), Daydreamer (in front of the fire in winter—stage 2), Eureka experience (bursting into spring—stage 3), Auditor/author (the fruits of summer—stage 4).

By role playing through these four stages of the creativity process you will be using your whole brain (and body) to experience what happens in each of these moments, exhibiting different character traits, and bouncing back and forth from your left brain to right brain as each uses its specialties in harmony to create the final product.

Whether you're a dominant left, dominant right, or mixed dominant, this process will force you to use the whole brain thinking pathway.

The four stages add up to the ultimate outcome of the creativity process: **IDEA**. They are as follows:

1. Info-seeker
2. Daydreamer
3. Eureka Experience
4. Auditor/Author of idea

IDEA

STAGE 1: INFO-SEEKER

In this stage, you are primarily in your left brain. You are gathering information, focusing on the problem, gathering ideas from various sources, researching through books, talking to people who are knowledgeable in the area of the problem or challenge you are facing.

The season is autumn. You are the squirrel you met on the path in your mindfulness exercise, gathering acorns for the winter. Pick up everything you can find—even if it is only remotely related. Play the part of the scavenger. Everything you find is a morsel for the mind.

In this stage, you are methodically plodding through the world of possibilities and depositing the ideas one by one into your brain, like coins in a piggy bank. These ideas are energy from your external world. Later on in the creativity process you will apply your internal energy to transform them.

The more energy you put into your brain, the more energy you will be able to release. This will give you creativity fluency—an ability to generate a large number of ideas. In the creativity process, where you never know the value of an idea until it has been explored from all angles, this ability to generate many ideas will ensure you have at least one winner. To help you increase your output, here are five techniques you can use to stimulate the flow of information into your brain.

• **Learn how to think differently by breaking the rules through the use of chaos, disorder, and ambiguity.** It's not easy to be a rule breaker. In order to live in our society, we are taught you have to "obey the rules." But to be creative you need to break "idea rules." These are not really rules, but patterns of thinking. Every great discovery, invention, or advancement in a field broke an accepted "idea rule." The following are just a few of the many examples:

- the idea that the earth is the center of the universe.
- the idea that if God wanted man to fly He would have given him wings.
- the idea that painting must mirror life and be as realistic as possible.
- the idea that people need to make bank transactions face-to-face with a teller.
- the idea that the computer was only for crunching numbers.

All these "idea rules" had to be broken before new inventions and new ways of living could evolve. Each new idea comes from a rule breaker. Columbus broke the rule that the world was flat. Henry Ford broke the rule that the internal combustion engine was impractical. John F. Kennedy broke the rule that a Catholic could not be elected President. The Beatles broke the rule that rock 'n roll was not an art form. Almost every advance in art, science, technology, business, medicine and other fields has occurred when someone challenged the rules and tried a different approach. This demands unconventional thinking. It is a key aspect in unleashing your creativity. To test your ability to use unconventional thinking, try the following exercise.

How can you use just three straight lines to connect the dots without lifting your pen? (see solution at the end of this chapter.)

When you train your mind to challenge the rules, new worlds of opportunity open up to you. Knowledge alone doesn't make a person creative. Creativity requires an outlook and attitude where you allow yourself to search for ideas. Even more importantly, your level of creativity allows you to manipulate your knowledge and experience to come up with new ideas and innovative ways of solving problems.

The earlier exercise on mindfulness was designed to help you do this by breaking you out of your normal patterns of routine, and allowing you to see the world from a new perspective. The act of doing this is very liberating and will foster unconventional thinking, and the ability to look at things differently. Because our minds are trained to think a certain way, it is difficult for us to create new channels of neural activity. Yet the most creative among us are able to do that by challenging the rules to find the new opportunities.

Part II

Mind Development Tools

114

• **Learn how to ask the right questions.** The key to obtaining the best answers is in knowing what questions to ask. One of the most powerful questions is the "What if?" question. Science fiction authors use this device all the time: What if human beings could be remolded to live under water? What if the South had won the Civil War? What if an alien race landed on our world? "What if?" is one of the best speculative games and a terrific exercise for creativity.

Just by exercising the "What if?" technique every day you'll discover that it conditions your mind to search your data banks for more options. Even if you don't have anything to put on the end of the "What if?" question, just by saying the words "What if..." out loud your mind will follow with something. It might be a crazy "What if?" response but that's not the point. Your goal is to create options and stimulate new ideas. The next time you are brainstorming for options, just say the words "What if..." and see if your mind doesn't start filling in the blanks with options.

The whole idea behind "What if?" questions is to be able to take another route or avenue to explore possibilities, or even, the impossible. The more you speculate, the more new ideas will come to you. Or the more you manipulate the knowledge you have, the more new ideas you will be able to generate.

For example, imagine you own a car manufacturing plant and you want to design a new car. Ask yourself "What if, instead of wheels, cars had treads like a small tank?" This odd image might lead you to new design ideas—or at least know what ideas you don't want to choose. You might ask yourself "What if, instead of four wheels, all cars had three wheels?" How would it work? Might it even enhance the design? Would it make the car slower or faster?

Gutenberg asked "What if a wine press was combined with a coin puncher?" and invented the printing press. Albert Einstein asked "What if I rode on a beam of light out into space?" and saw himself ending up back at the sun the further and further he traveled. This was the beginning of his theory of relativity. Creativity, along with discovery, is the ability to look at the same thing as everyone else and see or think something different.

Another approach with these type of questions is to involve yourself in the problems by asking "If I were a carburetor, how would I burn gasoline for maximum efficiency?" This "what-if" perspective, allows you to shift your thinking and add a new dimension of looking at the problem. It frees you from deeply ingrained assumptions and opens your mind to new possibilities.

• **Look for more than one answer.** As you are looking for creative solutions to problems, don't accept the first answer that pops into your mind. Train yourself to look for options and possibilities. Play with your wording to get different answers. Or try looking at the problem from the viewpoint of someone other than yourself. Force yourself to keep asking "What else? Are there other options? Is there another way to do this?"

• **Use analogies and metaphors to stimulate insights.** One of the greatest methods for stimulating new ideas is by making connections between unrelated ideas through some meaning they share. The following example shows how an idea from nature can be applied to a problem through analogy to create a solution.

While a man was walking in some tall grass, little seed pods attached themselves to his clothes, completely covering his pants legs. He pulled one pod off, examined it, and noticed it had a tiny little hook-like device on it that caught onto the fabric of his pants. From this, he came up with the idea of Velcro fasteners and made his fortune. The seeds had been there all along. Millions of people before him had experienced getting them caught on their clothes. It was his ability to make a connection between this idea

and an application that resulted in a new product, which lead to millions of dollars in profit.

This ability to make analogies is a specialty of the right brain. This is also the part of the brain that creates the thoughts that lead to metaphors by connecting two different universes of meaning through some similarity the two share. "Our mind is like a computer" is one example of a metaphor. Another is "launder the money." Metaphors develop your creativity by building an association between the familiar and the unfamiliar to facilitate understanding. For example, automobiles were once called "horseless carriages." And television could be explained as "radio with pictures."

Metaphors and analogies make complex or abstract ideas easier to understand while stimulating your own creative growth. Listen for and create analogies and metaphors as you go through your every day experience. Also, look for relationships between things that have no apparent likeness. In his book *The Act of Creation*, Arthur Koestler described the creative process as one of biassociation, which means to make something new and surprising, out of something unrelated, but familiar.

Most importantly, both analogies and metaphors can be fun. In a way, analogies turn us into storytellers and metaphors turn us into poets. Both help you look at things and ideas differently, and see the world with a new perspective.

• **Practice being eccentric.** In other words, learn how to play again. While this is covered under the tool of **Growing Down**, here are some quick suggestions you can practice now. Go to an art museum. Take a class in improvisational theater. Do things you wouldn't normally do. By doing these things and being eccentric you are training your brain to see things differently, and that stimulates the creativity process.

Another idea is to eavesdrop on a group of four-year old children, chattering as they play. You will be listening to the intelligence of the human mind before it has been chained and locked up with logic. As you watch them interact, rediscover your own naive childlike curiosity. Sing a song, do a dance. Act a little crazy every now and then. When you do this, two things are guaranteed to happen. One, you are going to have fun. And two, by recapturing your child within, the world around you loosens up and becomes freer and more relaxed. You are cultivating your mind to play and have fun. This will stimulate your thinking, and enrich your creative output.

These five techniques of generating ideas will fertilize and seed your mind with options and possibilities for increasing your creative output. It's all a part of stage one in the creativity process, where you are role playing as the info-seeker in the season of fall. This is the first letter of **I** in IDEA. Next move on to **D** for Daydreamer as you sit in front of the fire in the season of winter.

STAGE 2: DAYDREAMER

In this stage you are in your right brain. After doing the arduous and exhaustive research of idea gathering, you need to give yourself some time away from the problem. In this mode you are relaxing your mind, detaching yourself from the problem. Because your logical left mind has a difficult time in letting go, it is best to give your left brain an entirely different project to work on. Once you do, the artist right brain can invite the participation of your unconscious to play with the problem and the accumulated information. It is through the involvement of the unconscious that you make the creative connections and intuitive breakthroughs.

This is a period of creative relaxation. You are releasing the problem into the unconscious where it can examine the problem in light of your accumulated information, and make the connections and free associations, without the constraints of the critical conscious.

To ease himself into this stage, Einstein used to walk away from his blackboard, put his formulas aside, and play the violin. By removing himself from the problem and shutting down the analytical part of his brain, he allowed his unconscious idea processor to go to work on it. It is this process of the brain going "off line" to allow the ideas and problems to churn around in the mind that prepares you for the next step where the breakthrough connections are made.

So relax. Take a nap. Go for a walk. Let go of it. The ability to have quiet time away from the problem is a very critical step in the creativity process. What you are doing is giving yourself the space to create a solution. This space is the void (see **Void**) from where your creative thoughts will arise to send you into the next stage of the Eureka Experience.

Although this stage requires no conscious effort, it is often the hardest for most people to accept. The reason is that it requires us to do nothing while waiting for something to happen. Our society is not comfortable with waiting or doing nothing. Yet this stage is crucial. The left and right hemispheres of your brain are both trying to get at the problem. They are fighting for the chance to solve it. And, like a referee who breaks up a fight in a game between players of opposing teams, to give each one the space to calm down, this stage puts space or a mental peace between the two halves of your brain and hands over the problem to your unconscious to solve.

To allow you to access this mind-set, here are some techniques that will give you the sense of working the problem while actually freeing your focus so that you can "unwork" the problem on a higher level of awareness.

• *Super Intelligence* **soundtrack.** The first tool to use is your *Super Intelligence* soundtrack. It stimulates Alpha-Theta brainwave activity and higher states of consciousness allowing you to access unconscious imagery and accelerate your psychological information processing.

To give you the greatest benefit from this session, you should release the control of your conscious mind with this simple affirmation before you plug into the soundtrack: *I give permission to my unconscious to provide me with a solution to the problem of... (state the problem.)* Once you're finished with the affirmation, let go of it.

Another way to do this is to see yourself writing out a little note which says *"The problem of (fill in the blank) is a thing of the past"* and then put the note into a balloon. Imagine the balloon floating away, farther and farther up into the sky, until it can no longer be seen. After this, you've really let go of the problem and are ready to listen to the soundtrack.

Be sure to play the entire 28 minute session. It is composed of different segments which will sequentially take you from the waking Beta conscious state down through Alpha and Theta, and then bring you back to Beta consciousness a few moments before the soundtrack ends.

After the soundtrack has ended, take the next fifteen minutes to journal in your notebook. A very effective process, journaling is even more powerful after using this soundtrack because your brain is in an optimal state of creativity and mental clarity (see **Journaling**).

STAGE 3: THE EUREKA EXPERIENCE

From the Info-Seeker of the fall, to the Daydreamer and incubator of the winter, you are now passing into the Eureka Experience of the spring. Just as the seed planted in the fall breaks through the ground to reach out to the sun's rays in the spring, your breakthrough insight will emerge in this stage.

Creativity Workshop

This is the "Aha experience" of inspiration when your brain has made the connection which allows you to leap to a dramatic resolution of the problem. It is the climax of the process for which you laid the groundwork by reprogramming your unconsciousness idea processor, focused in on the problem, and let go of it on a conscious level allowing your unconscious to make the final creativity leap.

We are all capable of inspiration. What society calls creative genius is really the result of passing through these stages. The people who achieve the most success are those patient and trusting enough to endure stage two which contains the secret of inner listening.

STAGE 4: THE AUDITOR AND AUTHOR

The purpose of step four is to show that the solution you reached through intuition and inspiration can stand up to empirical proof. In this stage, you audit your results (and once satisfied of their effectiveness) release them to the world.

This is the summer of the process where you harvest the fruits of your planting and test your idea by putting it through a practical and workable plan. It is the stage where your left brain comes racing back in and shouts *"Look what I did everybody. Come quick. I have found the way."* It is the part of the creative process that brings you back to ground level. It uses words and numbers, plus principles, rules and logic to bring into realization what your intuitive mind uncovered.

In his book *Poetry and Experience*, Archibald MacLeish writes "We poets struggle with Non-being to force it to yield to Being. We knock upon the silence for an answering music." In this stage, you are taking the direct experience of knowing the answer from your right brain and passing it through to your left brain. It is as if the right brain, on having received the insights from your unconscious, throws it like a Hail Mary pass to your left brain, who in turn runs it through its specialties of language and numbers to give it an acceptable form that can be authored and hence communicated by you to the world.

The "non-being" is the raw idea in its sensory form that is impossible to communicate. It is the feeling. It is the hunch, the essence. It is an inner truth, but it is not proof. The scientific logical left-brained society we live in needs proof. It needs to see this idea laid out in a structure that can be analyzed. It requires form. That is the specialty of the left brain. Like a waffle iron that transforms batter into breakfast, your left brain jumps on the insight passed to it and presses it into a solution.

What is important to understand is that the answer, the solution, the idea, does not really come from you—it comes from the void. You, as the author, do not create the solution. You receive it. But it comes only after you encounter it, focus on it, struggle with it and then let it go. Only by holding your mind open can you really hear what is being spoken to you. This requires a high level of attention, of mindfulness. But this is not to be confused with passivity or laziness, which modern society equates with stillness. This is a mind-set of patient expectancy, of attentive reflection.

THE UNIVERSE DARES YOU TO BE CREATIVE

A famous quote from Seneca is: "It is not because things are difficult that we do not dare; it is because we do not dare that they are difficult." The universe DAREs you to be creative. It was a dare offered up to you on the day you were born. Embrace the four actions represented by the letters DARE as you progress through the four stages of creativity.

In stage one, as the info-seeker in fall, you **D**esire to find a solution. In stage two, as the Daydreamer in winter, you **A**sk your unconscious to find a solution through your deeper wisdom. In stage three, as you pass into the spring, you enjoy eureka and <u>R</u>eceive the insight through inspiration. Finally, in stage four as the auditor and author in summer, you <u>E</u>xperience the fruits of your intuition.

This multi-level approach to the creativity process can be viewed both sequentially and holistically in the following diagram.

STAGE	SEASON	ROLE PLAYING	CHARACTER TRAIT
1	fall	<u>I</u>nfo-Seeker	<u>D</u>esire
2	winter	<u>D</u>aydreamer	<u>A</u>ccepting
3	spring	<u>E</u>ureka Experience	<u>R</u>eceive
4	summer	<u>A</u>uditor/Author	<u>E</u>xperience
		IDEA	DARE

Creativity Workshop

121

We often hear the expression to dare to dream. But to succeed you need to do more. You need to grab hold of that dream and shake it like an apple tree to break the ideas loose. By using the left and right halves of your brain, you'll be able to generate new ideas and formulate a plan of action for those ideas as you pass through each of the four stages in the creativity process. The purpose of these four stages is to get you to another level where you can see things from a new perspective. From here you can see not only one solution, but many. This is not to say that the process is always a smooth one. By its very nature, it forces you through a drama of conflict and resolution to reach a solution.

The benefit of practicing everyday creativity is that it evolves from a process used to solve problems into an everyday mind-set. Problems become opportunities to express your creative powers. You discover a more active role in the events that shape your life. And life becomes more exciting and fun.

Breathing:
How to Take in the Energy
in Your Environment

"As we breath in, we know we are breathing in,
and as we breathe out, we know we are breathing out.
As we do this, we observe many elements of happiness
inside us and around us. We can really enjoy touching
our breathing and our being alive."
— Zen Master Thich Nhat Hanh

You cannot live more than a few minutes without taking in oxygen. And one-third of the oxygen you take in goes to your brain. Evidence suggests that the more oxygen the brain receives, the better it functions. And here's why: oxygen engages areas of the brain that are usually inactive from lack of blood and in so doing it retards the continual dying of brain cells—which die at the rate of 35,000 per day for a person over 30 years of age.

Working on the assumption that the deeper the breathing, the higher performance of the brain, psychiatrist Stanislav Grof began exploring the effects of deep and continuous breathing in the 1950s. He found that it produced psychedelic effects of spiritual experiences. Further research in the next two decades lead him to develop Grof Breathing or Holotropic Breathworks (holos meaning "whole" and trepein meaning "moving towards wholeness"). While modern medicine looked upon this as hyperventilation (and something to be avoided), Grof's experiments showed that hyperventilation was only a transient stage. What followed this stage was a feeling of expanded consciousness, euphoria, illumination and life-transforming experiences.

While Grof's Breathing may be a powerful method to bring more oxygen into the brain (and enter an altered state) it is not advisable to do this without an experienced Grof Breather. Another way to get more oxygen flowing to the brain is to do what Dr. Yoshiro NakaMats (the "Thomas Edison of Japan") does—dive deeply into the water and swim underwater for as long as you can.

NakaMats claims this method has given him the ideas for many of his 2,356 patents—including the floppy disk, the hard disk and the digital watch. And scientific research tells us why. Underwater swimming reenacts what scientists refer to as the "diving response," where our bodies interpret the increase in the level of carbon dioxide in the blood as a sign that our oxygen has been cut off. In response to this survival threat, the arteries that carry blood to our head open wide, flooding it with oxygen in the process. This response is what enables people (children in particular) to survive after being trapped underwater for far longer than anyone could hold their breath. And in the case of NakaMats, it is the response that delivers him the ideal brainstorming session.

But there's more. Breathing is not just a physiological process, it represents the vital energy of your spirit. Through breathing you not only take in vital oxygen for your body, you connect yourself with the world around you through an invisible energy force called "prana" by the Yogic traditions. Prana is the cosmic energy that enters the body through breath. Similar to the idea of qi or "chi" in China, prana is the life force that brings vitality to the body and sends healing energy to your vital organs. The practice of yoga teaches how to store and control this energy force.

Even Western scientists see the exchange of energy in breathing. They correlate the levels of oxygen in the brain to the hormone serotonin, which allows you to be alert. To breathe deeply brings in more energy to help clear the mind, thus making your brain more alert. By controlling your breathing rate you regulate the level of serotonin. That is why you take a deep breath to calm yourself to avoid an angry temper or to let go of nervousness before giving a speech. Breathing puts you into a more heightened state of awareness, where you are inspired (literally "breathe in") with ideas.

EXPERIENCE A NEW DIMENSION OF BREATHING

Because breathing is an automatic response, we don't think about how to do it. But here are three methods of controlling your breath that will give you immediate results to a situation you are facing.

• **Deep breathing.** To release yourself from tension, use slow, deep breathing. To do this, breath in slowly for a count of 10, being sure to fill your abdomen and your lungs from the bottom up. Then release the air (again to a count of 10). Deep breathing promotes Alpha brainwaves and relaxes your body and mind. The key is to hold your breath momentarily between breaths. It is the opposite of shallow chest breathing (where the rib cage only expands and contracts) which is associated with the fight-or-flight response where the nervous system is in a state of aroused anxiety.

• **The White Cloud.** Derived from the ancient Chinese practice of Qigong, in this technique you visualize (see **Visualization**) the air entering your nostrils as the energy of life in the form of a pure white light. As you inhale, you visualize the light flowing through your nasal passages, into your abdomen and on down to the base of your spine. Once there, the white light enters your spine (as if your spine were a tunnel) and moves upward through your spine into your head to circulate through your brain. You then exhale through your mouth. As you do, visualize the white light as appearing as a somewhat "polluted cloud" carrying away the toxins from your system. Repeat three to five times.

• **Breathing through alternate nostrils.** To help yourself come up with a solution to a problem, try this interesting and easy technique. According to the Chinese, the nostril you normally breathe through indicates which side of your brain is dominant. To achieve whole brain thinking, hold one nostril closed, breath in holding your breath for five seconds and then breathe out through the other nostril. Do this for ten minutes, with your eye closed and notice the calming effect as you slow your brainwaves from Beta to Alpha.

Breathing

125

Channeling:
Becoming a Conduit for
Breakthrough Insights

"Any creative endeavor is channeled,
whether it be music or art or theoretical science.
We have the capacity to tune into energies
and to convert them into reality for ourselves."
— Frank Alper

To channel your creativity means to simply bring it forth. Like a river that acts as a channel for water, your role is not to be the water, but to be the conduit that delivers it. It requires that you be open. Open to spontaneity. Open and trusting to your first thoughts and images. This idea asks nothing of you but to suspend disbelief and surrender your ego. In other words, get out of your own way.

As a conduit for your creativity, you are really acting as a facilitator doing a brainstorming session. Imagine yourself as simply the organizer of the event. Your job is not to create but to record the ideas. And as a facilitator you are never allowed to pass judgment. The benefit here is that your role as a facilitator eliminates your fear. It does so because you are not attached to the outcome—you're simply recording it. And by eliminating your fear you are free to create beyond the boundaries of your internal critic.

The point is that it's okay to not know. In fact, it is a requirement. (see **Void**) Why? Because if you knew the answer, there would be no need to create. By acting as a conduit you are freeing yourself to disengage your rational, linear left brain and tap into your intuitive, holistic right brain. The benefit here is that you replace the action of control with the action of play and in that mode you tap into your inner child (see **Growing Down**) and a larger dimension of energy.

Your role as a conduit is to be a receiver rather than a doer. That doesn't mean you don't care or are disinterested. Without care there is no feeling. And without feeling there is no connection between you and what you create. Feeling is the thread that links you to your creation. It is the conduit through which your energy passes.

All too often creativity is judged by the end result—the product—rather than the process. Feeling threatened about "not being creative," we try to reassure ourselves that we are creative by making an object that others admire. But rather than external praise, what we really are searching for is a sense of internal aliveness, of deep connection with the mystery of our lives. By focusing on process you lose any insecurities you have about being creative. You are able to give up attachment (and your fear) to the outcome, or the end product. This frees your creativity, turning off the voice of your critic.

EXPERIENCE A NEW SENSE OF CREATIVITY— THROUGH PROCESS

To enjoy the creativity process means to silence your internal critic. This exercise lets you do that by letting it know (before you even begin) that you are going to return this project to the earth when you are done. Because your critic won't attach itself to something that is going to be thrown away, this disengages it's power and lets you tend to the process.

In this fun exercise you are going to create a personal shield for yourself. Resembling a family crest emblem, your shield will contain words and symbols that describe the good characteristics you see in yourself. Before you begin, please gather markers or colored pencils and one sheet of 8-1/2" x 11" paper. Then follow these simple steps:

- Draw the outline of a shield onto the paper.
- Starting at the top middle, write your name vertically down the shield.
- Next to each letter, write the words "is for" followed by a personal characteristic of yours that begins with that letter (i.e. if the name was CHERYL the first line could be "C is for Cheerful.")
- After you have written one characteristic for every letter in your name, decorate your shield by drawing symbols, lines, shapes, or pictures.
- When you are finished decorating your shield, hold it in your hands and read it out loud to yourself. Thank yourself for the compliments.
- The final step is to burn the shield in a fireplace. As it burns, read the shield from memory. When nothing is left but ashes say "I know all this to be true".

Dream Workshop: Unlocking the Power of Your Fleeting Visions

"The dream is a small hidden door in the
deepest and most intimate sanctum of the
soul, which opens into that primeval
cosmic night that was soul long before
there was a conscious ego and will be soul
far beyond what a conscious ego could ever reach."
— Carl Jung

Humans need to sleep—so much so that fully one third of our lives are spent sleeping. Like food, air, and water, sleep is a necessary ingredient to health. When you sleep, only your conscious mind is resting. The unconscious never sleeps.

Much healing and growth takes place during sleep, as evidenced by the amount of time newborns and those recovering from illness spend sleeping. These activities are slowed during your waking hours because your waking conscious mind consumes a lot of energy. When you are asleep, however, there is no "noise" or interference from your conscious mind. Therefore your energy is freed to attend to the needs of the unconscious.

SLEEP DEPRIVATION

The ill effects of sleep deprivation are well documented. And they escalate as a lack of sleep builds up—from irritability to disorientation to bizarre behavior and death. Anecdotal evidence purports that a favorite torture of the ancient Chinese was to keep their victims awake until they went mad and died. The Spanish Inquisition had their own version of this, called "Tortura insomnia," which again allegedly ended in death.

Scientific studies support these horror tales with solid research. Experiments done on rabbits, cats, and dogs show that most animals die if kept awake for a period of four to 14 days. Before death sets in there are behavioral disturbances—restlessness, irritability, over-eating or under-eating and fearfulness.

Human subjects who have volunteered in sleep deprivation experiments have shown that any period of sleeplessness lasting more than four days results in hallucinations (dreaming while awake) and pre-psychotic behavior. In fact it's hard to keep people from taking cat-naps and those brief snatches of microsleep lasting as little as 10 or 15 seconds.

TO SLEEP—PERCHANCE TO DREAM

Not only do humans need to sleep, they need to dream. While much of the sleep period is dominated by rhythmic, slow electrical patterns, scientific experiments have concluded that between a fifth and a quarter of our total-sleep-time is spent in what is known as REM sleep—rapid eye movement.

This REM cycle occurs in bursts approximately every 90 minutes throughout any sleep period. During these periods the body is exceptionally relaxed, while the right brain is much more active, experiencing high-voltage, imagery stimulation.

It is during these REM periods that dreaming occurs. People wakened during REM phases have the highest ability to recall their dreams. And more importantly, people wakened during REM cycles repeatedly throughout the night don't function well the next day.

In a study contrasting the differences between those woken up during REM periods and those woken up during non-REM periods, the research showed that the group who had not been allowed to experience REM sleep (and thus not allowed to dream) began to show signs of severe psychological stress. Those that had been deprived of non-REM sleep, however, were just irritable. In addition, in the nights following the experiment in which the volunteers were allowed to sleep undisturbed, it was noted that those who had not been allowed to have REM sleep spent significantly more time in the REM phase than the average person—the increase being particularly high on the first night following the experiment.

The conclusion from these and many other experiments like them is that dreaming is vital to our health. But for what purpose?

The Native Americans believe dreams are a dress rehearsal for life. The Australian Aborigines, for the past 40,000 years, have taken walkabouts (see **Walkabout**) in the timeless Dreamtime dimension to alter their future by the way they dream "back" to it. Then there's the viewpoint of Segmund Freud, (who called dreams the "royal road" to unconsciousness) proclaiming that dreams are the fulfillment of "repressed wishes" that remain in your unconscious.

Yet another theory is presented in the book *Landscapes of the Night*. Written by Christopher Evans (an experimental psychologist-computer scientist—author and world authority on microprocessors), the book intriguingly uses the analogy between the brain and the computer. Substantiated with laboratory findings, Evans speculates that "dreams are remembered fragments of the brain's nocturnal data processing—those frenetically busy periods when, 'off-line', the mind is assimilating the day's experiences and using them to update its programs." These programs represent instructions for social survival that enable us to stay mentally and emotionally well-adjusted to play the many roles we lead. Like a computer, the brain uses experience (from the day's activities) as its input. But unlike a computer, it updates its programs automatically, modifying them based on experience to output a new program of behavior for the next day.

Dream Workshop

131

THE UNCANNY WISDOM OF DREAMS

Whatever the role that dreams serve in connecting our interior world to the outer reality, researchers agree that the power of dreams lies in their ability to access our unconscious—the vast reservoir of knowledge that connects us to our own inner wisdom and the knowledge of man since he first appeared on the Earth (see **Intuition**). To support this claim, history offers many stories of remarkable solutions to scientific challenges, creative breakthroughs, and uncanny predictions that come to people as they sleep.

A SAVAGE TALE OF SUCCESS

Elias Howe, inventor of the sewing machine, was given the missing information he needed as he slept to turn his worthless heap of wheels and gears into one of the most profitable inventions of all time—the sewing machine. Only his information didn't come through a dream. It came in a nightmare.

Howe was well on his way to completing his invention when he hit a snag—the placement of the eye in the machine's needle. At first he pierced the eye in the middle of the needle. But this resulted in stitches that were irregular. He tried other designs. But no matter how he positioned the eye, it did not produce a stitch as sturdy as a hand stitch. There didn't seem to be a solution to solve this problem. And without a workable solution, his invention would never make it to market.

Then one night he dreamed of being kidnapped by savages who were going to kill him. The only way he could save his life was to invent a sewing machine in the next twenty-four hours. In his dream he failed. And as he was led to his execution, the spears of the savages came down upon him. In his last moments of life Howe saw the eye-shaped holes close to the tips. Eureka! That was the missing answer he needed. Upon waking, Howe immediately went into his workshop and fashioned a needle with the eye at the tip. The result was a good lock stitch—250 a minute—which was far faster than any seamstress could produce. His dream provided the answer that he needed.

SNAKES DANCING BEFORE THE FIRE

The discovery of the molecular structure of benzene (whose liquid form is used in dyes and solvents) came to the German chemist Friedrch August Kekule in a dream, which Arthur Koestler (in *The Act of Creation*) credits as "probably the most important dream in history since Joseph's seven fat and seven lean cows." (see following in *Portal to the Future*.)

Benzene is a chain of six carbon atoms. But for many years chemists were unable to visualize how these atoms might lock together. Then one night Kekule cracked the code as he sat by the fire. He intuited that carbon compounds, like benzene, were not open structures, but closed chains or rings. With this insight of Kekule's came a revolution in the field of carbon-based (or organic) chemistry.

At a dinner commemorating his discovery he explained how he came upon his discovery: "I turned my chair to the fire (after having worked on the problem for some time) and dozed. Again the atoms were gamboling before my eyes. This time the smaller groups kept modestly to the background. My mental eye, rendered more acute by repeated visions of this kind, could not distinguish larger structures, of manifold conformation; long rows, sometimes more closely fitted together; all twining and twisting in snakelike motion. But look! What was that? One of the snakes had seized hold if its own tail, and the form whirled mockingly before my eyes. As if by a flash of lightning I awoke. I spent the rest of the night working out the consequences. Let us learn to dream, gentlemen, and then perhaps we will discover the truth."

MIDNIGHT TERROR WRITES WAKING TALES OF HORROR

As a child, Robert Lewis Stevenson woke up night after night screaming in terror from the nightmares that haunted him. Even as an adult these terrifying experiences would torment him at times, leaving him with "a flying heart, a freezing scalp, cold sweats, and the speechless midnight fear."

Dream Workshop

133

But for Stevenson, these nightmares turned into a profitable future. In an essay called *"A Chapter on Dreams,"* Stevenson invites the reader into his mind to meet his "Brownies"—the little people that, night after night, acted out the entertaining stories and intriguing dramas that he wrote about upon waking. At the end of this dreams essay, Stevenson credits the Brownies for the creativity of his stories, while saying his role in bringing them to print was to act as an editor to tighten up the story and smooth the details: "And for the Little People, what shall I say, they are but just my Brownies, God bless them! Who do one-half of my work for me while I am fast asleep...I am an excellent advisor; I pull back and I cut down; and I dress the whole in the best words and sentences that I can find and make. I hold the pen, too...On the whole, I have some claim to share, though not so largely as I do, in the profits of our common enterprise."

One of Stevenson's most well-known stories is *The Strange Case of Dr. Jekyll and Mr. Hyde*. Read what Stevenson says about the role of the Brownies in creating this master tale: "I had long been trying to write a story on this subject, to find a body, a vehicle, for that strong sense of man's double being, which must at times come in upon and overwhelm the mind of every thinking creature...For two days I went about racking my brains for a plot of any sort; and on the second night I dreamed the scene at the window, and a scene afterward chopped in two, in which Hyde, pursued for some crime, took the powder and underwent the change in the presence of his pursuers. All the rest was made awake and consciously, although I think I can trace in much of the manner of my Brownies."

In fact, so trusting of Stevenson in his Brownies that he would request them to give him profitable tales as he slept. In the book *The Power of Your Subconscious Mind*, author Dr. Joseph Murphy writes that Stevenson "had the persistent habit of giving specific instructions to his subconscious every night prior to sleep. He would request his unconscious to evolve stories for him while he slept. For example, if Stevenson's funds were at a low ebb, his command to his subconscious would be something like this: 'Give me a good thrilling novel which will be marketable and profitable.'"

A PORTAL INTO THE FUTURE

In addition to providing creative breakthroughs, dreams also can forecast the future. One of the earliest recorded dreams prophesying the future comes from the Bible. In this story, a pharaoh dreams of seven lean cows following seven fat cows. Unsure of what the dream is telling him, he goes to Joseph who interprets the dream as an upcoming famine. Accordingly, Joseph advises the pharaoh to store grain during the next seven years to avert famine in the subsequent seven. It was a strategy that saved Egypt from crop failure.

Not all dreams that predict the future are good visions. Such was the case of Abraham Lincoln who dreamed that he was awakened in the night and upon wandering downstairs in the White House found civilians and military guards surrounding a corpse. When he asked who had died, the response came "The President. He was killed by an assassin."

DREAMS AS PROPHETIC RIDDLES TO YOUR PERSONAL MYTH

So far, all the dreams retold here have been easy to decipher. Others require interpretation. In the book *The Courage to Create*, Rollo May said the value of dreams is not that they give a specific answer, but that they "open up new areas of psychic reality, shake us out of our customary ruts, throw light on a new segment of our lives." He likened them to the prophetic riddles given to the Greeks through the shrine of Apollo at Delphi. Often verbalized in poetry or wild vague riddles, these foretellings needed to be worked over to understand their meaning.

May writes, "like mediumistic statements of all ages, they were sufficiently cryptic not only to leave the way open for interpretation, but to require it. And often they were susceptible to two or many different interpretations. As in the case of many dreams, the sayings of the shrine were not to be received passively, but rather, the recipients had to 'live' themselves into the message."

As May suggests, dreams (like the divinations received at Delphi) are stimulants to look inside and seek counsel from your own intuition and wisdom. The dream merely restates the problem in a different way so that you can see it from a new perspective and with that perspective imagine new solutions.

Dream Workshop

In this way, dreams are like symbols or your own personal myths that invite your participation. The more you become involved, the more meaning, richness and interest unfolds as you wonder about and ponder on the dream. Again, quoting May, "a symbol or myth acts like a projective screen in drawing out the insight. Like Rorschach cards [showing splotches of black ink in no definite form] the oracle and its ceremonies are a screen that stimulates wonder and calls imagination into action."

135

This screen is not a blank mirror, but like the Zen koan, (see **Zen**) or a void of a white wall (see **Void**), it works to still your logical thinking mind, to lull it with its paradoxes and let you reach a deeper sense of knowing. It acts like the blank canvas to bring out the artist, or the silence that brings out the musician, or a blank sheet of paper to bring out the poet. As May writes, "The artist, the poet, and the musician dare to bring forth new forms, new kinds of vitality and meaning. They are, at least partially, protected from 'going crazy' in this process of radical emergence by the form given by the media— namely the paints, the marble, the words, the musical notes." (see **Channeling Creativity**).

Your dreams are your canvas. You use them as a tool to draw forth that which is you, to awaken new possibilities from a level of experience that is below your waking consciousness. Plato calls this process "the ecstasy of prophetic madness" which allows you to transcend your everyday existence and bring forth the life that is authentic to you. Dreams are a how-to for arriving at insights you would never otherwise feel or see. And, just as with the artist, the poet, and the musician who rely on their medium as a form to keep them from going crazy, dreams are the form that keep you sane.

Carl Jung believed the purpose of the dream was to make the person "whole" rather than "perfect." This idea of being whole meant to develop every aspect of the mind, every potential faculty of the mind, and using all the senses to their utmost—but never one at the expense of another. The dream was to ensure survival of the whole person by restoring a balance between the different aspects of personality so that they would enhance and not overcome.

While scientists will undoubtedly continue to research dreams and formulate new theories as to their guiding purpose, there is one point on which everyone agrees. Dreams are raw energy, being composed of the most primitive power we possess—visual images and emotions. And it is in this that we find their value. They are blatantly honest and downright embarrassing. They reveal true inner nature and actions that you would never "dream of" doing in public.

CRACKING THE CODE OF YOUR DREAMS

The question still remains, though, as how to interpret dreams. While earlier you learned that Freud believed you can view dreams as ways to fulfill your "repressed wishes," Carl Jung did not believe in generic formulas to interpret dreams by identifying the symbols and assigning a meaning to each one. Although a proponent of symbolism (Jung's groundbreaking book *Man and His Symbols* came about because of a dream in which he saw himself talking to the general public rather than to physicians), Jung remarked to his students to "learn as much as you can about symbols and then forget it when you analyze a dream." Why? Because as he contended, "No dream symbol can be separated from the individual who dreams it, and there is no definite or straight forward interpretation of any dream."

However, Jung also believed that the dreamer's individuality, intelligence and his own intuition were enough to interpret his own dreams. This is the reclaiming of your knowing when you suddenly get the idea behind the myth or the symbol. Again, in the words of Rollo May, "an element of ecstasy, however slight, is part and parcel of every genuine symbol and myth; for if we genuinely participate in the symbol or myth we are for that moment taken 'out of' and 'beyond' ourselves."

Is that not what a dream does—take you "out of" and "beyond" yourself? May calls this dreaming "a passion for form." A form that allows people the space to safely struggle with their world—to make sense out of nonsense, meaning out of chaos, coherence out of conflict. Through the medium of their imagination and the form of the dream they are creating new constructs and new relationships in their world in which they can survive with some meaning.

The universal truth for all dreamers of all ages in all cultures around the world, then, seems to actually come to the same conclusion: we are all dreaming for social survival. From the Aborigines creating their future, to the Native Americans participating in dress rehearsals for life, to the computer analogy of Christopher Evans, to Stevenson taking direction from his Brownies, it all circles back to the basic fundamental thought that the dream is a stage for our dramas. And, again, repeating the words of Kekule: "Let us learn to dream, and then perhaps we will discover the truth."

Dream Workshop

137

EXERCISE: CALLING FORTH THE POWER OF YOUR DREAMS

Just as the Greeks asked counsel from Apollo at the shrine of Delphi, you can ask your dreams for solutions to the challenges in your life. As you dream, you are in direct communication with your unconscious. By listening to your dreams you can enhance your emotional and intellectual performance during the day. The necessary intervening step is to remember your dreams and get them down on paper before they escape you forever. This exercise will show you how.

To begin with, keep a journal (see **Journaling**) by your bed so that you do not need to get out of bed to reach it in the morning. Then, before going to sleep, you might want to experiment with your *Super Intelligence* soundtrack. Its soothing audio matrix will unfold an Alpha-Theta state and stimulate REM activity. Imbedded in the soundtrack are affirmations to help liberate your creative visions.

In addition, try reading aloud the affirmations written below before you go to sleep.
I am able to recall my dreams.
My dreams reveal to me the solution I need.
My dreams give me a new source of direction.

My infinite intelligence guides me.
I am the answer.
I remember.
I feel love.
My dreams show me the way.
I am one with the universe.

As you use your soundtrack, or after reading these affirmations to yourself a few minutes before falling asleep at night, think about a problem that is puzzling you—for example, how to resolve a relationship, whether or not to find a new job, should you put the money into fixing up your car or buying a new one? Approach the problem in an open-ended way. You don't need to articulate it clearly. Just the mere suggestion of a question will be enough to engage the power of your unconscious mind and provide you with an answer through your dreams.

During your dream, interact with your dream Brownies. Ask them questions—why is this happening, what does this mean, what if I go about it in another way? Listen to their answers and ponder what they say. Like Apollo, they may not give you a straight answer. That is okay. By becoming involved with their response you will find the answer that is right for you.

When you wake up, try to stay in the dream state. Wake up gently. Use a soft light. Move as little as possible. Breathe deep and close your eyes to re-enter your dream. Then, opening your eyes, write as much of your dream as you can remember. In this phase, do not judge, do not interpret. Just record all the bizarre happenings of the night. Do not leave anything out, and (no matter how embarrassing) do not change, add or delete.

After writing as many details as you can recall, put your journal aside. Wait a few hours before you look at your journal again. At that point try to put the pieces together and listen to what it is telling you. Because of the high use of visual images in dreams, your waking mind needs to get involved to decipher the meaning. One way to do this is to record your dreams again, several hours after you awake, and then compare the two accounts. You will find that your second account will contain more logic and coherence, but is less revealing.

Above all, have faith that you will interpret the dream correctly. We all can. Research has shown that under hypnosis, most people decipher meaning from their dreams without any difficulty. The images in your dream are unique to you because they come from your own experience. To help understand the images, look for clues in the associations to them. For example, what do you feel when that incident, person, or event appeared in your dream? To do this, try to re-enter the dream state and become relaxed, opening your mind to all possible thoughts, connections and links. Using your emotions and intuition will help unravel the images and come to their meaning.

YOUR DREAM MINI-SERIES

More fascinating than any television program, your own nightly dramas will reveal even more to you if you interpret them in groups rather than as individual episodes. Often one will give you insights to another. And too, you may find that a dream will be recurring over months, or even years. Once you start interpreting your dreams, the images you come to understand can be used over and over again.

In fact, Carl Jung saw a definite structure (very much like a drama) in the context of many dreams. He used the following four phase process to help in analyzing dreams. Using this as a template will make your dreams easier to interpret.

PHASE I—scene of action, people involved, initial situation of the dreamer
- Statement of place. *I was at the coffee shop.*
- Statement about the protagonist. *My friend was listening to me as I told my story of how I got fired.*

PHASE II
- Development of plot—situation is becoming complicated and a definite tension develops because the dreamer does not know what will happen. *As I began to tell my sob story on how I got fired my friend poured some coffee for me.*

PHASE III
- Culmination—something decisive happens or changes completely. *As I continued complaining about my situation, my friend kept pouring coffee until it flowed out of the cup and all over the floor.*

PHASE IV
- Solution—result "sought" by the dreamer. *Suddenly I stopped telling my story and yelled at my friend—"Stop, you're spilling the coffee all over." Her reply was that she would stop pouring the coffee when I would stop spilling my guts all over and, instead, take action to find a new job.*

The best way to approach your dream analysis is as did Carl Jung, with the least expectations as possible. When asked what a dream meant, Jung would first say to himself, "I have no idea what this dream means." Only then would he begin to examine the dream. As he wrote in his essay *"On the Nature of Dreams"* Jung says to "admit your ignorance, and renouncing all preconceived ideas, be prepared for something entirely unexpected."

Emotional IQ:
A New Way to Be Smart

"If you want to draw a bird, you must become a bird."
— Hokusai

Howard Gardner, a professor of neurology at Boston University School of Medicine, was the first to define intelligence as "the ability to solve problems, or to create products that are valued within one or more cultural settings."

In his groundbreaking book *Frames of Mind*, he substantiated the existence of seven separate intelligences: linguistic (word smart), mathematical (logic smart), musical, spatial (art smart), kinesthetic (body smart), interpersonal (people smart) and intrapersonal (self smart). Hailed by educators throughout the world and applied in schools across the nation, this theory of multiple intelligences has challenged the value of traditional IQ tests, while giving new meaning to being smart.

In particular, it has spurred new thinking in the last two intelligences, which grouped together are called the personal intelligences. The subject of the popular book *Emotional Intelligence* written by Daniel Goleman in 1995, your emotional IQ includes your self-awareness and impulse control, persistence, zeal and self-motivation, empathy and social deftness.

Without these qualities, educators and psychologists predict you will have a difficult time making a living in today's society—even with outstanding educational credentials. The reasons are clear. Fast-growing companies need people who can manage and lead others to excellence. And corporations need team players that can orchestrate a product from design to implementation (where most products fail) and then onto market in record time.

For as we move from the information age to the age of services (often working in virtual offices around the world where people need to communicate across miles and cultural barriers) the challenge is to meet the service needs of the customer and not just create new products. This means value-added services that sell one product over another through a "relationship approach." To understand this takes a new kind of knowing. It takes emotional intelligence.

In her book *Clicking*, trend forecaster Faith Popcorn calls this "FemaleThink." But she's quick to add you don't need to be a woman to have this skill. Popcorn writes, "You just have to be awake, aware of the differences, and learn how to handle people in different ways." She says it's the kind of thinking that will change the world. And she explains why by describing what FemaleThink is not—not working through hierarchy (but using teamwork); not needing to know the right answers (but wants to ask the right questions); not single-minded (but multi-minded); not goal driven (but process aware); not to a destination (but on a journey); not transaction-oriented (but relationship oriented) not resists change (but seeks change). While these are all right brain specialties, it's the last one that's important.

Part II

Mind Development Tools

142

We all know society is changing faster than ever before. With that comes new careers. It is estimated that people entering the job market today will change careers (not just jobs) at least five times before they retire. And that takes a new mind-set that is not only open to change but also creative in applying old skills to new requirements.

As it relates to creativity, several of the emotional IQ characteristics named above are important, including persistence, zeal and self-motivation. It was Albert Einstein who said that "Creativity is 1% inspiration and 99% perspiration." While the creative process does involve inspiration, the rewards come as a result of focused work disciplined by persistence, zeal, and self-motivation.

Again, from the book *Emotional Intelligence*, comes this ability to motivate oneself: "Marshaling emotions in the service of a goal is essential for paying attention, for self-motivation and mastery, and for creativity. And being able to get into the 'flow' state enables outstanding performance of all kinds. People who have this skill tend to be highly productive and effective in whatever they undertake." (see **Flow**)

As it relates to whole brain thinking, your emotional IQ resides primarily in your right brain. It's the domain of relationships and connectivity. This is where your feeling for empathy resides. To be creative means to transcend yourself and become that which you are focusing on. The more empathy you have, the easier it is for you to make this transition. And for those who do, the future is wide open.

EXPERIENCE THE EMOTIONAL IQ TEST: ARE YOU READY FOR KINDERGARTEN?

A report from the National Center for Clinical Infant Programs stated that readiness for school is determined more by emotional and social standards, rather than traditional intelligence. Almost all students who do poorly in school, says the report, lack one or more of the following seven key ingredients, all of which are related to emotional intelligence. Read them and see how well you score!

1. Confidence. A sense of control and master of one's body, behavior, and world; the child's sense that he is more likely than not to succeed at what he undertakes, and that adults will be helpful.

2. Curiosity. The sense that finding out about things is positive and leads to pleasure.

3. Intentionality. The wish and capacity to have an impact, and to act upon that with persistence. This is related to a sense of competence, of being effective.

4. Self-control. The ability to modulate and control one's own actions in age-appropriate ways: a sense of inner control.

5. Relatedness. The ability to engage with others based on the sense of being understood by and understanding others.

6. Capacity to communicate. The wish and ability to verbally exchange ideas, feelings, and concepts with others. This is related to a sense of trust in others and of pleasure in engaging with others, including adults.

7. Cooperativeness. The ability to balance one's own needs with those of others in group activity.

Emotional IQ

143

Flow:
Your Connection
to the Universe

"No longer conscious of my movement,
I discovered a new unity with nature.
I had found a new source of power and
beauty, a source I never dreamt existed."
— Roger Bannister on breaking
the four-minute mile.

In the natural world, flow is easy to see. A river flowing to the sea. The flow of blood through the bloodstream. Qualities associated with flow are many. Movement. Energy. A natural force. Continuous. Easy. A recycling force that allows the energy to be used again and again. Yet an invisible force.

And taking a broader view, for what purpose does each flow? The river flows to give life to the fish, animals and plants. It flows to irrigate the land. Blood, too, flows to bring nourishment and oxygen to the rest of the body. Each then flows to support a surrounding community. By its action it unfolds its environment. In performing its role it is part of a larger whole. Through this action the environment attains its potential—fish, animals and fauna flourish. Your body grows strong and resists disease.

In your life, flow acts the same way. It is an easy, natural force that keeps you moving ahead so your life can unfold in a way that allows you to reach your potential. Yet it too is invisible. You can't see it. You can't touch it. You can't control it.

It is natural—like the flow of blood through your body, it just happens. Like the flow of a river, it is easy. The difference is it is occurring outside of you and connecting you to a larger whole. Through its energy you move in harmony with the people and events in your life.

In a state of flow you are alert but relaxed, focused but open to possibilities. You are connected to the moment. In his national bestseller *Flow*, Mihaly Csikszentmihalyi defined flow as "an optimal experience, a state of concentration so focused that it amounts to absolute absorption in an activity."

He goes on to say that flow happens most notably when a person's body or mind is stretched to its limits in a voluntary effort to accomplish something difficult or worthwhile. The task is neither too easy or too hard. If it's too easy, the person gets bored. If it's too difficult, the person becomes frustrated. This frustration results in noise that interferes with the person's focus and begins a negative internal dialogue of defeat.

People in flow are completely absorbed in what they are doing. They lose track of time. Everything around them fades into the background as they become intent solely on the work they are performing in that moment.

You probably already know the feeling. When you are "in the flow" you feel as though everything is going right for you. Obstacles melt away. Things fall into place. You are moving ahead with full speed. Favorable happenings and coincidences abound (see **Synchronicity**). But even better, you feel a connection with what you are doing.

At these times there is more meaning to your life because you are moving toward your uniqueness, while at the same time you are feeling part of a greater force. This is known as the process of differentiation and integration. It allows you to grow by becoming united with other people, while you are authentic to you. You feel more together. And you have an intuitive sense that you're not alone.

You feel exhilarated and filled with a great sense of joy, totally involved with life in the moment. You reclaim a sense of involvement with what you're doing.

Flow is a state of mind that is harmoniously ordered not only within you but with the larger pattern of the universe. Whatever you are doing in flow is your authentic pattern that aligns you with your purpose and so gives you greater meaning. Like the river that unfolds the potential of the land as it flows to the sea, so you nourish those around you by being true to your inner pattern as you play your part in life.

The universe is a flowing web of consciousness in which everything is connected. By aligning ourselves with our own underlying patterns, we come into harmony with our environment. As Zen (see **Zen**) tells us "Let your nature blend with the Way and wander in it into harmony free from care."

EXPERIENCE YOUR PERSONAL FLOW ENVIRONMENT

Activities that produce flow vary from person to person. While one person may feel in flow when reading or painting, another person would feel bored. It's all a personal choice.

Flow

What are your flow activities? For the next week, try keeping a record of when you felt in flow during your daily actions. Use a chart similar to the one below. Set your watch alarm to beep once every two or three hours. When it does, make entries on the chart as to your activity and your frame of mind.

147

At the end of the week take the time to review your chart. Highlight the flow producing activities. Once you know what works for you, make a point to set aside time for these activities each week.

Day/Date	Time	Activity	Level of Flow (low/medium/high)

Growing Down:
Understanding by Unlearning

"Every child is an artist. The problem is
how to remain an artist once he grows up."
— Picasso

To grow down means to let go of expectations. To live in the
moment, guided by your own inner visions and feelings. And, to
boldly say "ME FIRST!" Living a life that's more authentic to you,
instead of making someone else's dreams come true.

Artists don't care much for rules. They are guided by their inner
visions. Like a child dumping a whole bucket of blocks onto the floor
(instead of taking them neatly out one by one) artists feel at home
surrounded by chaos. A child has yet to learn the limit imposed by
routines and schedules that control adults. While a schedules can be
effective in the adult world for meeting deadlines and accomplishing
tasks, it has the negative effect of putting your mind on auto pilot,
which in turn dulls the senses. Without the pressures of deadlines
and expectations, children and artists are free to play.

Growing down is reclaiming the energy of play by relying on
your senses not your intellect. For example, take an orange. You see
its roundness. You feel its dimpled texture. You smell its pungent
aroma. And you taste the intense flavor in your mouth. This is an
experience of direct knowing, as opposed to learning with your
intellect which depends on words to convey meaning. Direct
knowing has a simple intelligence that is instinctual.

A child's world is not ruled by the logical left brain. And because
this is the domain of our critical voice, children are free to create
without fear of failing. Like artists, children are free-wheeling and
creative, who love to play with forms, shapes, colors and think in
patterns. In this state of mind they are adept at making new
connections, bringing together different ideas to create new
meaning. They are directly involved in learning, creating knowledge
from play rather than through intellect.

By growing down you can reclaim that part of you that is absorbed by and enjoys life moment to moment. You will be more involved with the moment because your senses will become more acute. The artist brain is the sensory right brain. It is the brain you used as a child when, unable to read or write or comprehend a large vocabulary, you took in information through your senses.

At that time, you were in touch with the physical world around you. The feel of wet grass under your barefeet. The magic of a butterfly floating mysteriously from flower to flower. Everything was new and amazing. This was a time when you skipped down the driveway, bounded down the stairs, and sang songs freely as you went through your day without any fear of being criticized.

As adults we have responsibilities to people other than ourselves. But to grow down means to put some balance back in your life by nurturing your spirit. In her best selling book *The Artist's Way*, author Julia Cameron suggests to make an "artist date" with yourself once a week to nurture your inner artist. During this suggested two-hour block of time you go on a field trip and fill your sensory right brain with images and feelings triggered by sight, sound, smell, taste, touch. This is the "compost material" (see **Creativity Workshop**) from which the seeds of creativity and insight can bloom.

Go to a garage sale, a second hand store, a five-and-dime or craft shop. Or get out in nature—a lonely stretch of beach, a walk through the woods or even a park in a big city. The main thing is to be alone with your inner artist, as you would spend quality time with a lonely child. The emphasis is on fun, not duty.

EXPERIENCE GROWING DOWN BY GETTING DOWN

Children play and approach learning with their whole bodies. The next time you're working on a challenging problem, don't reason it out sitting at your desk. Instead, sprawl out on the floor and assume a more playful position: prop up your elbows and support your head in your hands, bend your knees up and kick your feet up and down or completely roll over and just stare at the ceiling with your hands behind your head (see **Void**). You'll be surprised at how this body position frees up your mind to new ideas.

Humor:
A Trapeze Swinging from
the Left to Right Brain

"At the height of laughter, the universe
is flung into a kaleidoscope of new possibilities."
— Jean Houston

Whether listening to a joke or telling one, your mind needs to go through mental acrobatics. To understand the surprise of the punch line, the mind needs to get away from the typical routine of thought and operate on more than one plane of thinking. It needs to detach itself from everyday logic, to stand back and get a broader view. For only then can you see the ridiculous ironies that would otherwise be overlooked.

To spontaneously see the silliness of the situation, humor parallels the seeing of paradoxes. A true paradox represents a baffling and inexplicable situation. Like the mysterious riddles of the Sphinx, paradoxes push the mind beyond the obvious. The value in training yourself to see paradoxes associated with the challenges you face opens the mind to new possibilities. A fun way to do that is through telling jokes.

The left brain is logical, linear and concrete. The right brain is the poet. Able to create metaphors and similes, it sees the humor in two contrasting thoughts that cause a mental jolt delivered by the joke. Whether presented in a cartoon, a skit, or a one line joke, the brain needs to take a mental leap from the literal plane to the metaphorical to get the humorous meaning. If you pay attention you can actually feel the shift going on in your head.

For example, try to feel the shift in your thinking as you think of an answer to this joke: "If April showers bring May flowers, what do May flowers bring?" Give yourself a moment to think before reading on. The answer is "Pilgrims." Whether or not you solved this on your own, you probably felt the shift in your thinking as you heard the answer. And here's why.

The two contrasting statements are "May flowers" and "Mayflowers." This juxtaposition of the two creates a dynamic tension, a paradox, to the common expression "April showers bring May flowers." What exists is a chaotic scenario, one that has no logic. The answer follows the logic of the question (May flower) with a surprising answer that makes the statement true in a different plane—for the Mayflower, as a name of a ship, mirrored the language in the expression and it also met the second criteria of "bringing something." With the understanding of the punch line, reason is deserted and laughter rushes in as an emotional response.

This is a creative act. For it momentarily unites two traditionally incompatible poles. It involves original thinking in either the solving or in the understanding. To get a joke, the listener must fill in the gaps, complete the hints, mentally follow the hidden analogies. By doing so the listener is lifted out of a passive role and actively involved to some extent in the inventing of the joke as a visual (see **Visualization**) in the imagination.

EXPERIENCE A HUMOROUS JOLT EVERY HOUR

Humor acts as a whack on the side of the head to break up the grueling routine of rational thought hour after hour. It's a mental break that helps restore the balance in your brain, stimulating positive brain chemistry. And as a bonus, the laughter eases tension plus causes you to take in deep breaths of air and bring oxygen to your brain (see **Breathing**).

To capitalize on these benefits, try giving yourself a joke break every hour. It takes less than a minute. All you need is a book of jokes at your desk, or one of the popular Shel Silverstein books, such as *Falling Up*.

Imagination:
Transforming Chaos into Form

"It is the imagination that gives shape to the universe."
— Barry Lopez

To imagine is to let your mind out on a kite string and have it run freely with the wind. It is the ability of the right brain to reach out to ideas, images and feelings. It is also the ability of the left brain to hold the potential of each idea, image and feeling in attention long enough to shape it into a concrete form.

This is creating order out of chaos (see **Channeling**). Both forces are necessary—one to push out and the other to reel back in. In order to soar, your imagination needs to be let go from rigidly-held preconceived notions. Yet in order to bring meaning, it needs to have form imprinted on the vitality it feels—much like the waffle iron is needed to turn batter into waffles.

Form is a way of setting limits. The limit may be a deadline. Without deadlines would you ever finish your work? The limit may be a budget. Often projects that are the biggest successes are the ones that are underfunded. To creative people, form is actually an ally because it is a way to sift through the endless possibilities and help hone in on a most likely possibility. Like the river banks that channel the river (and without which the river would spread out across the land), the form channels the spontaneity and intuitiveness (see **Intuition**) of the creative person into a useful end result.

In addition to this dynamic balance of reaching out and reeling in, the ability to imagine requires the faith to leap into the unknown without fear of failure. The only hard part in using imagination is anxiety, or the fear of not being imaginative enough. It's taking a risk that something better will come out of your searching for the new. But it's a risk that comes with rewards. As Andre Gide said, "One does not discover new lands without consenting to lose sight of the shore for a very long time."

EXPANDING YOUR POWERS OF IMAGINATION

Look at the figure below. How many triangles do you see? Can you see eight? Do you also see a six pointed star? Actually there are no triangles or star in this picture. Your imagination has created them by filling in the information that is not there. Your mind sees this image as a whole, and creates the missing information. This is one of the ways the imagination works, taking bits of what is known and extending it beyond to create or reveal something new.

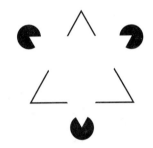

Imagination is one of those fundamental tools that becomes a foundation for everything else. It is the fountainhead of creativity. The force that drives ideas. As we get older we tend to rely more on logic and left brain activities and so the tendency is to let our powers of imagination diminish. Almost all children 12 and under when asked to close their eyes and "see" a particular object in their mind, report being able to do so. In adults that number drops to about 25%. The ability to see images in your mind is an important element in visualization, creativity and accessing right brain awareness. How can you recapture this capability? Through exercises that stretch your imaginative forces and allow you to "see" again.

Below is a simple exercise that trains you in mental imagery, giving you practice in stretching your imagination. Choose from the list below, each item one by one. Close your eyes and imagine you can picture that image in your mind with as much clarity as possible. Allow five minutes for each of these. As you'll notice each item on the list goes from the concrete to the more abstract. As you keep practicing with this list you should notice that each time you do the exercise the images get a little clearer and a little more focused. This is good. You are beginning to stretch and expand your imagination powers.

As you close your eyes repeat the entire phrase as written below, and let the image appear in your mind's eye. Look at it from as many angles as possible, adding as much sensory input as you need to flesh out the details.

- Allow me to see a red apple.
- Allow me to see a TV set.
- Allow me to see a blackboard.
- Allow me to see the see the ocean.
- Allow me to see my mailman. (this could be any person a teacher, cab driver, some neutral person you don't really know that well.)
- Allow me to see such-and-such person. (this would be someone who you do know well.)
- Allow me to see the letter Z.
- Allow me to see the letter A.
- Allow me to see someone writing each letter of the alphabet on a black board, and erasing it before writing the next one.
- Allow me to write the word C-A-T on the blackboard.
- Allow me to write the word I-M-A-G-I-N-A-T-I-O-N on the blackboard.

Imagination

155

Intuition:
Your Personal Inner Compass

"It is always with excitement that
I wake up in the morning wondering
what my intuition will toss up to me,
like gifts from the sea. I work with it
and rely on it. It's my partner."
— Jonas Salk

Often called the sixth sense, this natural but traditionally elusive power can provide you with the crucial edge in an increasingly chaotic hurry-up world where the facts that logically lead you to a decision change continuously. It's a vibration, a "feeling in your funny bone" as Ray Kroc felt when he decided to go against the advice of his expert advisers and buy McDonalds.

Intuition reveals "inner truth" to guide your daily actions with an uncanny sense of direction in an instantaneous experience that brings together many patterns of meaning. These flashes of insight, independent of logic, appear like quasars out of nowhere to leave you with a fuzzy feeling of knowing what you don't logically know. Whether you call it intuition, a hunch, or a lucky guess, there is more going on here than your logical brain can handle.

Research shows that brainwaves change when subjects are exposed to subliminal stimuli. While they are not consciously aware of the information, their intuitive mind takes the material in and creates analogies by drawing on bits and pieces from areas that are totally unrelated to the incoming material. A characteristic of exceptionally intuitive people is a high level of receptivity to this type of information. In addition, they usually have a diverse range of interests that expose them to unusual experiences, and get their information from a wide variety of sources—books, magazines, even courses that have nothing to do with their occupation.

Unlike rational thought which takes place over a logical sequence of steps or events, intuition is experience you receive all at once, suddenly and inexplicably. Sometimes it arises out of the need for a solution when you have insufficient information or too little time to gather it. Intuition lets you skip the many steps required by logic and leap to a conclusion. Like a spontaneous hunch, it feels right even in the absence of proof.

Where does intuition come from? It wells up from the unconscious. It is your connection to a vast source of knowledge and wisdom that Jung called the "collective unconscious." Like a huge library of knowledge, this level of awareness holds all the information and knowledge since man's first appearance on this Earth. Your tool to access that level is intuition.

Intuition works best when you don't have all the pieces to the problem. In fact, thinking gets in the way of intuition. You don't figure intuition out, you simply let an answer appear. Then, if you need to, you can work backwards to "prove" it with logical thinking. As Albert Einstein was quoted, "I knew the answers before I had even asked the question."

EXPERIENCE THE VOICE OF INTUITION

A primary benefit of intuition in problem solving and decision making is generating alternative choices. While the facts may lead to one solution, there is almost never just one right answer. Intuition allows you to stretch out to an innovative solution. While brainstorming is a popular way to generate alternative solutions, the following intuitive twist takes brainstorming one step further.

This method was coined "random stimuli" by Edward de Bono. First, you state the problem that you are facing. Then chose a random word or object to associate with the problem (open a page in the dictionary and without looking place your finger on a word). Next, let the chosen work trigger associations with the stated problem. These associations are allowed to connect with aspects of the problem, regardless of how remote the connection may be.

The result is a bevy of innovative ideas for solving the problem. In effect, random stimuli inserts a piece of new information that is unrelated to the problem. The rational mind can't deal with it, and this shakes up the mind creating a new structure of thought that invites the participation of your intuition. After the ideas are triggered, you then evaluate them for practical application.

Journaling Workshop:
Transforming Thoughts into Action

"So the point of my keeping a notebook
has never been, nor is it now, to have an
accurate factual record of what I have been
doing or thinking. How it felt to me: that
is getting closer to the truth about a notebook."
— Joan Didion

Every day you have thoughts, feelings, experiences, and observations. The act of writing these down is called journaling. Each page represents a cross section of your life, while the collection of pages represents your life's work in progress.

The purpose of journaling is not to keep a record of your daily activities. Rather, is it a void (see **Void**) to be filled with your emotions and feelings, both joyous and disappointing. Journaling can expose the real issues in your life. It will allow you to get in touch with the deep things that affect you. Through this writing you arrive at a deeper understanding of yourself. And this can pave the way for action and change to occur.

The two-fold challenge is to "show up" to the page (once a day) and allow yourself to write freely without being censored by your critical voice. The critical voice is your ego, your editor. It is a control freak and censors everything you write. It will try to hold you back from writing something that is impolite, embarrassing, or shocking— even to you. Yet these emotional issues are what you most need to hear on these pages. So let them flow. You can handle them safely here. If not here, then where? If not now, then when?

Plato said, "The life which is not examined is not worth living." Come and examine your life—privately, ploddingly, persistently. This is the voice of your inner needs, your long ignored complaints, your silent longings, your unfaced fears, your failures and fiascoes as well as all the successes great and small that you didn't take the time to congratulate yourself on. The reward is that through this process you will learn what you really want and ultimately be willing to make the changes needed to achieve it.

HOW TO JOURNAL

In her empowering book *The Artist's Way*, author Julia Cameron refers to the journaling process as "doing your morning pages." She suggests that this stream-of-consciousness writing be performed every morning by filling three sheets of a yellow pad with longhand writing. The purpose is simply to drain your brain.

Instead of using a yellow pad, you might enjoy using a spiral bound notebook. And instead of having a quota of pages to fill up, give yourself a time limit. Begin with ten minutes each day the first week and work up to 20 minutes a day by the third week. Depending on your time available you could increase it to 30 minutes, or even an hour. Timing your writing adds pressure to keep your hand moving. Knowing the clock is ticking is an effective motivator to keeping the words flowing. And to start your words flowing, follow these suggestions from Natalie Goldberg, author of *Writing Down the Bones*:

1. Keep your hand moving. Don't pause to read what you have written. That's stalling and trying to get control of what you're saying.
2. Don't cross out. That is editing as you write. Even if you write something you didn't mean to write, leave it.
3. Don't worry about spelling, punctuation, grammar. That is bringing out the perfectionist in you and you want the messy person.
4. Lose control.
5. Don't think. Don't get logical.
6. Go for the jugular. If something comes up in your writing that is scary or naked, dive right into it. It probably has lots of energy.

The purpose of these rules, says Natalie, is to burn through to first thoughts, uncensored by the critic who wants to be right, polite and admired. In journaling you need to write from the sensory right brain (the creator) that sees and feels directly, not how the logical left brain "thinks" you should see and feel (the editor).

First thoughts have tremendous energy, and freshness. First thoughts fly right past ego, that mechanism that "tries to be in control, tries to prove the world is permanent and solid, enduring and logical. It's not. It's ever-changing as you are," asserts Goldberg.

And she continues, "The editor is the person who wants to control things and look good. The creator is the one who wants to say it as it is. On the deepest level, the editor is the ego, which is trying in the face of impermanence to create solid ground and ignore death. And the creator is trying to speak the truth of existence."

What is the truth of your existence? What are your gifts? Who is the authentic you through which your gifts will flow? This is what journaling will tell you. When your first thoughts are present you will connect with what is authentic in you. It is an inspiring process that allows you to become larger than yourself. Inspiring meaning literally "breathing in" (see **Breathing**). Through journaling you are breathing in the spirit of the universe.

But this is not to say you are writing as an art. Just the opposite. This is most likely the worst crap of the universe. So lose your nervous fears and doubts about journaling. As Julia Cameron says, "it's simply the act of moving the hand across the page and writing down whatever comes to mind. Nothing is too petty, too silly, too stupid, or too weird to be included."

The key is to write without stopping, not even for a second. Don't put your pen down to take a sip of coffee. If you do you'll either censor what you just wrote or think about what you're going to write next. Don't think! Just write. Write fast. Create from the immediacy of the moment. Keep moving your pen across the paper. Your pen is like an oar that takes you to the other shore of your mind.

In her book, *If You Want to Write*, Brenda Ueland gives this motto: "Be Bold, Be Free, Be Truthful." You do this not by blocking out, but by allowing everything to come to you. You simply show up at the page with a beginner's mind (see **Zen**) every time you sit down. The more impulsive and the more immediate the writing, the closer it gets to feeling and the deeper it goes. With every sentence you write, you will learn something. It will stretch your understanding.

You need to be willing, but not willful. Don't will the writing, just let it come. And in the same way you write today, you will write tomorrow and the next day. Do not strain to write something good. If you get stuck then write "I am stuck...out of luck...this really sucks..." Keep a rhythm, keep a rhyme and like an inward dancing, the motion of the moving pen will get your right brain moving again.

Do not worry what comes out. It will be clumsy. Awkward. Misspelled and grammatically incorrect. And that's wonderful. Because that means you are getting past your ego, your critic, your censor. You are doing well when this happens. Listen to what William Blake said: "Improvement makes straight, straight roads, but the crooked roads without improvement are roads of genius."

Let the genius in you fill these pages. Writing this way is "feeling" on paper. Listen to what comes next. Like running, swimming, walking (see **Walkabout**), it becomes a rhythmic automatic response. There is no separation between your mind and body. The connection between your pen and paper is paralleling the connection between your hand and heart and out of this cooperation flows meaning.

Don't think. Listen. Listen deeply. And trust the process if you can't trust yourself. The deeper you listen, the more you let go. You will feel the void around you fill up with visions and voices and only writing can vent this vital aliveness. There is no judgment. There is no perfection. There just is.

HOW TO USE YOUR JOURNAL

However tempting, please don't read what you wrote for six weeks. When the time comes, take this tip from Julia Cameron and read it with two different colored markers in your hand—one to highlight insights and the other to highlight actions needed.

You may discover that many of the actions you needed have already been taken care of unconsciously. That is the power of journaling. "Words are a form of action, capable of influencing change," writes Ingrid Bengis. And your journaling will cause you to take action. Writing is your experience shifting through your consciousness. It's bringing your thoughts, ideas, emotions and wishes into the concrete world. This makes them real and tangible. And it gives you more conscious control over your life.

This process of going inside and writing opens an inner door through which the universe helps and guides you. Your willingness (not willfulness) swings this inner door open. This is the energy of the universe moving through your hand as you write. It can be very powerful.

If you look over the time that you have been journaling, you will see that many changes have entered your life. And not all of them will be easy. This is a direct result of your willingness to be open to the actions of a higher energy. You will feel a higher sense of personal energy, plus bursts of anger and sudden points of clarity. People and objects may take on a different meaning to you.

There will be a new sense of direction in your life as you surrender to moving with the flow (see **Flow**) of the universe. You may also experience a sense of both bafflement and faith. There is a paradox going on here—you are no longer stuck, but you cannot tell where you are going. That is as it should be. On the one hand you may feel that you can't continue with this—that, dull as life used to be, you just wish it would go back to the same old routine. Then on the other hand, you wonder how you could have accepted that dull existence when just making a few simple changes could improve your life so much. That is the full circle of your power—the journaling to recognize the changes you need and the actions you take as a result to give you the life you want.

Journaling Workshop

163

EXERCISE: BEGIN JOURNALING TODAY

Starting a journal is easy. All you need is a notebook and a pen. A spiral bound notebook works well because it can open up flat. Be sure the pen you choose allows the ink to flow easily and smoothly so you can write quickly.

An ideal time to journal is immediately after a *Super Intelligence* session. You are fresh. You are relaxed. And you are close to your emotions. Decide the length of time you want to write for, or how many pages you want to cover. Always start by putting the date at the top of your page.

Before you begin, review Natalie Goldberg's rules:
- Keep your hand moving.
- Don't cross out.
- Don't worry about spelling, punctuation, grammar.
- Lose control.
- Don't think. Don't get logical.
- Go for the jugular.

Remember too that the way to silence the censor is to go with your first thoughts. Quietly ask yourself: "Now...now. What am I feeling **NOW**?" Then listen and let your hand start flowing as you surrender to your emotions. Let your words take you from one peak emotion to the next. If something comes up in your writing that is scary or naked, do not shut it off. As Natalie Goldberg says, "dive right into it. It probably has lots of energy. Be glad for this emotion. It will get you writing."

Above all, have faith in the process. A Chinese poet once said "We poets struggle with Non-being to force it to yield to Being. We knock upon the silence for an answering music." By showing up at your page you are knocking upon that silence. The answering music is the voices and visions rising from this void. Let their words sing through the motion of your hand writing. Breathe. Yield. Feel. Write. Their gift is the power of being you.

Meditation:
Finding Your Space in the Infinite

"All of the many meditative methods for
modulating the inner voice begin with the
desire to hear it. The clearer the desire, the
clearer the hearing."
— W.A. Mathieu

While meditation has its roots in the religions of the East, it is
practiced today by many people all over the world who have no
affiliations with these religions. The reasons for meditation are many,
as are the forms of meditation. Those who meditate regularly report
that they have a deep sense of inner calm, and are more positive and
patient.

In addition to the obvious health benefits of this, meditation also
enables practitioners to connect with a deep inner self which leads to
heightened mental awareness, enhanced immune systems, a deeper
creativity and being psychologically more centered.

But there's more. Experienced meditators are drawn to more far-
reaching goals as they begin to pursue the search for an
understanding of the nature of reality. We meditate to discover our
place in the universe. Meditation is our connection to an inner power
source that has the ability to transform not only our inner world but
our outer world as well. The ultimate purpose is to expand the mind
to a level where you transcend consciousness and experience a state
of pure awareness.

Just how does meditation work? There are many forms but each
has essentially the same three objectives. To calm the mind. To open
it. And third—achieve awareness.

This can begin by focusing the mind on a mantra. A mantra is a
special sound or word you repeat. The simple repetitive sensation—
the hearing of a word over and over again, or visualizing (see
Visualization) your breath going in and out of your nostrils, the
sound of waves or distant tolling bells. Any of these could be a
mantra. The purpose of the mantra is to have the mind focus so

intensely on it that other thoughts disappear. The most famous of these is the single sound mantra OM (pronounced A-U-M). Through concentration and the narrowing of your focus to one theme, you remain awake but your mind state changes, moving you deeper and deeper into calmness, until your mind becomes opened and eventually you acquire awareness. It is this enlightened state of awareness the meditator seeks, where you experience transcendence and the feeling of oneness with the universe.

In his book *Complete Meditation*, Steve Kravete wrote, "By practicing meditation and being completely who you are, you will become more than you are now. You will be able to cross the next evolutionary bridge and begin to develop the full potential of your creaturehood."

Meditation alters your consciousness by changing your brainwave patterns—those wavelike ripples of electrical energy that correspond to certain states of consciousness. Artists, musicians and athletes are prolific producers of Alpha-Theta brainwaves. Creativity and strong Alpha-Theta activity appear to be linked. Meditation greatly increases the production of Alpha and Theta brainwave activity as well as synchronizing the left and right brain hemispheres. In addition to being able to maintain high amplitude Alpha and Theta levels even while not meditating, Zen Masters, Yogis and Swamis also demonstrate exceptional whole brain symmetry. What does it mean? Through meditation they have learned the correct physiological responses necessary to achieve and sustain these higher states of consciousness.

HOW TO MEDITATE

You own an extremely powerful meditation tool in your *Super Intelligence* soundtrack. Instead of having to take classes or go through any training, you can plug yourself in for 28 minutes and **it will meditate you**. The goal as we discussed in great detail throughout the first section of this book is to stimulate whole brain synchrony and the production of Alpha-Theta brainwaves. The use of this tool will help you reach a meditative state much more quickly than with any other method. However you might find it valuable to study these other methods as well. It's like eating multiple flavors of ice cream. You may have your favorite but it's sometimes useful to taste other flavors.

Mind Mapping Workshop: Breaking Down the Barriers to Creativity, Learning, and Memory

"When the two halves of our brain exchange their disparate experiences, pool their viewpoints and approaches, the resulting synthesis brings to problem-solving a whole symphony of talents."
— Albert Rothenberg

Mind maps were developed in the early 1970s by Tony Buzan (author of the book *Use Both Sides of Your Brain*) for use by students as a visual note taking process which was easier, quicker and more effective than traditional notes.

Since then, the process of mind mapping has caught on with virtually every group of people (from first graders to millionaire executives) as an effective, efficient means for brainstorming, planning meetings, organizing projects, writing books, giving speeches, preparing for tests, self-analysis or even "To Do" lists.

Mind mapping breaks down the barriers that block free thinking to reveal a wealth of ideas for making quick decisions to solve problems in innovative ways, while better organizing the information flow within your brain to boost your concentration and increase your recall of knowledge.

HOW TO USE A MIND MAP

A mind map is a visual outline. Rather than using the traditional format of outlines with Roman numerals and capital letters, the information in a mind map radiates from a main idea in the center of map. This central point acts as a starting place for the eye and the brain.

On the following page you'll find an example of a mind map. This one shows something you are familiar with—the mind

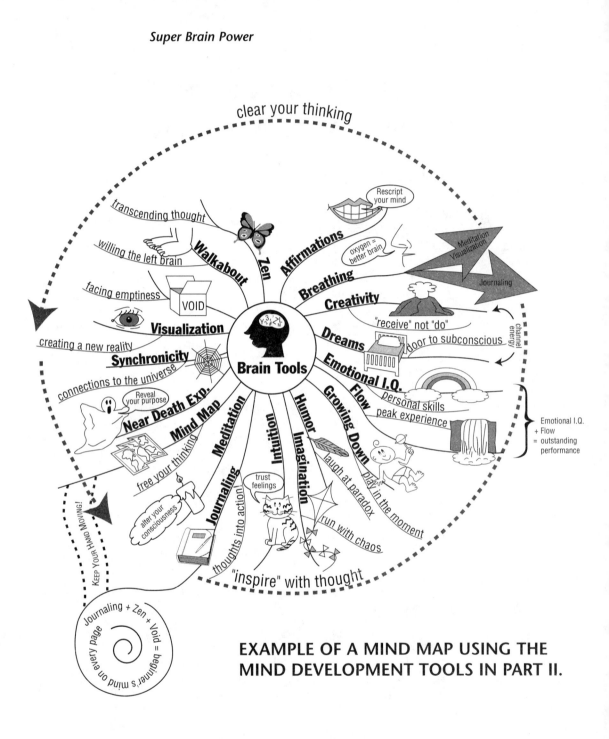

**EXAMPLE OF A MIND MAP USING THE
MIND DEVELOPMENT TOOLS IN PART II.**

development tools and workshops in this section of the book. In this example, you see a picture of a brain in the middle with the words Brain Tools, which is the two-word description of Part II in this book.

Connected to this central point are branches of thought arranged in a free flowing self-organizing manner. In the example here, there are 19 branches. Each branch contains a one or two-word description (Affirmations, Breathing, Creativity, etc.) and a picture, both of which relate to the main idea in the circle. Connected to these branches are stems and off-shoots that support it with details and more specific information. By arranging the information in this manner you see the natural progression of a main idea to a specific detail quickly and easily while, at the same time, seeing the "big picture" as well. This ability to see the "big picture" is encouraged by the dotted lines and arrows that connect one branch to the next.

Mind maps enable your brain to achieve optimum performance by engaging both hemispheres. It offers the linear left brain words and details plus an organization of thought, but it does so in a free flowing manner that gives the holistic right brain the freedom to make associations between the branches of thought and explore the patterns as it attends to the information provided by color and images.

Mind mapping gives you these advantages:
- Fun and easy to create yet even faster than traditional note taking to ensure you don't miss information while writing nonessential words.
- Works with your memory—through association which links one thought to another in a nonlinear fashion and through visual images for easy recall.
- Provides a hierarchy that highlights main points clearly, while allowing you to add information easily to a previous point.
- Acts as quick, easy and effective way to review information before a test.

Michael Gelb, who collaborated with Tony Buzan on mind mapping said, "The greatest power of mind mapping is that it trains our brain to see the whole picture and the details...to integrate logic and imagination" (see **Imagination**).

By engaging the whole brain, mind mapping improves your creativity by allowing you to generate better ideas and more of them with relative ease. Psychologists refer to it as "ideational fluency" and it gives you a supreme advantage in everything you do. The reason is because it's impossible to judge creative solutions at their onset as to their appropriateness. What at first sounds like a great idea may turn out to be impractical and can't be implemented. Likewise, sometimes a solution seems so obvious that it could be easily overlooked—but the more it is mulled over, the better it fits into the picture. With the ability to throw preconceived notions out the window and be open to generating many solutions you improve your odds of having at least one creative solution that works.

In addition to breaking down the barriers to creativity, mind mapping dramatically increases your ability to recall the specifics more easily, because it encourages you to envision the whole picture in a glance as you absorb the specific details. The mind map, in essence, gives you a "multiple focus" allowing you to learn simultaneously on different levels.

In her book *Mindmapping*, author Joyce Wycoff compares the process to "pinball thinking," or keeping information "in play." She writes, "Think of a pinball machine. The steel ball rolls through the playing field bouncing off rubber barriers, lighting lights, setting off bells, jumping out of holes, racking up points with each move. A skillful player will be able to flip the ball back into play when it approaches home and thus start the ball through the playing field scoring more points. The longer the ball is kept in play, the higher the point count. The mind is similar in that the longer we keep information in play, the more opportunity that information has to make new connections, to bounce off other ideas and information and to score new ideas."

HOW TO CREATE A MIND MAP

There are no right or wrong mind maps. Each mind map is a unique expression of the individual who made it. Yet while every mind map looks different, they all follow a similar pattern. This is a pattern that works with your mind, letting information flow in a manner that is natural and easy to your mind.

You begin in the middle by writing one or two words or drawing a picture (or both) that captures the essence of the topic, problem or situation. What you're doing here is defining the focus of your attention. If you are using words, print it (in upper/lower case) rather than using script writing. This is more readable and memorable. It's important to use as few words as possible—just enough to capture the idea. Better yet, use colorful symbols and pictures that will make your map "speak" to your right brain. This is the language of the right brain, which is quick to perceive images and patterns.

The main ideas radiate from the center, much like branches radiate from the trunk of a tree. On these branches you put key words/images to capture the essence of the idea. Don't worry about the order of your ideas. Just let your hand flow as they come to you and put them down wherever they fit. Remember, that is the beauty of a mind map—you can use arrows, dotted lines, or other visual icons to show links between the different branches, and thus give it order.

Keep your hand moving—don't judge the quality of the idea (see **Journaling**). And if you feel yourself getting stuck, try drawing another line to trigger a new idea. If you run out of room, simply tape another piece of paper onto your mind map. Keep going—you're breaking boundaries and that's what mind mapping is all about.

Connected to the branches are stems. These contain the details that relate to the branch idea. And, if more specific information is needed, each stem would have the particulars written on an even smaller line. Think of these as off-shoots. The result is a free-flowing canopy of information. It is your knowledge tree.

Mind mapping pulls together all of the information and gives you a multiple focus allowing you to see the specific details and the bigger picture at once. The free-flowing structure allows you to add new information easily. Plus the open sides encourage you to explore the information creatively, making new connections and seeing a pattern of information emerging off the page.

Each of these aspects represents a different level of learning.
• On one level of learning you take in key points, organizing principles, and major categories describing the central theme.

- On another level you get specific facts and details that support the above.
- In the final level of learning you launch your mind into a new dimension as you look at the information with greater insight from a higher perspective. This allows you to see patterns or trends that emerge from the relationship between the branches to the center of focus.

Through your mind map you are actively involved with the information, not simply recording it. You are a creator of your own knowledge, and we tend to remember better what we create. Through mind mapping you are taking the information and by filtering it through your brain, creating a structure for it. The specifics become locked into memory while the broader meaning retains an elasticity that's useful to creation.

Known as "transference," this elasticity allows you to move knowledge to a channel and build upon it, enabling you to tackle new skills or knowledge with ease. It is this channel that also allows you to "speed think" the future by quickly activating an entire channel of knowing from just a trickle of incoming information. In essence, mind mapping gives you the groundwork for incoming information so that as the project, meeting, speech, book (or other purpose of the mind map) begins to unfold, your intuition picks up the patterns of new incoming information and extrapolates it into reality. You are able to better envision the whole (or the future) with an uncanny ease. This is a powerful ability you can develop through this process.

EXERCISE: USING MIND MAPS AS A VISIONARY COMPASS

You've learned about mind mapping. You've seen a mind map. Now it's time for you to create one on your own. The fun, easy exercises that follow will let you experience the mind mapping process as it introduces you to various ways to use mind maps.

Before beginning each mind map, have some sheets of blank paper handy, as well as several different colors of pens or fine tipped markers. Be sure to play your *Mozart Brain Boost* soundtrack (Track 3) from your *Super Brain Power* CD. It will relax you and allow you to focus as the information flows smoothly from your hand to the paper.

As you create your mind map, remember to follow these simple guidelines:
- Begin in the center of your paper with the central idea (words or images). Print your words in upper and lower case letters.
- Draw lines from this center for each branch idea, using as few as words as possible (or images) to convey the idea.
- If needed, connect more details to the branch idea in the same manner.
- Add arrows, dotted lines, or other visual icons to link branches together.

Like a visionary compass that intuits the future from the white void of the paper (see **Void**), a mind map is an easy way to capture fleeting thoughts that are waiting for you on the peripheral of your consciousness. Over the next few days, try creating a mind map for each of the following uses.

• **Problem solving.** Whether it is a personal or a professional challenge, a mind map gives you a snapshot of all the issues. It "telegraphs" these issues to others and shows your viewpoint by illustrating the relationship of one issue to the other.

• **Organizing and Planning.** Because a mind map does not require you to prioritize the information before writing it down, it is the ideal way to gather all your thoughts in a free flowing manner independent of linear thinking that may block ideas. Once all the actions necessary to carry out a project are down on paper (on your branches) you can then go back and number each one in a logical order.

• **Personal Growth.** Like a portrait of yourself in words and icons, mind mapping for self-analysis presents your deepest desires in direct, simple images and words. A helpful hint is to not label your branches in left brain terms such as "Long Term Goals" "Immediate Goals." Instead, try drawing a branch for each role in your life (such as mother/father, wife/husband, occupation, hobbies, etc.) and see what plays out from there.

Mind Mapping Workshop

Giving the branch a more personal label will allow you to use your emotions to discover what you really want for yourself in each area.

• **Writing Speeches, Reports, Novels.** The very process of creating a mind map opens up your floodgates to creativity. Centered by your main focus or idea, you are free to strike out in any direction. Keeping your hand moving continuously lets you fly right past the critic in your left brain before it can pass judgment and allows you to overcome writer's block before it sets in. You'll find a new depth and perception to your writing.

Plus, as a bonus for speech givers, you'll find that a mind map enables you to give a speech without the use of notes. To do this, write every major point of your speech on a branch. Then use the whole brain technique known as a "mental movie" to easily review the entire mind map in your mental eye. Use the following guidelines to help you.

1. After mind mapping your speech, hold up your mind map and squint your eyes. What do you see? If nothing jumps out at you, pump up the visual aspect of your mind map to engage your right brain. Add pictures, or go over the words on the branches with a bolder pen and use a yellow highlighter. Then hold your mind map up again as you squint your eyes. By now, some information should pop right out to the front. This helps to organize your mind map and give contrast and clarity to the details.

2. Begin reviewing the mind map by reading the words or images in the center. (Play your *Mozart Brain Boost* soundtrack in the background to help you recall the information.) As you read the words out loud, trace the circle with your finger, taking special notice of the picture or symbol. This will engage your sense of hearing and your kinesthetic sense to improve your memory of the information. Do this several times.

3. Next, run your finger along each branch and onto each of the stems and off-shoots, again, verbalizing the words or pictures on each line.

4. Repeat this review of the entire mind map several times. Then turn your mind map face down and replay a mental movie of the map by mentally seeing and feeling your finger going over each of the branches as you hear the information on the map pop into your mind. This movie will become very real. As you watch it in your mind, the images are instantly linked to the words. It is as if someone were narrating a documentary on the information contained on your mind map. When you can clearly visualize the movie, you are ready to give the speech from memory, without the use of the mind map.

This technique of creating a mental movie will give you instant and easy recall with the powers of your own mind. It puts you "on scene" with the information, and does not require anything except your own imagination. The reason it works so well is because it is the essence of whole brain thinking—combining the right brain's natural ability to easily recall visual images with the left brain's powerful ability to reconnect with specific words.

Mind Mapping Workshop

175

Near Death Experience:
An Incredible Journey for You

"Whatever prepares you for death enhances life."
— Stephen Levine

In their book *Death, the Final Stage of Growth*, authors Joseph and Laurie Braga write, "Death is a subject that is evaded, ignored, and denied by our youth-worshipping, progress-oriented society. It is almost as if we have taken on death as just another disease to be conquered. But the fact is that death is inevitable. We will all die, it is only a matter of time."

By ignoring death, our society learns to fear death, which causes us to turn away risks and opt for a safer ground. But by seeing death as a friend you can cut through this fear. The Bragas go on to say that, "If you can begin to see death as an invisible, but friendly, companion of your life's journey—gently reminding you not to wait till tomorrow to do what you mean to do—then you can learn to live your life rather than simply passing through it." For many people this viewpoint comes only after a near death experience (NDE). But it's a viewpoint you can cultivate now by gleaning wisdom from the stories of near death survivors.

A 1982 Gallup Poll estimated that at least eight million adults in the United States have had an NDE. Today, this figure is expected to be close to thirteen million. Down through the ages, experiences have been reported from many cultures and religious traditions. And now scientists have documented an area in the brain which allows us to have the experience. Something is definitely happening to cause a NDE, and when it does, this experience changes people's lives.

While the NDE is a tool and an experience unlike any other, the process reveals a secret that is strikingly familiar to the lessons learned from other tools (see **Meditation, Visualization Workshop, Journaling Workshop, Dream Workshop**). It is a secret that great prophets have tried to tell us for years. That secret is not about death, it is about life, and how to live it in an enlivened way that is filled with meaning.

In the best selling book *Embraced by the Light*, author Betty J. Eadie writes of the message she received form her NDE: "Love is supreme...Love must govern...We create our own surroundings by the thoughts we think...We are sent here to live life fully, to live it abundantly, to enjoy in our own creations, to experience birth, failure and success, to use free will to expand our lives."

The importance of NDEs is in what they teach about living. To some, the NDE defines a value system based on care for others, knowledge, and service. Others report they have glimpsed the meaning of life and the universe. This includes seeing the pattern of the universe—knowledge beyond ordinary human consciousness. The commonalty between NDE reports is a revealing of issues that hold deep significance to not only the life of the individual but to humankind as well.

Often an NDE permanently alters a person's attitude of what is real and important. Some kind of transformation has occurred within themselves. While sometimes the NDE is joyful, other times it is a hellish nightmare. Like ancient myths whose heroes enter a terrifying underworld in order to fulfill a god-inspired mission, NDEs fulfill people with a mission to return to the world and complete a service or bring back a gift from the deep that will serve humanity.

Ironically, it is this terrifying experience that is the gift, for it has the potential for moving the person toward genuine wisdom and maturity. A frightening NDE shocks you into seeing life's deepest issues—Who are you? What is important? Who or what is running your life? Many report seeing a shallowness in themselves, in their goals. With new ideas for life's purpose and value they return with a deeper understanding and renewed sense of purpose.

THE GIFT OF A NEAR DEATH EXPERIENCE FOR YOU

Although this exercise cannot take you to the edge of a real NDE, it can reveal to you the important inner truths you hold for yourself that you may be ignoring. What is your purpose? What do you want to do with your life? What experiences do you want to have that you have been missing?

These are not easy questions to answer. But by imposing a "deadline" on your life, the answers come a little quicker. (Imagine you are going to die in five days...how would you spend your remaining time?) And by imagining you're past the "deadline" you get the added incentive of urgency to find the answers for you.

In this exercise imagine you have already died. Visualize your funeral (see **Visualization Workshop**). In your mind's eye imagine the people at your funeral—did you have a big turnout, or just your immediate family? See the casket draped with flowers—is it open (what are you wearing?) or closed? Read your obituary in the paper. See the writing on your tombstone. Then ask yourself the following questions:

- What would you want to hear people say about you at your eulogy?
- What would you most like to be remembered by?
- What characteristics and qualities of you, your work, your relationships are leaving an impact on the people you knew?

Near Death Experience

179

The answers to these questions will reveal what is really important to you. Then you can use your findings to evaluate how well you are living your life in accordance with your inner truths and make changes that will better align your reality with your desires.

Synchronicity:
Tapping into a Power
Greater Than You

"A thousand unseen helping hands."
　　　　　　　—Joseph Campbell

As defined by Carl Jung, synchronicity is "the coming together of inner and outer events in a way that cannot be explained by cause and effect and that is meaningful to the observer." In other words, it is being in the right place at the right time, without any prior planning.

It's discovering that the one remaining can of paint on the shelf is the very color you need. It's reaching for the phone to call an old friend just as the phone rings with their call. It's walking past the magazine rack in the store and seeing the car you are about to buy emblazoned on the cover with the headline "Lemons for Sale."

There's more going on here than pure luck. But as a culture we are more likely to believe this is good timing more than anything else. Educated with a very left-brained scientific viewpoint (grounded in cause and effect relationships), we deny that unforeseen factors can play a role in our success. But they can, and they do. And if you're doubtful just look into your past. The evidence of their presence is revealed in the positive outcomes in your life—or in the negative ones that paved the way for better things for you (otherwise known as "blessings in disguise").

On one level, synchronicities serve as gentle nudges to guide you, plus subtle signs to assure you that you are heading in the right direction. Like the childhood game where your friends clapped louder as you got closer to the hidden object (and clapped more softly as you moved away from it), synchronicities reaffirm your intuitive feelings (see **Intuition**), giving you the confidence to continue along your chosen path despite the fact that it has yet to reward you with the physical signs of success.

On a deeper level, synchronicities connect you with the greater whole—even if the idea of a greater whole has long lost its meaning for you. Synchronicity embodies the benevolent spirit that you stopped believing in when you learned that Santa Claus, the Easter Bunny and the Tooth Fairy really weren't real. Once fooled by these fictitious fakes, the grown-up in you refuses to ever risk being naive again by believing in a higher unseen power that acts in your favor. But that power is as real as the love you feel for another person, and yet, like love, just as impossible to prove its existence.

Part II

Mind Development Tools

━━━

182

Your left brain goes looking for proof, while your right brain goes looking for truth. The truth about the meaning of life. The truth about who you are. The truth about your purpose in life.

Every living thing offers a unique gift of excellence, yet the excellence is only manifested in the giving away of that gift. Just as no two snowflakes are alike, no two people share the same gifts. This is your innate creativity that was unmistakably emblazoned on your neurons the day you were born. What are your gifts? You need to experience them for yourself, before you can send them out into the world. Again, the universe DAREs you to be creative—Desire your gifts, Ask for them, Receive them, Experience them, and then Send (or Share) them with the world. Once you do you can reap their rewards.

You can write the most beautiful song in the world, but until you let someone hear it, it cannot give them joy and you cannot receive the joy of having given that song to the world. This is a catch-22 situation that asks you to commit and invest yourself into a direction before you have any proof that it is going to pay off for you.

To get to the end of your life and regret having not followed your passion (see **Near Death Experience**) is not having really lived a complete life. That's the benefit of using synchronicity as a tool to finding the path that is right for you. It supplies you with the support you need in your quest to find your authentic self. Like the clapping of hands in that childhood game, that lets you know you are closer to the hidden object, synchronicity shows up more and more when you are on the right path, even if the rewards of success are not yet in view. Be patient. What you desire could be around the next bend.

EXPERIENCES OF SYNCHRONICITY ABOUND IN YOUR LIFE

Establishing a belief in the existence of synchronicity is easier if you first think in terms of the past, rather than the future. In your past you'll find the proof of synchronicity—even though you may have labeled it as a lucky break, or good timing.

As you think about your past experiences, how many positive outcomes can you attribute to synchronicity? Think about these: How did you meet your spouse? How did you finally land a job? When you were in need of a large sum of money or a new car or a place to live, what suddenly occurred to rectify the situation? Look at little things too—such as hitting all green lights as you race to an appointment, or finding the only open parking space in front of the building you are entering.

Once you can validate that synchronicity has helped you in the past, keep on the lookout for ways it works for you in the present. Post a chart in a visible spot and make a simple entry every time a synchronistic event happens to you. Awareness of these interesting occurrences will help bring more of them into your life.

Synchronicity

183

Visualization Workshop:
Creating Your Future with
Mental and Sensory Imagery

"It is interesting that visionary and
mystical inspiration are behind many
of the world's greatest inventions and
scientific breakthroughs: even those of
such giants of the mind as Albert Einstein
and Nikola Tesla."
— David Tame

Most of us have heard the idea that "our thoughts somehow shape the reality we experience." While negative thoughts influence the world around us and bring about negative circumstances, positive thoughts somehow bring about positive circumstances. In other words, when you shift how you think about yourself and your circumstances, both you and those circumstances begin to experience a change. A way to harness and focus this energy is through the tool of visualization.

Visualization uses your imagination to form a mental picture in your mind of what you want to experience in your life. But it's more than just "envisioning" your future. It's goal setting with all your senses. It's playing a movie in your head that allows you to see, feel, hear, smell, taste and touch the outcome you desire.

Used by Olympic champions, stock market experts, actors and more, visualization lets you tap into your natural ability to imagine in a more conscious way. And in doing so it focuses your mental energy and helps bring about the events you want to experience in life—from prosperity, to a stable relationship, to meaningful work, to health and beauty and more.

The power of visualization was proved convincingly in an experiment conducted by the Russians in the 1980 Olympics. They split their team members into four groups. Group A used 100% traditional exercise, group B used 75% physical exercise and 25% visualization; group D received 75% mental visualization and 25%

physical practice. After the Moscow Olympics and the Lake Placid Olympics, the largest number of medals went to the team members in group D. The group that used visualization.

The power of this tool, like so many others, lies in directing the energy of your right brain through the power of your imagination (see **Imagination**). And while we use this power everyday (as exemplified by the expressions *You get the picture. Now you see what I mean? Stop daydreaming!*), the tool of visualization allows us to direct this power into the depths of our subconscious.

Arnold Schwarzenegger, five-time Mr. Universe and four-time Mr. Olympia says, "As long as the mind can envision the fact that you can do something, you can...I visualized myself being already there—having achieved the goal already. It's mind over matter."

Yet, visualization is far more than positive thinking.

THE PITFALLS OF POSITIVE THINKING

An entire industry of motivational speakers has been created around the tenets of positive thinking. However, the millions of people who attend positive thinking seminars receive little, if any, lasting benefits from them. Basically, they get high from the motivational uplift for about two days. Then they go back to their old self again.

The reason for this is that the "old you" will do everything in its power to prevent change. It will procrastinate and make excuses for not using new ideas and programs, even if they are good for you. Why? Because the old you is comfortable. It has a built-in survival mechanism to protect the status quo. That's why change is so difficult. That's also why positive thinking on a surface level always fails—because these motivational stories deal only with your conscious mind—and the conscious mind is not the engine that powers your life.

Visualization goes far deeper than positive thinking because it works on the unconscious part of your mind. And it's the subconscious, or the unconscious portion of your mind, that determines your behaviors, beliefs and attitudes. Your thinking on a unconscious level is what affects your wealth, health, and success (or failure) in any undertaking. By going directly into the unconscious and rewiring your beliefs, your attitudes and how you think about yourself and your future, visualization offers the key to permanent, lasting change.

HOW TO RESCRIPT THE PROGRAMMING IN YOUR MIND

A friend of mine is a very successful, wealthy real estate entrepreneur. Yet he started without a single dime in his pocket. In just a few years he was able to create a great fortune with a simple philosophy of "faking it until he made it." He convinced himself on a subconscious level that he had already acquired a great fortune, when in fact he was really broke. Through the power of visualization he became a millionaire first in his mind. And then his unconscious auto-pilot brought about the reality that followed.

There are many similar stories that illustrate this self-fulfilling prophecy. Each one demonstrates that what we take to be true on a unconscious level becomes our reality. This is not to say that skill (and even luck) do not play a role in wealth and prosperity. Money-making skills are learned, yet they begin with a desire and a belief that it is possible. It's the positive expectation of success that matters, all the rest can be acquired.

You've probably seen this happen to you—but in reverse. When you tell yourself you're going to have a bad day, what happens? You have a bad day. Likewise, if you've been told all your life that you'll never amount to anything, or if you believe that being wealthy is something beyond your grasp, this becomes the mind script that is welded into your subconscious. Computer programmers have a term they use called "Garbage in—garbage out." A badly programmed computer is doomed to spit out bad information. It's the same with your mind. The reality you are experiencing for the most part is a mirror image of what's going on in your mind.

Through visualization you can work with the issue of beliefs and behavior at the deepest levels of your being. To create lasting change, you must rescript this core set of beliefs that form how you think and perceive your world. You need to anchor new beliefs into your unconscious, at the source where your beliefs are formed, and

Visualization Workshop

187

reinforced by your perceptions and experiences. Only then can a new reality become true for you.

Philosophers and great thinkers have been saying it for thousands of years. Roman philosopher Marcus Aureoles said, "Our light is what our thoughts make of it." Napoleon Hill said exactly the same thing in *Think and Grow Rich*. But before you can think and grow rich you need to break through an encrusted mind script created by years of negative programming. The tool of visualization gives you this power.

VISUALIZATION IN 4 EASY STEPS

With visualization you mentally rehearse future events adding positive emotions about those future events linked to successful images from your past. Through this mental programming you are rescripting your subconscious to bring forth a desired goal into reality.

The four steps of visualization only need to take five minutes a day. Use this five minutes as a mini vacation to escape your regular routine, and use this time to work on your desired goals. Here is a breakdown of the four steps and how to do each one.

• **The First Step** is to get into a comfortable position, close your eyes, and focus on your breathing (see **Breathing**). With your eyes closed, roll them upwards slightly, as if you're trying to see the center of your forehead, and listen to yourself breathe. Focus your attention on slowly taking deep breaths, and on the sound of the air coming in and out of your lungs. Feel yourself relax. Do this breathing exercise five times. It will only take 45 seconds or so as you focus on your breathing. This simple relaxation exercise will immediately alter your consciousness, putting your brain into a light Alpha state.

• **The Second Step** is to select an image of a past memory where you were extremely happy. Really get in touch with that experience. It doesn't matter what it is, or when it happened. The point is to conjure up a "winning feeling" or a positive emotion that you can connect with your image of a future event. Perhaps this is an image of a moment you remember falling in love. Or receiving a standing ovation during a high school play. Go back into your past and pull out a very specific event that you can relive in every detail.

As you recreate the event in your mind's eye, feel the pats on your back. The loving adulation. Remember the voices, the smells, the colors. As you recreate this scene, let yourself re-experience all of those winning feelings. What you are doing here is bringing forward a positive emotion into your consciousness that will psychologically become linked with the future goal you want to achieve. Emotions are the key to anchoring the desired goal and giving energy to your unconscious.

• **The Third Step** is to envision the future goal you desire as vividly as possible. As you do, be sure to continue to feel those winning feelings welling up inside of you from that previously lived experience. You can envision your future through a mental picture, a word, a musical note, even a taste. Some people respond better to pictures, while others to words or different sensory images. The key point here is to see yourself as if you already achieved that goal, whether it is in the form of a picture, a feeling, or words.

Visualization Workshop

189

For example, if your future goal is to create more wealth you would visualize yourself as already having it. See yourself going to the bank with a big deposit, or sitting at your desk piled high with $100 bills. Smell the money. Roll in it. Throw it in the air. See yourself walking down the street in the finest clothes or driving past your friends in your dream car. Also, hear the whispers and comments of your friends, wondering how you ever became so successful.

If you're a student taking a test, see that big, red, A+ marked across the top of your exam. If you're a salesperson, see yourself actually closing the sale. If you're giving a speech, see the audience clapping for you, and telling you what a wonderful job you've done.

Perhaps your goal is to own a vacation home. Picture yourself walking through the front door into an expansive entry way. Feel the slate floor beneath your bare feet, and hear the landscapers cutting your acre of grass outside your door. Go ahead and walk through the entire home in your mind, filling in the details exactly as you would like them to be in your reality. Smell the fire in the fireplace in your master bedroom, taste the fine wine in your wine cellar and touch the computer screen that lets you see who is ringing your front bell. By focusing on your desire with your every sense you are creating a mental blueprint for your success. (Remember your inner mind doesn't know the difference between a real or imagined event. It uses the energy of your emotions and your mental blueprint to alter your perceptions and set up the conditions to bring about this new reality.)

• **The Fourth Step** is to open your eyes and say out loud: "I now allow myself to have _____ ," filling in the blank with whatever it is that you want. Then say, "So be it. It is done." This simple but powerful statement affirms the goal that you just programmed, and then releases it into the universe so that you do not dwell on it. Dwelling on it only creates mental doubt that you believe it's really not possible.

Dwelling on it would be similar to wanting something so badly that you try too hard and you choke. It's an easy trap to fall into. However, if you've visualized it, and energized it, you've already created it. Now release it, and let it go. By letting go of it, you're actually programming into your unconscious a belief that you expect it to happen.

Does this sound too simple?

Visualization works because it's using the energy of your imagination to reshape the contents of your unconscious. By taking yourself through this four step program on a regular and consistent basis you are training your unconscious to focus your mental energy on your goals. You will be amazed at how powerful this simple tool is for helping you achieve your dreams.

EXPERIENCE THE PROVEN POWER OF VISUALIZATION IN SPORTS PERFORMANCE

Visualization is a great way to improve your game—no matter what the sport. From golf, to tennis, to high diving, skiing and more. If you can visualize yourself performing great in your mind, you will carry out that performance in real life. The secret is to involve all your senses and imagine the positive outcome of the event through the four step visualization process.

Before beginning, select the goal or objective of your visualization session. Then take yourself through the four steps, as summarized for you here:

- **First Step**: Get comfortable, close your eyes, and roll them upward, focusing your breathing for five breaths.

- **Second Step**: Recreate a winning feeling by bringing forth a positive image from your past, and reliving it for a minute.

- **Third Step**: Envision your future goal as if you've already achieved it, and do a mental rehearsal of that event or goal with as much power and detail as possible. The more details you add, the clearer the picture will become. And the clearer your picture, the better your outcome.

> *See the clothes you are wearing.*
> *Hear the voices of the people who will be there.*
> *Smell the sunscreen you're applying.*
> *Feel the sun on your face, the way the club or*
> *   racket or ski pole feels in your hand.*
> *How tight are your shoes or boots?*
> *What is the time on your watch?*

Visualization Workshop

———

191

Feel your weight shift as you move, see the ball (or your skis) move in exactly the precise direction and feel the rush of victory as you are declared the winner.

- **Fourth Step**: Open your eyes and affirm the goal you just programmed (by saying "I now allow myself to _____.") Then release it by saying "So be it. It is done."

Through visualization you give your imagined reality as much richness and detail as you possibly can. Yet don't worry if at first your images are a bit fuzzy (see **Imagination**). The process improves with practice. Tie in sounds, smells, and touch. In fact, the more senses and the greater the specificity, the more ammunition you're giving your subconscious to believe it and then act on it. Practice this visualization exercise on some goal you have for five minutes every day. It will create a neural pathway of success in your brain and your life!

The Void:
A Place of Beginning

"The secret of the receptive
Must be sought in stillness;
Within silence there remains
The potential for action."
— Zhou Xuanjiing

Like an empty canvas or a blank sheet of paper, the "void" is the source of creation. It is the nothingness from which you spring forth the birth of ideas and wisdom.

The void is a place of beginning—one that offers no immediate direction but rather a well-spring of possibilities. The purpose of entering the void is to let go of expectations, which also means letting go of control.

Although a difficult concept to a Western mind, the void can be an exciting place for those who do not fear the unknown. It is the playground for the artist in you. Your willingness to go there without panic or fear can be your partner in your life-long success.

In Zen, (see **Zen**) the void is the emptying of the mind of all thoughts. This is a clearing process that can be accessed by meditation. But you don't need to meditate to access the void. As the below exercise will show, simply looking at any blank wall will let you glimpse the power of the void.

EXPERIENCE VISIONS FROM THE VOID

An easy way to access the void is to stare at the canvas above your head—the ceiling or the sky. Next time you have a problem to solve, or are searching for the right phrase in a letter, or simply can't decide what direction to choose, try finding your answer by accessing your void. Here's how.

Simply gaze softly (at the ceiling or the sky), breathe deeply and let go of your thoughts by concentrating on the nothingness before you. This disengages your rational left brain and allows your intuition to tell you what you need to know. Don't "will it" to happen—allow it to happen. Let go and the answer you need will come to you.

YOUR INNER VOICE

The answers you receive may not only surprise you, you may discover there is a real voice attached to them. This inner voice can be an immensely powerful source of insight, and so it may be beneficial for you to develop this tool even further. Use the principle of the void to access your inner voice. Ask your question and listen. Really listen. It's there. That little voice that's been talking to you all your life. It may be quiet because you are not allowing it to speak.

Here is an exercise you can use to help awaken your inner voice. Using your imagination (see **Imagination**) create an imaginary person that gives your voice a face. Give it a name and a personality. Perhaps it's a real person, someone who really existed in the past or the present. It could be a historical figure like Abraham Lincoln or Albert Einstein. It could be a fictional character like Superman or Yoda. Or it could be an entity who is entirely self-imagined. I have two of these inner voices (my inner advisors) who are very lifelike with real personalities and different sounding voices. They each have names, and particular personalities. I use them to bounce ideas off and to ask for direction when I'm stuck. I see these inner voices as very potent sources of intuition. Every time I've gone against their advice about a decision I was making, events went badly. When I do listen and make choices according to the direction they provide, even when the advice is counter to my reason and logic, more often than not, it turns out to be accurate. Why? Is it because of some higher power? Your inner voice(s) are your intuition (see **Intuition**). They are in direct contact with sources of information that your rational logical mind cannot grasp. These insights are unconscious data bits that don't fit into categories or logical patterns. So it is these intuitions or hunches that more often than not, turn out to be highly reliable, even in the face of logical evidence to the contrary.

Test this idea out for yourself. Enter the void—give an imaginary face and personality to your inner voice(s), and ask questions. Validate the answers you receive. I think you'll be surprised at how "right" this information turns out to be.

Walkabout:
Networking with Nature

"Solvitur ambulando...It is solved by walking."
— St. Augustine

In its traditional sense, the walkabout is a prolonged and dangerous journey into the wilderness required for male Australian aborigines at about age fourteen. Made popular by Marlo Morgan's book *Mutant Message Down Under* (a 4 month journey with a tribe across the Australian desert), she describes her experience of "releasing of attachment to objects and certain beliefs" as a "very necessary step in my human progress towards being."

The walkabout immerses the individual in nature, a world where the senses rule over the intellect. Through the hardships across the rugged geography, the aborigines survive by calling forth deep collective inner knowledge inherited from the ancient wisdom and philosophy of their 40,000-year-old culture.

Although on one level, this life-or-death initiation seems very far removed from our modern day world, on another level, a walkabout is a timely tool that has especially important benefits to our hectic lifestyle.

As you walk, you open up into the space around you. As you listen, you reawaken neural reward pathways while the sights and sounds of nature replenish your sensory right brain. With your logical left brain "off-line" you give yourself important downtime to unconsciously work on solutions to challenges you are facing. The rhythmic and repetitive motion of walking acts as a massage to your spirit. It literally grounds you into the moment and frees you from distracting thoughts of the future.

The message received from walking can solve a problem, or fill you with a great sense of purpose. But more importantly, it's the experience of the walk itself. The sensual pleasure of physical movement while the meditation of nature energizes your spirit. Walking lets you directly experience and interact with the world, making you feel more connected—more alive. You know this because you've already experienced it many times in your life. It's just that you forget and need to be reminded.

The more you feel your own personal aliveness the greater your connection will be to everything else. This greater vision will be a recurring theme as you do these exercises, that all living things are part of the same whole, sharing this planet. It's a message echoed by native people of our own country, as expressed in this quote by Chief Seattle: "Man did not weave the web of life, he is merely a strand in it. Whatever he does to the web, he does to himself." You just need to go for a walk and pay attention to the splendorous Eden that is all around you.

EXPERIENCE A WALKABOUT FOR YOURSELF

Educators in some schools around the country have adapted the idea of the walkabout in urban areas. In this version, students develop their own programs of study in preparation for a great task of their own choosing. You too can design your own walkabout. While not putting yourself in a life-or-death situation (as did the Australian aborigines), the simple process of going on a camp out, driving across the country or simply sitting quietly on the ground facing the sun from dawn to dusk will allow to focus your attention on areas you would not ordinarily think about. The insights you gain could be the beginning of a whole new direction in your life.

Zen:
Breaking Through The
Barriers of Consciousness

"If the Angel decides to come it will
because you have convinced her, not
by tears but by your humble resolve to
be always beginning; to be a beginner."
— Rainer Maria Rilke

Zen is an ancient art that uses intuition and introspection to seek out the answers to the age old questions of enlightenment: Who are we? What is our purpose? What is the meaning of life? Unlike other religions or philosophies, Zen does not use traditional thinking to figure out the answers. Instead, it relies on "koans," or unanswerable puzzles designed to break through the barriers of consciousness.

A familiar koan is **"What is the sound of one hand clapping?"** The purpose of the koan is to stretch a person beyond "thinking." Logically, there is no answer. And that is the point. To solve the riddle you must transcend logic and reason. The koan drives you into, what has been described as "feverish concentration," from which arises "supreme frustration" until you transcend conscious thought into the deeper level of the unconscious. It is the process of transcending the confusion (a state of chaos in which you were frustrated) into wisdom. To do so you need to access a total state of concentration where you are eventually awakened into enlightenment.

Instead of "figuring out" a koan, you use intuition (see **Intuition**), insight and contemplation. In essence, you look at the koan from all sides and focus on it so greatly that you become the puzzle. This is the time the solution reveals itself to you. In arriving at the solution you have caused your conscious mind to become empty and open to a new wisdom beyond what your rational thinking mind could offer.

There is a famous Zen story about the emptying of the mind. It tells about a prestigious professor who visited a Zen master at a temple in Japan. The professor was taken to the master by an attendant. Another attendant brought tea. After being seated, the professor immediately began talking about his knowledge on Zen philosophy. The master kept silent as he poured tea into the professor's cup. The professor continued to talk until he suddenly realized that the Zen master was still pouring tea, even though the cup was overflowing onto the floor. As the master still continued to pour, the professor cried out "Master, please stop, the tea is overflowing!" The master looked up and spoke for the first time during their meeting. "Just as the cup can hold no more tea when it is already filled, how can I give you anything when your mind is already filled?"

So too with your mind. In order to learn, you must first empty your mind of preconceived notions and assumptions you hold to be true. This is the beginner's mind. It is an open mind—one that is uncluttered, flexible and curious. The acknowledgment that you don't know is the first step on your journey toward knowledge. Do not confuse your not-knowing with being ignorant. Instead see your mind as pure innocence. Like the artist facing an empty canvas (see **Void**), it is filled with infinite possibilities.

EXPERIENCE ZEN FOR YOURSELF

Remembering that the purpose of the koan is to drive you beyond logical thinking, here is a koan for you to ponder: **"What was the appearance of your face before your ancestors were born?"**

To contemplate the solution, sit on a cushion facing the wall in a simple crossed-legged position with both feet on the floor. Keep your back straight (but not tense) and let the stomach muscles relax. Your head, neck and body should all be in a line so that the center of gravity passes from the base of the spine through the top of the head. Rest your hands lightly on your knees. As you close your eyes, banish all thoughts except for the koan.

As you will soon find out, this koan will defy your logical thinking process. To arrive at a solution, you will need to use your higher reasoning which often comes to you in a small intuitive voice. The "Aha" voice, it will whisper softly into your ear. The more you practice listening to it, the louder it will become. One day you will realize that it is your constant companion, ready to support you with knowledge and solutions you need.

PART III:
Questions and Answers

Some Questions & Answers On Using Your CD

"No more words.
Hear only the voice within."
— Runi

The process of transforming the energy in your brain is an exciting high. But like any growth process, it is also arduous, demanding, and can raise conflicting emotions in you. Know that this is normal. Many before you have gone through these same highs and lows. For that reason I have included this section. It is filled with the questions and issues you may encounter as you begin to use these tools on a regular basis. In addition to the Q & A segment, I have added a number of letters received from users of the Brain Supercharger technology. I am sharing these with you so you can see how others have used and benefited from this technology.

Q. The CD packaged with this book has 2 soundtracks on it. What are they and what is the purpose of each one?
A. The two unique soundtracks included on your Super Brain Power CD are called *Super Intelligence (28:01 minutes)*, and *Mozart Brain Boost (27:19 minutes)*. Although the philosophy and technology incorporated into these soundtracks has some similar elements, each is used in a different way. The first soundtrack, *Super Intelligence*, is used to induce a deep meditative state. It is 28 minutes in length. Through a process of whole brain synchrony and mindscripting techniques, it is designed to program your unconscious with a new set of beliefs about creativity, imagination and awareness. It is designed to meditate you, and allow you to experience altered states of consciousness.

The second soundtrack on your CD is titled *Mozart Brain Boost*. It takes advantage of the unique properties of certain musical forms to stimulate learning. It is designed to help you focus and concentrate on an activity whether that's reading, studying or just thinking.

Q. What kind of feelings can I expect?
A. When accumulated tension flows out of your muscles and other parts of your body, you can expect a number of sensations.

Some of these feelings may be new to you. These can include tingling, a floating sensation, momentary numbness, mild muscle twitches, or feelings of warmth or heaviness in certain areas of your body. You may find your mind wandering to unexpected thoughts that startle you, or even experience a lucid dream. This is entirely natural since a common result of this altered state of consciousness is increased mental alertness.

Some people may feel themselves dozing off during a session. You are probably not actually sleeping as the audio matrix is holding you in a Theta pattern which is just above the threshold of sleep. But because you've lost all "time sense" it may feel as if you've been sleeping. If you are physically or mentally exhausted, you may find it desirable to turn off your CD player and drift off to sleep after your session.

Q. How should I use these soundtracks?
A. The *Super Intelligence* soundtrack (on Track 2), must be used **with stereo headphones only**. Put on your headphones, cue up Track 2 on your CD player and push play. (Track 1 is a brief introduction that gives you instructions in its use. You may want to listen to it once through and then you can skip it in future sessions.) Adjust the volume to a comfortable listening level. Close your eyes and lay back in a comfortable arm chair or firm sofa or on a bed that keeps your spine straight.

Slowly, as the soundtrack unfolds, the audio matrix will automatically take you from a conscious Beta brainwave state down through a relaxed Alpha state and into a deep Theta state of relaxation and altered consciousness. This will last for about 25 minutes. As the session winds down, the matrix will slowly bring you back to a Beta conscious state at the end of your 28 minute session, and wake you up automatically.

Since relaxation is the opposite of tension, the best way to approach the experience is to just "let it happen." The matrix layered within the recording will automatically synchronize your brainwave patterns and unfold a deep state of relaxation without you having to do anything except just relax and let yourself go.

You should keep a written journal of your experiences. After each session take 15 to 20 minutes to record your thoughts, feelings, and experiences. Not only is this a valuable process that gives you a formal record of your progression, but the short time you devote to contemplation has many rewards. You'll find this time highly creative and useful for problem solving in every area of your life.

This *Super Intelligence* soundtrack should be used on a regular basis, daily if possible, for a full 28 minute session. Just as with any exercise program, you can only receive the full benefits when you do it on a frequent basis. Once you've experienced the pleasant sensations of deeper relaxation and higher states of consciousness, you'll look forward to these short sessions as a welcome "time out" from your busy life. To establish a consistent use of this program, it is helpful to designate a set time and physical location for listening to this soundtrack. Choose a place that is quiet, dimly lit and away from any interference or distractions.

The *Mozart Brain Boost* soundtrack is designed to be used as background music while you read, study or relax. It does not require the use of headphones. Simply set up your CD player for continuous play and allow it (Track 3) to play repeatedly in the background while you go about your other activities.

WARNING: DO NOT USE ANY OF THESE SOUNDTRACKS WHILE DRIVING A CAR OR OPERATING MACHINERY AS THEY MAY CAUSE DROWSINESS.

Q. **What kind of results can I expect from using these soundtracks?**
A. Each person is different and it will depend on how often you play them as to how quickly you see results. Many people feel an immediate difference in their attitudes and behaviors, while for others the shift is slow and more subtle. It is highly recommended that you record your feelings and experiences in a daily journal. This gives you a formal record to review at a later date that can reveal the subtle shifts in your attitude and how you perceive the world. Within 90 days of continuous use, everyone should have noticed some positive effects.

Q. **Is this the same as "positive thinking" or "self talk"?**
A. No. The concept of positive thinking and self talk deals with your conscious mind. And because it only addresses you at a conscious level it is not as effective in changing behavior or

modifying self-image. Positive thinking, while good, really only scratches the surface by only addressing your conscious mind.

The problem with telling your conscious mind, "I am wealthy" or "I am thin" is that it knows you are telling yourself statements that aren't true. And too often, positive thinking exercises can actually backfire. Why? Because they establish a negative feedback loop of anxiety and fear due to the fact that you don't really believe what you're telling yourself on a conscious level. The unconscious mind will take your fears and in its own way create obstacles and limitations that prevent change from occurring.

The mindscripting technology incorporated into these soundtracks succeeds because it bypasses the critical conscious mind and therefore does not produce the same degree of mental conflict. The subconscious then goes about acting on this new experience using these scripts as a guide. The most important fact about the unconscious is this:

THE UNCONSCIOUS MIND DOESN'T KNOW THE DIFFERENCE BETWEEN A REAL AND AN IMAGINED EXPERIENCE!

By bombarding your unconscious with new internal images and experiences you are able to rewrite your internal mindscripts. Gradually your outward experiences are realigned to match these new inward images of reality. In other words, your unconscious auto pilot will follow whatever instructions are placed into it. It doesn't pay any attention to whether or not it is acting in your best interests—it just follows the script it receives from your experiences and internal dialogue.

Q. What is the *Brain Supercharger* Technology Based On?
A. The *Brain Supercharger* technology (*Super Intelligence*) is based on altered states research and the study of meditation. There is now a tremendous amount of interest by Westerners in the ancient practice of meditation because of the known health benefits. But much more is going on than just relaxing and dealing with your thoughts and emotions. Meditation is a powerful technique for expanding consciousness.

For most of us it is difficult to grasp the concept that our so called "normal" waking state is neither the highest nor the most effective state of which the human mind is capable. There are other states of vastly greater awareness that you can enter briefly and then return to normal living feeling enriched, enlivened, and enhanced.

To discover such insights we have to go very deeply into meditation. This is usually quite difficult for those who have not internalized the physiological responses required to induce these mental states. Eastern masters have long known of these difficulties. That is why the so-called "enlightenment state" is so rare and difficult to achieve.

The *Brain Supercharger* technology offers a solution. By physically driving the brain of the listener into the desired mind-state it allows almost everyone to experience an altered state and enter into those higher states of consciousness. The relevance of this level of awareness becomes clear when you remember that the aim is not just to become relaxed and dreamy, but rather to expand (as far as possible) the range of states over which you have mental control.

Both soundtracks on your CD are designed to open a window into the unconscious and to affect attitude and behavior through positive suggestion. However the actual process is different, as well as the brain states of the listener in each one. The *Brain Supercharger* technology (*Super Intelligence*) is more like a meditative process that drives the brain into a specific state of consciousness. By using a special frequency matrix, a random sound harmonic overlay and mindscripting techniques, the mind is placed in an optimum state for psycho-physical stimulation. First the frequency matrix alters your mind-state to stimulate Theta consciousness. In this special mind-state, you are extremely relaxed and receptive to new ideas and experiences. Then the random sound harmonic overlay helps to nudge your brain into greater whole brain synchrony. As your left and right brain become more synchronized, your brain functioning reaches a new level. At this stage you are primed and ready for behavioral programming. Finally, using mindscripting affirmations (directed at your inner mind) you are able to map new habits and behaviors into your unconscious.

Q. How often should I listen to these soundtracks?
A. Daily if possible. The point of the soundtracks is to expose your unconscious to as much positive programming as possible. Use *Super Intelligence* soundtrack for the full 28 minute session once a day if possible. It may seem difficult at first to fit this half hour into your

Q & A

205

busy schedule. But it is well worth your time. The benefits of stress reduction, heightened well-being, creativity, and mental clarity in addition to any psychological rescripting benefits make this as important as physical exercise for your body.

Q. Can I decrease the amount of time (or the number of times per week) I use the *Super Intelligence* soundtrack as my brain "becomes more fit?"

A. It is believed that through continuous use, your psycho-physical state will be altered in such a way that you may not need to use these soundtracks as frequently. Like physical fitness, once you've achieved your fitness goals, a maintenance program allows you to sustain your edge. Assuming you have reached that peak you may decide to cut back on your usage to once or twice per week.

Part III

Questions and Answers

206

Q. Do I need any special equipment or a special CD player?

A. No. Any quality CD player will work. However the better quality stereo players and headphones have a better frequency response and will reproduce the matrix and tones with greater precision. You don't need the most expensive equipment in the world to get results with these soundtracks, but a quality system can enhance the experience significantly. **NOTE: YOU MUST USE STEREO HEADPHONES** (for *Super Intelligence*). A special binaural audio phasing process is used in this soundtrack to direct specific sounds and frequencies to areas of your brain. The new ultra light headphones that sit on the surface of the ear are not as effective as those that completely cover your ear, blocking out all noise distractions.

Q. How will these soundtracks affect my sleep? What happens if I fall asleep during a session?

A. Some users may experience changes in their sleep cycles. Many require less sleep while others initially (first few weeks of use) feel a need for more. These soundtracks help to induce states similar to that experienced during dreaming. It is believed by many psychologists that the true purpose of sleep is not so much the body's need for physical rest but for psychological information processing. Because these soundtracks can provide a replacement for some dream activity, it may decrease the need for psychological sleep. The reason some users may feel a need initially for more sleep may be due to increased information processing activity stimulated by the soundtracks. As this need is lessened so too will be the need for excessive sleep.

Q. Can listening to these soundtracks become addicting?

A. No. However, as with any positive experience, you'll look forward to your "escape time" provided by these soundtracks, as a welcome time out from a hectic lifestyle.

Q. What is the content of the mindscripts?

A: listing of the affirmations incorporated into *Super Intelligence* is listed on pages 102-103.

Q. Why should I keep a journal? What types of observations should I be writing in my journal?

A. Keeping a written journal of your feelings and experiences is a good way of measuring your progress. Because the shifts are subtle and cumulative over a period of time, it is difficult to notice changes from day to day. However, keeping a journal gives you a record you can refer to months later and you will be able to easily see the shifts in attitude and behavior. After a *Super Intelligence* session it is important to take a few moments to write down your feelings and thoughts—no matter how strange or insignificant your ideas may seem at the time.

Q. Sometimes I feel uncomfortable or uneasy during or after a session. What's going on?

A. These soundtracks use a powerful mindscripting process that allows you to shift your thinking about yourself. Initially, this new programming may be in conflict with your current belief systems and comfort zone. As a result you may feel uneasy, anxious, or restless. These feelings are generally temporary and are an indication of your progress into a new level of self-awareness, which when achieved, can be a very empowering experience.

Negative thoughts and feelings, although uncomfortable, can provide great insight if you are willing to look at them and understand their source. The *Brain Supercharger* technology is a tool which can help surface those negative feelings so they can be looked at and addressed. The ideal environment in which to examine these feelings is in your journal where you can record your thoughts and establish a record that you can review and analyze.

Q. Can I use these soundtracks while I'm driving?

A. NO! Under no circumstances should you listen to these soundtracks while driving or operating machinery.

Q & A

207

Q. When is the best time to play my soundtracks?

A. *Super Intelligence* requires 28 minutes of undisturbed relaxation. Plan a time when you can give yourself a half hour each day. Take the phone off the hook and close the door. Many busy people get up a half hour early every morning to do a session. It not only gives them the extra 28 minutes, but the resulting mental clarity and focused attention remains with them throughout the day. Other people use it after they get home from work and find it helps them relax after a busy day. It is recommended that you listen to *Mozart Brain Boost* whenever you are involved in a learning activity. This does not interrupt your schedule as it is used as background music.

Letters From Users Of The Brain Supercharger Technology

What follows are reprints (uneditied) of several letters from users of the *Brain Supercharger* technology. This is just a sample of the thousands I've received since 1988. I've included representative examples so you might gain some perspective from their experiences.

Dear Mr. Spotts,
I purchased some tapes this past fall and received them on December 13th. They are the Ultra Success Braincharger with the Booster. I thought you might be interested in my experience with these tapes.

First of all, some background: I am a 40 year old woman, definitely a product of the sixties, and a practitioner of TM for more than 10 years. Although I love TM and have reaped many benefits from it, I have frequently had difficulty finding the quiet place, stilling my thoughts, etc. which is necessary in TM in order to go down into a Theta state. In 1988 I made several major lifestyle changes: ending a 20 year relationship, moving to a new city, buying a business, etc. The business was failing and, by autumn, I was panicking. So I ordered your tapes after seeing an ad in Psychology Today or maybe it was Omni. Before they finally arrived (Canada Post managed to lose them for a month) I was feeling close to suicidal. I was literally having very detailed fantasies about going for a swim in icy Lake Ontario. (In Canada it's cold in December.) I was even making plans. By this time, I was unable to meditate at all. There was no stillness inside me at all. Then your tapes arrived. I decided to try them before swimming. After all, they were paid for.

I remember it was a Friday and, after dinner, I took my headphones and ghetto blaster up to my bedroom with warnings to my teenagers not to disturb me. ZONK. That tape just sucked me down into Theta and kept me there. The release of stress was exactly what I needed and I needed it badly. I used the Brain Supercharger tape 10 or 12 times that weekend. Electronic meditation sedation.

I began to think more positively from the first time I used the Brain Supercharger. It helped me to put things into perspective and to find some light in my life. I settled into a routine of playing it first thing in the morning and last thing at night. I have given up TM. My business is better but has not turned around as quickly as I wanted. I had expected a dramatic turnaround and improvement has been steady but slow. Yesterday I ran across the page of affirmations that was enclosed with the tapes and I realize that over the past two months I have integrated most of them. When I first read them, they were affirmations; now they are me. Now I KNOW that my business will continue to improve and so will all areas of my life.

Each time I use the tapes my experience is different and I like that. Altered states of consciousness can be fun. I have not experienced any psychic phenomenon but have encountered lights (often) even when not using the tape and occasionally a male entity is in the "background" while the tape is on. I feel some resistance to these things. Who knows what the results might be if I was able to relax a little more?

Although I bought the tapes to improve my business and self-esteem, that is not the primary benefit that I received from using them. As a stress management tool, the Brain Supercharger is unparalleled. Bonne chance and much prosperity to you, Mr. Spotts.

Very truly yours,
L.P.
Canada
P.S. Was able to give up coffee, alcohol + white sugar since using the tapes. Cigarettes were already gone.

Dear Dane:
My friends are all asking me what has happened to me! I can't be selfish, so I'm rotating my tapes among them on a one week trial basis to see if they help them. I get phone calls every day, about their improvements, and they all want their very own tapes!

The reason they have made such a difference in my own life, is because of the stress I have been under since January 1990. Before that time and for a while afterward I was able to keep it together because I could meditate and have O.B.E.s. In January 1990, my Dad was diagnosed with cancer. Shortly after, so was my grandmother.

I worked two jobs at the time. I have a fierce dedication to my family, and after months and months of hospital visits, and shifts at home, I realized I was living on borrowed energy. My father + my grandmother were in two different hospitals. But I spent hundreds and hundreds of hours with each. My Dad's battle with cancer ended 14 1/2 months after diagnosis. My grandmother's, 4 months after that.

The stress and exhaustion, hampered my ability to relax enough to meditate. When I plugged in the tapes, it was like a visit to my old self! I thought I had lost her strength and courage forever. Up until this point, the stress was working away at my nervous system. I went days without eating, I couldn't sleep for more than 3 hours straight. I had pains cropping up all over my body for no apparent reason. I was having shooting pains from my elbows to my wrists and hands to the point where I couldn't even pick up a glass of water or hold my nephew for fear of dropping him.

My brain instantly remembered the path to my inner self where there is enough love to help me through. Days after I started listening to the tapes, my friends were excited about my state of mind. They kept saying, "What happened to you? I've missed this in you!" So, I showed them the tapes. They were all impressed and wanted to borrow them. After the expenses of 18 months of two relatives with cancer, I can't afford to buy everyone tapes, but I would if I could. But somehow, I know, that you never get something for nothing, and if they buy the tapes they will listen to them. Especially after listening to mine.

I have spent the last 2 weeks thanking God for the peace I've found again. Although I know it's up to me to turn that peace back into strength. I've been on the phone with peers and mentors thanking them for their ears, patience and love through my pain.

I wanted to especially thank all the people working on this for their labor of love that resulted in these tapes. Thank you very much!
May the Blessings Be,
L. M.

─────────────

I purchased your "Ultra Success" Brain Supercharger tapes a little less than a year ago. It was a risk on my part because I had already invested a lot of money on so many tapes from other companies and had experienced little results (if any). In other words, I was very skeptical. I've been listening to your tapes on a regular basis since I received them and know, without a doubt that they work!

Before I purchased your tapes, I was feeling a bit down and out because I wasn't getting anywhere in life. I was broke all the time. I had a job that had no future — the company was on the verge of bankruptcy and I didn't know what direction to take because I didn't think I qualified to do much — my self esteem was low! Today, not only do I feel more confident but I am also holding a position as an Assistant Director for a successful private school and I am earning a very comfortable income. A couple of weeks ago, I was told that I would be getting a promotion to Director which means that my income will also increase — and it hasn't even been a year! In addition, I am in the process of buying my very first house. This alone, is a major feat because of the high real estate cost in California.

My life has totally changed (for the best) during the past year and I can surmise that it had something to do with your tapes. Of course I had to take control of my own life but with the help of your tapes, the process was made effortlessly. I still need to accomplish a bit more and there's no doubt in my mind that it will all be realized.

As part of my job, I have to conduct workshops every week. The topic: "How to Increase Success." Guess what I discuss? The students are wide-eyed when I explain this new concept to them.

Thank you and have a Happy Holiday!

Sincerely,
V. C.

I always had a wish to write a screenplay, but it had always been a wish. Never something I believed I could actually do. I just sat down for one extended weekend. And I wrote it. I needed a trigger, a catalyst...and I think the tapes have been instrumental in that. Within a week, I had actual proof that I was doing something different. There was some transformation happening inside of me. It's strange because it's a completely different experience than anything I've ever tried. These tapes bring about benefits without the kind of effort that normally you would have to make to change self limiting behavior...they take you by the scruff of the neck and literally force you to do what you want to do.

Sincerely
D.B.

Reprints of Letters

Someone very dear to me purchased your "Brain Supercharger" series and gave it to me as a birthday gift. I have been using the tapes now for well over two months and find them to be truly outstanding! I look forward to the time that I allot each day so that I may listen to my tape and sail away into a universe of bliss and understanding. I want to thank you from the bottom of my heart for developing this wonderful system. I would also greatly appreciate a catalogue of your other productions, so that I can order for myself in the future.

Thank you for your time,
S. M.

Dear Dane:
I received my "Ultra Success" Brain Supercharger kit about 6 weeks ago. I ran right down and bought a new auto-reverse cassette player and some Sony headphones (I called it my Mother's Day present to myself), ran back to my one-person office and plugged myself in.

I was truly not prepared for the feelings I experienced the first time I heard the soundtrack. At times I felt as if I were listening to the soundtrack of a science-fiction movie, at other times I felt almost as if I was visiting another dimension! In any case, by the time the tape finished I knew this was something special. Now that I know more what to expect, my reactions are not as startling to me, but I am able to let the tape "do its work" while I relax and take a mini-vacation. I use the Brain Supercharger every morning when I get to my office. I go into the back room, lie down on a little chaise lounge and use the tape to start my day off right. When the tape is done, I take the cassette player into my main office and start the subliminal booster tape. People coming into my office like the sound of the waves. When possible, I lock the door and turn off the lights at lunchtime and repeat the Brain Supercharger in the back room again.

Some very interesting things have taken place in the last several weeks. Perhaps it would help you to understand that my spouse is a very negative man who insists that my business is failing and we should move back to the mainland so I can make money easier. We married five years ago, he is an immigrant and has yet to work a day since our marriage. (That's my problem, I know.) Be that as it may, in the last few weeks I have designed a dynamite new business card which will be ready in a few days, I started a series of spots on the local radio station about better bookkeeping tips, and I have started attending psychic development classes (which never interested me before). Last week with no apparent cause I had four new clients contact me for regular monthly bookkeeping.

Maybe it's coincidence. Maybe not. I can look past my husband's negativity and I don't buy into it any more. I have channeled my creativity and I'm acting on it. I am believing in myself for the first time.

Your form letter that comes with the Brain Supercharger Kit says "Thank you". Now it's my turn. Thank you, Dane. I may not become the most famous bookkeeper in the world (is there even one famous bookkeeper?), but I know that I will be successful. Thank you again for the Superbrain Technology. I have felt a change taking place, and as I continue the Ultra Success program I can't wait to see what's going to happen to my business and my life!

Peace and love to you,
C. C.

(11/15/92)

Dear Mr. Spotts:
On February 2, 1992, I for the first time used your Brain Supercharger tapes and after that enlightening experience I knew from that moment on my whole life would be much more fulfilling and enjoyable. I have kept a journal from the first time up until now of all my thoughts and emotions experienced after every session and let me tell you that there is a big difference from who I was at the beginning of the year and who I am now at the end of the year. Just to demonstrate how much I have changed for the better I would like to tell you of my on-going evolutionary process.

Before listening to your tapes I was 25 pounds overweight, had low self-esteem, and was a very depressed soul. I let every little thing bother me and I didn't enjoy my life. I was always negative and just wandered through life without accomplishing anything. I usually spent several hours every day just contemplating about what life meant or was and why I was put here. I believed that my life was a total waste and disaster and not worth a dime.

But now I can't even imagine being in such a terrible state of mind as I was before I used your program. Your tapes have helped me to reignite a once wet spark now into a flaming torch! My weight is now 133 pounds and I have gone from a 34 inch waist to a 30 inch waist. My thinking is so positive that I can detect negative thoughts and eliminate them before they know what hit them. I feel confident, attractive, and happy. I have given up watching T.V. because I have discovered a new and fascinating world in my mind. Before I would let driving in general irritate and upset me, but now when I'm confronted with a challenge like a traffic jam I, in your words, just think that it is another deal in a world full of deals and I move on to the next one without having it bother me.

I once again just want to congratulate you for the excellent work you have done with this program. Thank you for a new and successful life and may your program help other people just as it has helped me.

Sincerely yours,
J. P.

Dear Dane Spotts,
Using sound frequencies to unleash the great forces of your mind has got to be the most phenomenal discovery of the decade.

In the last year or so I've come upon the discovery of the human body having an electro-magnetic field surrounding several vortex's in the body which channel the vital life force into reproductive energy. By doing several special exercises you are able to keep your body in balance which gives the body greater stamina, strength, harmony, and just a total rejuvenation. This is all fine and good but I'm too lazy and after a hard day at work, my body wasn't able to perform these exercises.

You could imagine the awe I was in when you sent me your letter & eight page insert describing all of the research, testing, & producing of these special combinations of sound frequencies that synchronizes your brainwave patterns of electrical energy into an optimum state of awareness. The ancient physical exercises that I was doing was just too much to handle when all I really wanted was to be able to be in charge of my state of being. If your tapes can rescript my sub-conscious, then you will have fulfilled my desires to be in perfect harmony.

Personally speaking, I went to a psychiatrist for six weeks during & after my divorce, which had me totally out of control, in which time they were able to get my breathing under control, but there was still an emptiness inside.

Since then having to raise two girls (9 1/2 months & 2 1/2 yrs. old) after 2 1/2 years, I have read over 100 books and bought several tape programs which is just a lot of opinions in print & audio. I want to be me! Help! I think you have the answer I'm looking for. I want to be whole again after 2 1/2 years of research & raising kids I'm ready. Let's use this open-minded leverage to rescript my dysfunction's and "Find My Purpose In Life". I'm not dead, but I feel I have no direction or energy to fulfill my goals & objectives that I wish to obtain. I want to alter my state immediately with your tapes and go beyond my expectations! I want to blaze a path for others to follow (without the ego trip) & create a total confident winning attitude that will transpire others to follow.

I also want to congratulate you & your colleagues for having the insight to pursue this program for the mental & physical health of mankind. I know that you want to share this technology with the world, but I'm kinda selfish coming up in a way of life of going down all of the backroads through the hardknock school of life, also being a concerned parent that thinks the school system is on the brink of disaster, but all I want is myself & my daughters to be the "Best of the Best", out in front with the successful intellects conquering the world, & "Enjoying The Thrill Of The Journey."

Sincerely,
Fellow "Mind Development Warrior"
C. G.

Reprints of Letters

213

Dear Sir,
Hi, I am a customer of yours. There are a few reasons why I am writing this letter. The first is one of thanks. The subliminal research team you have there are incredible. They should be given a Nobel Prize. They have done their research well and leave other companies in the dust. The service is also terrific. As a result of using your tapes I feel terrific and recently picked up a great job. It seems to me other companies mean well but they don't get down to the very critical nitty-gritty. Your company is very good with that and since you work out the kinks your tapes really work!

Sincerely,
J. R. G.

To Whom It May Concern,
I am writing to inform you of the results of my listening to your tapes. After listening to the first tape I noticed that colors seemed more colorful, pictures seemed to stand out more, I was more relaxed.

After listening to tape 2, I was even more relaxed and achieved a sense of peace of mind I could never achieve before. Colors are very colorful and my thinking is clear and deep. I have a very stressful job. Your tapes have made it so much easier. I used to have a bad temper and was rude to family, friends and passengers but now I'm Mr. Mellow. Your tapes are so effective that my wife has come back home. We were going to get a divorce due to my hostility but after she saw how mellow I had become she came back home and we have canceled the divorce.

With my stressful job I put your tapes to the ultimate test and they passed with flying colors. Hope to see you in the future.

Metaphysically,
V. A.

(7/26/90)

Dear Dane:
I received my ULTRA MEDITATION tapes today. I have always been skeptical about audio and video tapes that supposedly induce any specified state of mind. I chose not to read the literature about the effects of the tape so as to not be predisposed to any condition.

I turned the tape on at 3:03 p.m. and got into a comfortable position. Almost immediately I felt very relaxed. Within about 4 minutes the awareness of my physical body was completely gone, I didn't hear the music, and I was off in a completely different realm of being. If this is a state of ultra meditation (especially for the first time of playing the tape), it is all I need to keep balance in my everyday life.

I looked back at the clock at 3:19 p.m. and realized that I had been in a meditative state for about 12 minutes and was absolutely amazed at the total peace of mind I felt. I really look forward to keeping this feeling for the full 30 minutes and also to listening to the second set of the tape (if it's half as good as the first one, I'm in for a really nice treat). This tape will definitely be an important part of my daily life.

Sincerely,
S. H.

Part III

Questions and Answers

▬▬▬

214

(3/13/91)

Mr. Spotts:
Let me begin by stating that I have never written to a company to compliment them on their product before. By telling you that your tape system has saved my life—I am not exaggerating.

A little over a year ago I was diagnosed with a terminal illness. Little by little less significant things in my life began to go wrong (my car was stolen, my lover left me, my mother became disabled, etc.). Needless to say, I had gone into a severe state of depression. I began to avoid everything and basically, when not at work, I sat in front of the television and ate junk food. Prior to this, the only time I ever spent at home was when I was entertaining or asleep. I made three unsuccessful attempts at suicide at this time.

One evening while inhaling potato chips and chocolate milk, I happened to catch your "infomercial." I had worked with tapes before so I knew they worked, and the stress reduction your program offered seemed like it might be what I needed to help me out of my depression. As I stated before—your tape system saved my life. I sleep only a few hours a night. I have more energy than ever before. I have quit smoking. I have stopped procrastinating. The ironic part is that really nothing around me has changed; how I perceive it has. A good example is that I still dislike my job, but I no longer mind going to work.

Another reason for my writing, other than to thank you for such a wonderful product, is to say there is a whole market out there which you may be neglecting — the terminally ill. You could possibly devise a live seminar which could be presented in hospitals, hospices, and to groups and organizations which deal with terminal illness. I am sure your "immunity" Brain Supercharger tape would be of particular interest to many. It is the one I use most often. It's better than an extra dry martini.

Well, thank you very much for taking the time to listen to my ramblings. Thank you very much for such a fine product, and I hope the weight loss tape is as effective as the others I've used are—I've got fifteen pounds to lose!

Sincerely,
G. G.

(4/12/89)

Dear Sir,
Recently I came across your ad in *Psychology Today* and it fascinated me. Since I had come to a wall in my exercise program, I decided to try your tape on Peak Performance in Sports.

It would be an understatement to say that it literally "woke me up" from my lethargy and stimulated me to exercise more vigorously. As a physician you can imagine my surprise in that it not only worked, but did so after only 3 sessions. I am thoroughly impressed!

Sincerely,
W. Z., M.D.

(10/26/88)

Dear Dane,

As I told, you I am very impressed with your tapes. Until listening to your tapes the only tapes that I could achieve a Theta state were the Monroe Institute tapes. But yours are much more powerful. No need to go through mental exercises or countdowns — just lay back, relax and there I am—Theta bound. What a joy!

I have been on the path to enlightenment since the 60's. I've used many different tapes and attended many seminars, trainings, etc. I recently completed 10 rebirth sessions in which I gained a lot of insights. The first time I listened to your tape was in some ways similar to the aftermath of my first rebirth session. Both times I felt a clarity of mind and real sense of experiencing the present moment to the fullest. I felt very powerful, joyful and ready to take on the world.

Since that first tape encounter I've listened to the tape at least 3 times a day. Each experience is different but always worthwhile. Sometimes I feel I'm in a lucid dream and am controlling the action. Who needs Disneyland with that kind of fun!

The times I experienced Theta are usually early morning sessions. Theta for me is very similar to the way Stuart Wilde describes it in his tapes. I perceive in my 3rd eye location objects or words through a brown-black hazy film. Things move in and out of view very quickly. Many times I don't understand what I see.

You did a careful and thoughtful wording on the affirmations. I do sense a spiritual quality to them. And some make me think of messages in A Course of Miracles.

I was wondering if it is important to have the earphone speaker that is labeled "left" on the left ear? Sometimes I've switched and the energy of that session seems different. Speaking of energy, I usually feel a tingling sensation in waves rolling through my body from head downward. I do lie north to south and as suggested by Stuart Wilde extend my energy body beyond my physical body. Since using your tapes my other non-tape meditations have been more powerful. In fact it seems that my tape sessions are charging my "batteries" for my meditation sessions.

Thank you for creating these tapes. You've given many struggling people a real opportunity to take a big step in their personal development. I appreciate it.

Sincerely,
D. M.

———————————

(9/24/88)

Dear Dane,

I talked to you several times on the phone. I am the fellow who's been in T.M. several years and is presently going to law school. You requested that I send you a letter concerning my evaluation of the Brain Supercharger Kit. I can't emphasize my pleasure with this Kit enough. I think you have created something that is unique and very special. You've done an excellent job in its design, purpose, packaging, and effectiveness. I receive stronger, faster, and deeper states of meditation with this tape. My body unloads stress much faster. When in a deep state of T.M. my body at times will twitch, indicating stress relief. With your tape I immediately and always get to this deep state. I've noticed my eyes after a meditation have a sparkle and shine that wasn't there before, after use of this tape.

Your tape has been a real "Godsend" for law school. Law school is nothing but hard work and stress. Anyone involved in any type of school or serious study should own these tapes.

I can't wait to receive your experimental learning tape. Please be sure to send me one. I'll send you regular reports on its effectiveness. I feel I can be a special help to your organization. As a T.M.er, and having done rather extensive research in the field of brainwaves, I feel, I'd be able to interface with you quite well. (By the way, I'm having a friend of mine build me a small experimental EEG machine for experiments.)

Reprints of Letters

215

Please feel free to reproduce any part of this letter or future letters in future advertisements as an endorsement to your products. You have my total support and help. Please feel free to call me, if you would like to discuss your tapes on the phone.

Sincerely,
B. F. D.

Dear Mr. Spotts:
I received and began to use your mind-scrubbing ULTRA-MEDITATION TAPES on September 29, 1988. They are, indeed, in this world, but they are not of it. In the past three or four years I have ordered many, many audio and video tapes; now that I have the ULTRA-MEDITATION TAPES all of the others are useless.

Since beginning listening to the ULTRA-MEDITATION TAPES my blood pressure has normalized; my eating habits have become nutritional rather than tastebud oriented; my drinking, smoking and other multitudinous bad habits have normalized and I feel centered. Specifically, I am physically relaxed, emotionally calm, mentally alert and spiritually awake.

Thank you.

Very truly yours,
C. M. D., P.A.

Dear Sir,
I bought the tapes of Millionaire's Mind along with all the others, in August 90. For a period of about 30 or 40 days, they stayed on the shelf and then last Sept 20, I started listening to them. I started with the audio tapes and then pursued with "The Brain Supercharger". When the tape was over, I felt a little bit better. On Monday the 24, I listened to it again plus "Self Confidence and Success Motivation" I actually heard a female voice; faintly. I heard some of the phrases she softly spoke, "I CAN DO IT," "I AM CONFIDENCE," "I RADIATE ENTHUSIASM," "I BELIEVE IN ME," and some others I could not completely make out.

But all this, just to tell you the feeling I got when I got up was like you know the feeling when you go bowling, and you just played 5-6 STRIKES IN A ROW. That's how I felt. GREAT, and ready to CONQUER THE WORLD.

Thank you so much
M. P.

(11/20/88)

Dear Dane,
Thanks for the prompt service in sending the tapes that I ordered, and for taking the time to talk with me about your own experience with these tapes. I appreciate the tapes more, now that I have a better idea of where you are coming from.

In September of this year, I had my worst month of the year in generating income through commissions. I decided I had to make a major commitment to improve my performance, beginning with the resolution of any subconscious conflicts about achieving success. After reviewing available advertisements from various magazines, I purchased tapes from several sources.

But...none of the tapes from these other companies even approaches the threshold of radical transformation evoked by the Theta brainwave entrainment of your Brain Supercharger series. There is absolutely no doubt in my mind that your tapes are the most powerful, effective tools for self-transformation that I have tried so far. The inducement of Theta brainwaves as a prelude to subliminal rescripting is a clearly superior approach to altering subconscious thought patterns, and your tapes achieve what many others have talked about but have yet to accomplish. Congratulations and thank you!

In October 1988, my first month of using subliminal tapes, I quintupled my income from September 1988, and made 20 percent more than my previous all-time high for monthly income. In my second month of using subliminal tapes, including your Brain Supercharger Ultra Success Conditioning tape, I tripled my income again, from the prior record-breaking month. I remain amazed at the effects of subliminal rescripting! The only thing that I did differently was to listen to tapes for 4-6 hours per day.

There was a quantum leap in consciousness during the second month, which I attribute principally to your Brain Supercharger Ultra Success Conditioning tape. It is more powerful than all the other tapes combined. However, I still use other tapes because some of them have affirmations specifically related to my profession, while others have pleasant, relaxing background music which I can listen to all day. But unequivocally, the title of "King of the Subliminal Tapes" goes to the Brain Supercharger.

The Ultra Meditation tapes indeed produce altered states of consciousness of a profound nature. I believe that they would be of immense assistance to people who lack concentration or experience in disciplines involving mind-control. As such they would be invaluable tools to enhance the developmental and learning processes by providing controllable, repeatable entry into states of mind which are rarely accessed consciously. In addition to the therapeutic value of deep relaxation through synchronization of the brain's hemispheres, these tapes provide a veritable space/mind platform from which advanced adventurers in consciousness can blast off into even subtler spheres of perception, to explore the furthest inner depths of the ultimate frontier—the human mind, which is but a mere reflection of something much greater.

My only concern is that the Theta experience would be beyond the capacity of certain people to holistically assimilate and integrate, thus perhaps causing an exacerbation of previously existing conditions. Tools misused can destroy as well as create, so there should be a note of warning for those people who have a history of, or propensity toward, psychological imbalance.

In conclusion, I am deeply appreciative of your service in making tapes like these available to the general public, and wish you all the best in your future endeavors. Please keep me informed of any new developments. I would be most pleased to be available to review any new, experimental products. Thanking you again,

In Wholeness and Light,
S. M. Q.

(10/10/88)

Dear Dane,
First of all, I must say I'm really fed up with all the hype and exaggerated claims used to sell most of the self-improvement tapes on the market. I have an extensive collection of such tapes, and while some of them are very good, most of them just don't live up to their advertising. Some were so bad I returned them immediately for a refund. Others I kept, hoping they might eventually do what they were supposed to, but more often than not they never did. Such disappointments cause one to become somewhat skeptical after awhile, and indeed, when I placed my order for your tapes, it was with considerable doubt that they could be as good as your ads made them sound. Can you imagine my surprise and utter delight when your tapes turned out to be even better than your enthusiastic endorsements in the ad had led me to expect! After listening to the Ultra Meditation tapes only one time, I knew without a doubt that these were the tapes I had been searching for. (Actually, one doesn't just listen to your tapes, one experiences them. And what a pleasurable experience it is!)

Again, your tapes did not disappoint me; in those 28 minutes, they do indeed give me a complete meditation, and you're so right... it is like a vacation. At the risk of sounding corny, I like to think of your tapes as my "mind spa"... they take me firmly by the mind and lead me gently to a fabulous resort on the outskirts of time and space. No two visits are ever alike — each one provides something new and fascinating. The sounds on your tape may be "intentionally boring", as you say in your literature, but the feelings and experiences they induce never are! By the way, I think both soundtracks are quite beautiful, but the first one is especially interesting. I really get into trying to listen to everything that's going on in it! Even my roommate who is not easily impressed by such things says it is very enjoyable and well done, different from all the others he has heard. As a matter of fact, yours are the only tapes I can get him to use regularly; he would just as soon not bother with any of the others.

No other tapes (or techniques) relax me the way yours do. It amazes me the way I can actually feel the tension leaving every part of my body, shortly after I start one of the soundtracks. It's a real physical sensation, not something I have to "visualize" or suggest to myself. The tension just flows out of me, like water down a drain. It's great.

In the short time I've been using your tapes, I've noticed a subtle change in myself. Ordinarily, when some little thing upsets me, like a bad experience in traffic, I have a tendency to fly off the handle. I try to control my reactions, but the other day, something interesting occurred. I was in rush hour traffic when another driver did something rude that I didn't like at all. I could feel anger starting to well up inside me, then all of a sudden, POOF — it was gone! I didn't even have to think about it or make any effort to control it, it just vanished, leaving me smiling and amazed. This has happened a couple of times now, and I feel it's the use of your tapes that's providing me with this very welcome "side effect". I'll be looking for other improvements in my life as I continue to use your tapes daily.

R. G.

_____

Part III

Questions and Answers

▄▄▄▄

218

Hello.
I would like to take this opportunity to tell you how much fun your Ultra Meditation tapes have been. I have meditated for about 15 years and had attained the "mind awake body asleep" state only occasionally. I'm referring to a deep "Floating" state here. With Ultra II I have been going in regularly and have learned to find that bodily feeling even without the tapes. I count Ultra II as the key for me to have stored the memory of deep meditation so as to be able to go back to that state at will. It is truly a great teacher and guide to meditation.

Thank you
R. W.

_____

Dear Dane:
I've used the Brain Supercharger once and I must write to you. The info tape was great, especially what you said about having joy in the present. You know many people, in hope, can believe in a better future but if you tell them they can have joy now, there may be difficulty in believing. Even though many paths bring one eventually to a whole state, it's still in the future. To experience that joy, that wholeness, brings back the memory of what we once were and what we will again be. Like a cell who's memory is stimulated will return to wholeness, and must to remember its evolutionary promise.

I listened to both sides, so I want to share my experiences. At first I just plain enjoyed the tones. Then I found myself slipping into another state of consciousness. It seemed to greatly affect the child within me. It was fun. After all, as a child, I went there all the time and since then, have been seeking to reunite. I would suddenly, but smoothly, find myself slipping into a thought — something from the day or the past. Then I'd hear a little click and it was as if the worrisome thought went up in a puff of smoke. In fact I'd forget what it was and didn't want to bother to try. It didn't matter!

Side 2 was even better. I had a beautiful past life recall which brought deep meaning to my present conditions. I made contact with entities, "old friends", and to my delight perceived we would work together again. I felt joy and excitement. I've been celibate for a number of years and have been addressing issues of sex, and I admit, judging myself. As that issue came forth, I found my consciousness in my 2nd chakra. What a wonderful place to be! I could see how divine and powerful sexual energy was, and how "it" totally loved and accepted me. So I then proceeded to enter each of my chakras whereupon I perceived my gifts and status of energy. I've never felt my Spirit before — not like that.

Right now I'm at such peace. All is well. I feel so in tune with everything. You know how they say there are many paths and the joy of finding one that works for you. Well, I know I'm on the right track. I would recommend your tapes to anyone. Before I opened them, I could feel the high energy emitting from them — a Cosmic source.

Thank you, Dane, and to your co-workers for sharing your path with others.

Love in Light - L. C. B.

(8/15/88)

Dear Dane,

Last week I experienced a healing. This occurred on the fourth straight day of use of tape 1, side 1. I saw a beautiful scene. My husband and I were standing in wedding garment. When I looked at the preacher it was Jesus. He put a crown of flowers on both our heads. At this point in time I became a spectator. Me and my husband then blended into one person. We split apart again and Jesus put a white lily in my hand and spoke to me about the meaning of Easter. Jesus handed my husband a scepter. At this time we were turning around and walked away. Jesus said, "Lo I am with you always." The floor, ground, behind us back to Jesus turned a florescent pink. I really was crying when I came out of the meditation. Then my body experienced a quickening. This condition lasted about 15 minutes. I'm sure this was a healing for my marriage and who knows what else.

There is a question I'd like to ask: Four of my friends over a two day period had listened to tape 1 side 1. I didn't tell them any of my experiences. Each person, including self, experienced some sort of O.B.E. situation. Two of the four broke out in the sweats. Question: Are you aware of this from others? Does this happen often?

If you would like more details feel free to contact me. All four of the others were very impressed. We all have been working in metaphysics for about 10 years or longer. I hope this information is helpful to you.

Peace and Joy
B. C.

Have a good day!

Dear Dane Spotts,

I also want to thank you and your corporation for the wonderful experience your tapes are giving me. I have been feeling my way along the path of inner experience, struggling with insight meditation and seeking the "great path of awakening" without really knowing if what I'm finding is what I'm looking for, or if I've lost the way before really finding it. I'm reaping undreamed of benefits; I felt I was on the right track, and your tapes are serving as solid reinforcement that my struggles are not in vain. My blind faith in you is justified. I'd been stung before, but not lately. Positive results from my efforts!

You might also be interested in knowing, your tapes arrived on July 11. I buried my mother on July 13. Without the tapes, which served as a sort of touchstone, I'm sure I would have skipped my meditation sessions and thus lost this lifeline. Would you say, Jung's synchronicity?
I thank you.

Peace.
D. H.

(4/16/89)

Dear Sir or Madam;

For the last 6 months my Step-son Tim Kuring, a long time customer of yours, has been kind enough to share his Ultra Meditation tape set with me. The tapes have caused me to have many very clear, lucid, and vivid dreams. During the time when I am using the tapes I have visions. Some of the visions have been; I have had an ancient Hopi, in an Eagle mask, dance around me shaking medicine rattles. Another time, a horse that I was very fond of, that died three years ago, appeared and talked to me. Just last week Mandelbrot sets formed in the air' about me and flew around flapping their bodies like giant manta rays.

Sincerely Yours
M. N.

Dear Dane Spotts

I think your tapes are the best tapes in the entire world. All my life I have been searching for tapes like yours that put you in an altered state and then feed subliminal affirmations into your subconscious mind. I have tried other company's subliminals but they were not effective in producing change but I know your tapes work. Your company is the only company that I trust. Your company is the only company that I will do business with.

Thank you very much Dane Spotts and may God bless you for your wonderful contribution to the human race.

K. S.

Dear Mr. Spotts:

I wanted to congratulate you and your company on an absolutely first-rate product that will bring the benefits of meditation to many people who might otherwise miss out. I have practiced Transcendental Meditation routinely since my induction in 1975. My experience, in the three weeks that I have owned and used your ultra-meditation tapes, is that the quality of the meditative experience is apparently comparable to that which a traditional meditator of my experience level can achieve unaided. I have loaned the tapes to both my wife and co-workers without previous meditation experience, and all have reported positive results. The most general reaction from people who have not had prior experience is a sense of profound relaxation, and renewed energy.

My own experiences have been more profound. I have had out-of-body experiences, using the second tape, and combining traditional meditation techniques with either of the two tapes produces a pronounced, exquisite sense of relaxation and relief from stress. I have also found that the tapes can be used prior to sleep, without any detriment to the sleeping experience; in addition, both tapes can be effectively employed after eating meals, which is not always possible with TM.

I have ordered two additional set of the tapes, based on my experiences and the quality of the product. My wife will get one set, and I plan to make the other available to co-workers, because I think the experience will help alleviate stress and improve interpersonal relations and productivity. You and your associates should be proud of your achievement, and I hope that you will have the success which this product, and your future productions, deserve.

I would be very interested in any additional work you do in this area; please send me word of what's available. I'd also like to ask you to consider an extended-play version of your current series, which would provide 45-60 minutes of the meditation experience for those who are more experienced with meditation.

Thanks for a quality product, and I hope to hear from you as you progress with additional developments.

Sincerely,
Dr. W. Y.

Dear Dane,

I am a graduate student in studio painting who happened late one evening to see you on TV. I ordered your products the next morning. I have concentrated on just three of the tapes; the creativity and problem solving, communication, and the prosperity tape. In a few weeks I noticed I was reading more and making more trips to the library. I found myself speaking out in class more often and my self-confidence grew. All of this from the communication tape. Lately I have been listening to the prosperity tape. This has helped me to widen my perspectives on careers. I am reaching higher and am making plans to reach goals that before were only dreams. I now realize that anything is possible. Still there are days that I get a little down. When this happens I use the tapes twice a day and find that it perks me up and I am back on track. The changes were subtle and it was only a short time before I was able to see a correlation between the tapes and my changing attitudes. At any rate I feel my initial purchase was an investment in me that is paying off, by awakening my mind to the great potentials that await me.

Sincerely,
C. Q.

Appendix A

THE BRAIN SUPERCHARGER
An Empirical Study

Prepared for
Mr. Dane Spotts, President

by

Lawrence G Cory, Ph.D., F.I.A.B.M.C.P.
Center For Transpersonal Studies
and
PSI/Metrics, Inc
Venice, California

October 10, 1990

BACKGROUND

Many instruments, currently available on the market, purport to entrain and balance the right and left hemispheres of the brain, while simultaneously lowering its alpha rhythm. They achieve these states by visual, kinetic, and/or electronic stimulation of the cerebral cortex. On the other hand, the BRAIN SUPERCHARGER is the first device to facilitate whole-brain synchrony entirely through sound, thus representing a major breakthrough in safe, inexpensive, and potentially effective psychotechnology.

The question, of course, is whether this innovation delivers what it promises. That is, does the BRAIN SUPERCHARGER, as its name suggests, increase such aspects of mental functioning as INTELLIGENCE, ALERTNESS and EMOTIONAL STABILITY? And if so, do these functions improve to a greater extent than they would by listening to a recording of merely pleasant, meditative music?

OBJECTIVES

With these considerations in mind, the present study was designed to determine:

- The extent to which listening to the BRAIN SUPERCHARGER is more
  psychologically effective than listening to an identical "placebo" sound track.

- The "critical" psychological dimensions which the BRAIN SUPERCHARGER alters.

- The effect of these "critical dimensions" on the overall personality of people who
  listen to the BRAIN SUPERCHARGER.

- The pattern of conscious responses to the BRAIN SUPERCHARGER compared to that of a
  placebo tape.

These objectives were addressed through an empirical, "double blind" experiment in which respondents believed they were evaluating a new "meditation tape". Nevertheless, half the sample listened to an unmarked copy of the BRAIN SUPERCHARGER (the "Experimental Group") while the other half listened to a "placebo" tape, identical in every respect except for the absence of the SUPERCHARGER technology (the "Control Group"). The details of these methods are described in the following section.

METHODS

This section discusses: 1) Sample; 2) Psychological Measurements; and 3) Analysis of the Data used in the study.

Sample
An invitation to participate in our study (see Appendix A) was sent to the following institutions:

- Ryokan College (Los Angeles)
- International Academy of Behavioral Medicine, Counseling and Psychotherapy
- Bedanta Society of Southern California
- Southern California Counseling Center
- Family Study Center of Southern California
- The Center for Transpersonal Studies

In addition, respondents were solicited on the street, by fliers left under the windshield wipers of cars, and by random mailings. This resulted in a sample, as of this writing, of 52 respondents—a surprisingly large number considering the two-week listening requirement and associated daily questionnaires. (A cutoff date of September 30, 1990 was set by PSI/Metrics for data collection.)

Respondent Groups. Each respondent received an unmarked "meditation tape" which he or she was asked to use every day for two weeks. Of these, roughly half (58%) were the BRAIN SUPERCHARGER, while the remainder (42%) were PLACEBO tapes, identical to the Supercharger in every way except for the underlying, brain-synchrony sound track. Thus, any differences between the SUPERCHARGER and PLACEBO groups would be due primarily to the whole-brain technology present in the former, but lacking in the latter.

Sample Demographics. Table 1, on the following page, is a breakdown of the sample by its demographic characteristics. It shows that our respondents, on the average, are affluent ($54K a year), well educated (75% post-graduate degrees), professional (90% professional/managerial occupations) women and men (58% and 42% respectively). Significantly, for the objectives of this study, the vast majority are also religious, affiliated primarily with the Eastern/New Age denominations (45%) in which meditation plays such an important role. Moreover, these characteristics, for the most part, are equally represented in the SUPERCHARGER and PLACEBO groups, once again suggesting that any differences between them, after listening to their respective "meditation" tapes, could only be due to the Supercharger soundtrack present in one but not the other.

Psychological Measurements. A significant feature of this study is its measurement of the personality structure of respondents in the SUPERCHARGER and PLACEBO groups both before and after listening to their unmarked, "meditation" tapes for two weeks. This design permits us to determine which psychological dimensions, if any, are affected by the Supercharger technology to a greater extent than its PLACEBO counterpart.

Personality Measurement. Respondents in both the SUPERCHARGER and PLACEBO groups completed a standardized psychological test before and after listening to their tapes. This instrument, the "16PF", was developed by the renown psychologist, Dr. Raymond B. Cattell, and his associates at the Institute for Personality and Ability Testing in Champaign, Illinois.[1] For the past forty years, it has been the instrument of preference in studies of normal personality functioning. In this regard, it has several advantages. First, it was developed scientifically rather than intuitively; secondly, it has different but parallel forms, thus permitting uncontaminated "before" and "after" measurements such as used in this study; third, it measures a broad spectrum of personality dimensions, including INTELLIGENCE, which may or may not be related to the BRAIN SUPERCHARGER tape; and finally, a vast body of psychological literature on the 16PF over the past forty years has permitted the development of computer programs for actuarial analysis of its profile results, the significance of which will become clear later in this report.[2]

---

1 For a technical discussion of the 16PF, see *Handbook for the Sixteen Personality Factor Questionnaire (16PF).* Raymond B. Cattell, etal. champaign, Illinois: Institute for Personality and Ability Testing, 1970.
2 This study uses the best of these programs, one developed by Dr. Bruce Duthie for Applied Innovations, Inc. of Wakefield, Road Island.

Table 1

Demographic Characteristics of the Sample

	TOTAL (N=52)	SUPERCHARGER (N=30)	PLACEBO (N=22)
GENDER			
Male	42%	47%	36%
Female	58	53	64
EDUCATION			
Ph.D.	40%	30%	50%
M.A.	35	40	0
B.A.	15	30	--
H.S.	10	--	20
OCCUPATION			
Professional	75%	70%	80%
Managerial	15	30	--
Student	5	--	10
Retired	5	--	10
RELIGIOUS PREFERENCE			
Catholic	5%	--	10%
Protestant	30	30	30
Jewish	10	--	20
Eastern/New Age	45	50	40
None	10	20	--

Brain Supercharger Study

223

The dimensions of personality measured by the 16PF are as follows:

- Warmth
- Intelligence
- Emotional Stability
- Dominance
- Impulsivity
- Conscientiousness
- Boldness
- Sensitivity
- Skepticism
- Creativity
- Awareness
- Insecurity
- Liberality
- Self-Sufficiency
- Self-Discipline
- Tension

As indicated earlier, the psychological meaning of these dimensions are described in Appendix B. At this point, it is sufficient to note that any or all of them could be the "critical factors" related to the impact of the BRAIN SUPERCHARGER on its listeners.

Daily Listening Diary. In addition to completing the 16PF before and after listening to their tapes, respondents in the SUPERCHARGER and PLACEBO groups were asked to complete the same "Daily Listening Diary" on each of the fourteen days of their participation in the study (see Appendix B). For each day, this specially designed instrument measured the respondent's:

- *Reaction to the tape on that occasion*
- *Reaction to the tape compared to the previous day*

Thus, this instrument measured conscious reactions to the SUPERCHARGER and PLACEBO tapes, while the 16PF measured their unconscious influence, if any, on the listener's personality.

FINDINGS

The statistical findings of this study are presented under three headings: 1) Individual Components Analysis; 2) Actuarial Profile Analysis; and 3) daily Listening Diary Analysis. The meaning of these will become clear when we discuss them under later headings.

Individual Component Analysis. Table 2, on the following page, shows the average scores on the 16PF before and after listening to the SUPERCHARGER and PLACEBO tapes. These differences were analyzed to determine which, if any, are statistically significant. Briefly, "statistical significance", in this research context, means that the difference between two average scores on the 16PF is LARGE and STABLE enough to occur by chance factors alone in 3 only 5 cases out of 100—i.e., the ".05 level of confidence" universally accepted as "significant" in most psychological research. These differences can be summarized as follows:

STATISTICALLY SIGNIFICANT CHANGES

Supercharger Group	Placebo Group
Intelligence	
Emotional Stability	
Alertness	
Self-Discipline	Self-Discipline

TABLE 2
Psychological Impact of Supercharger and Placebo Tapes

AVERAGE 16PF SCORES

	SUPERCHARGER GROUP (N=30)			PLACEBO GROUP (N=22)		
	Pre	Post	Dif	Pre	Post	Dif
Warmth	3.6	4.0	+0.4	4.5	5.0	+0.5
Intelligence	6.8	8.0	+1.2*	6.4	5.9	-0.5
Emotion. Stab.	5.9	7.0	+1.1*	6.3	6.4	+0.1
Dominance	5.9	6.0	+0.1	6.1	6.1	---
Enthusiasm	4.8	4.1	-0.7	4.6	4.5	-0.1
Conscientious	5.6	4.9	-0.7	5.3	4.9	-0.4
Boldness	5.5	5.6	+0.1	6.1	6.6	+0.5
Sensitivity	6.4	6.8	+0.4	6.7	6.3	-0.4
Skepticism	5.7	5.5	-0.2	5.1	5.4	+0.3
Creativity	6.8	7.5	+0.7	6.3	7.2	+0.9
Alertness	4.9	5.9	+1.0*	5.3	5.4	+0.1
Insecurity	5.6	5.5	+0.1	5.0	5.6	+0.6
Liberality	6.3	5.5	-0.8	6.1	6.5	+0.4
Self-Sufficncy	7.9	8.5	+0.6	6.6	6.9	+0.3
Self-Discipline	4.9	5.9	+1.0*	5.1	6.3	+1.2*
Tension	5.8	5.4	-0.4	5.4	5.6	+0.2

NOTE: This difference is statistically significant at or beyond the .05 level of confidence previously described.

The fact that SELF-DISCIPLINE increases in both groups (and, therefore, cancels each other out) is not surprising since the requirement to listen to the tapes every day for two weeks in itself could increase this dimension. On the other hand, there are no other significant changes in the PLACEBO group, while INTELLIGENCE, EMOTIONAL STABILITY, and ALERTNESS improve markedly among listeners to the SUPERCHARGER tape.

These findings strongly suggest that the SUPERCHARGER technology does what it claims to do: that is, it provides the human brain with a psychophysical "workout", as it were, that improves its mental functioning. Furthermore, a PLACEBO tape—identical to the SUPERCHARGER in every way respect except for its psychophysical technology—has no such effect on its listeners and, in fact, has little if any effect at all.

Profile Analysis

An obvious question, of course, is how do the psychological gains a person realizes from listening to the SUPERCHARGER tape alter his or her total personality? Recent advances in computer technology have made possible actuarial analyses of 16PF results. That is, the profile for an individual or group can be interpreted in its totality, rather than as a collection of individual scores. Just such an actuarial analysis was conducted for the SUPERCHARGER and PLACEBO groups, and the results are reported below.

The Profiles. Figures 1 and 2 on the following pages graphically represent the previous data in Table 2 from which the actuarial analysis in Appendix C was made. As discussed earlier, the SUPERCHARGER group showed statistically significant gains in INTELLIGENCE, EMOTIONAL STABILITY, ALERTNESS, and SELF DISCIPLINE, while the PLACEBO group only increased on the latter dimension. The question, however, is what do these changes mean in terms of the overall psychology of each type of respondent? That is, as mentioned earlier, who do the psychological gains results from the SUPERCHARGER tape translate into new personality structures for its users? The Actuarial Analyses reported in Appendix C answer this question.

Chi-Square Analysis. Before discussing them, however, another analysis of Figures 1 and 2 is can be most revealing. Putting aside, for the moment, the issue of each dimension's statistical significance (as described earlier), we can look at the overall patterns they from before and after exposure to the SUPERCHARGER and PLACEBO tapes. That is, the question can be raised, "How many personality dimensions show a positive increase of one or more points in the SUPERCHARGER vs. PLACEBO groups—and is this multi-dimensional difference statistically significant, without reference to the significance of each of its individual factors? Table 3, below, shows the results of this procedure.

TABLE 3
Overall Profile Changes

DIRECTION OF CHANGE

	Positive	Negative	TOTAL
Supercharger Profile	10	0	10
Placebo Profile	4	3	7
TOTAL	14	3	17

The data in Table 3 suggest that SUPERCHARGER listeners, on the average, experienced more positive changes in personality than their PLACEBO counterparts. And, indeed, this is the case. By applying the appropriate test of statistical significance to this distribution[3], we find that the differences between the two groups is significant at and beyond the .05 level of confidence.[4] Moreover, the actual dimensions summarized in Table 3 are as follows:

TABLE 4
DIRECTION OF CHANGE

SUPERCHARGER Positive	Negative	PLACEBO Positive	Negative
Intelligence		Boldness	Sensitivity
Emotion. Sta.		Imagination	Insecurity
Seriousness		Experimen.	Tension
Sensitivity		Self-Discip.	
Imagination			
Alertness			
Self-Sufficent			
Self-Discipline			
Tension			
Less Conforming			

---

3 That is, the Ci-Square Test of Statistical Significance.
4 Chi-Square= 5.36, significant at the .02 level of confidence, with 1 degree of freedom.

Thus, on an overall basis, SUPERCHARGER users appear to become more Intelligent, Emotionally Stable, Serious, Sensitive, Imaginative, Alert, Self-Sufficient, Disciplined, Relaxed, and "hand loose". PLACEBO listeners, on the other hand, while becoming more bold, imaginative, experimenting and self-disciplined also become less sensitive, secure, and relaxed. And finally, these differences, on an overall basis, are statistically significant in favor of the SUPERCHARGER experience.

Actuarial Analysis. Turning now to yet another level of analysis, the psychological scores in Figures 1 and 2 were submitted to a computer interpretation developed by Dr. Bruce Duthie. (See Appendix C for the results of this procedure.) This shows that both groups were unremarkable in their personality structures before listening to their respective tapes. That is, they were solidly average in their overall, pre-exposure personalities. What emerges as significant, however, is that the PLACEBO group remained average after listening to its tape, while the SUPERCHARGER group showed marked changes in its overall personality structure.

The Supercharger Effect. How do the four psychological dimensions effected by the SUPERCHARGER tape alter the overall personality of its listeners? The computer reports in Appendix C answer this question. Compared to the PLACEBO group, whose reactions remain essentially the same, the SUPERCHARGER listeners, as a result of its psychotechnology, experience a "high morale", also "persevering under difficult circumstances." They become "more efficient" and "insightful" as well as "quick learning and intellectually adaptable." Moreover, listening to the SUPERCHARGER promotes "better than average judgment" and an "imaginative inner life". The "intuitive" and "feeling" functions also increase, along with a deepened concern for "theory, art, philosophy and other abstract interests." On the other hand, a certain amount of "impracticality" accompanies these interests, but these are compensated for by an "independent, resourceful and self-sufficient" point of view which results in the SUPERCHARGER listener "making his own decisions when at all possible".

The Daily Listening Diary. Respondents were asked to complete the "Daily Diary" in Appendix B. The results of their entries are shown in Table 4 on the following page. These data show that the overwhelming difference between the PLACEBO and SUPERCHARGER groups was that the former was "agitated", "restless" and "put to sleep", while the latter had a more "peaceful" "spiritual" and "hallucinatory" experience. As one experienced meditator, a male member of the Hindu religion put it (See Appendix E for other typical comments):

"[I] felt an incredible lightness of body & mind. My mind traveled up and out, beyond the limits of the world. Almost an out-of-body experience. Felt very peaceful for some time after."
(Respondent No. 47)

Appendix A

226

TABLE 5
Verbatim Daily Diary Comments

RESPONSE	PERCENT TOTAL (N=52)	SUPERCH (N=30)	PLACEBO (N=22)
Relaxing/Peaceful/Soothing	24%	27%	20%
Unusual Body/Visual Experience	10%	14%	7%
Agitated/Restless/Mind Wandered	4%	9%	--
A Spiritual Experience	5%	8%	1%
More Centered/Less Stressed	5%	7%	3%
At Peace/Happy/Joyous	5%	8%	1%
Alert/Aware/Less Tired	6%	5%	7%
Quieted the Mind	2%	4%	--
Fell Asleep/Became Sleepy	17%	4%	29%
Had Personal Realizations	2%	3%	1%

Reaction to the PLACEBO tape, on the other hand, was more negative. In the words of one participant, also and experienced meditator:

"[I felt] agitation, disgust. Wished it to be over soon." *(Respondent No. 11)*

Thus, on an objective basis, as well as a subjective level, reactions to the SUPERCHARGER tape were more favorable than those of the PLACEBO.

DISCUSSIONS AND CONCLUSIONS

The findings of this study are sufficiently clear to suggest several important conclusions about the SUPERCHARGER. These are discussed below, first in general and then in terms of their marketing implications.

General Conclusions

To begin with, it appears that the BRAIN SUPERCHARGER "works." That is, it does what its name implies it does: daily usage seems to have a profound effect on the mental functioning of its listener, increasing his or her...

- INTELLIGENCE
- EMOTIONAL STABILITY
- ALERTNESS

Conversely, a comparable group of people, exposed for the same period of time to a PLACEBO tape—,identical in every respect except that it lacked the SUPERCHARGER technology — showed essentially no changes at all.

These psychological gains from the SUPERCHARGER, in turn, translate into increased judgment, greater creativity, a broader occupation outlook, and a generally more relaxed view of life—as indicated by an actuarial profile analysis of the data. Once again, the PLACEBO group showed no such modifications in their personalities. Instead, they found their tape "agitating" and "annoying" causing their mind to wander and making them "restless."

<u>Marketing Implications</u>. In conclusion, the BRAIN SUPERCHARGER appears to alter the personality of its users in essentially positive and life-enhancing ways. Therefore, although not "therapy" it is therapeutic. Its impact on EMOTIONAL STABILITY, as noted earlier, an essential factor in the ego strength of normally functioning men and women, testifies to this fact.

These findings correspond nicely with the growing trend toward short-term and/or "self-help" psychotherapy. The traditional models of extended, one-on-one counseling are giving way to new and innovative technologies -- including even computerized psychotherapy—and it might do well to position its product somewhere along that trend, as indicated below.

<u>Mental Health Professionals</u>. In such a marketing effort, the EST model should be kept in mind. That is, the service offered is "therapeutic" without claiming to be therapy. Within that context, the BRAIN SUPERCHARGER could be offered to mental health professionals as an adjunct to, rather than a replacement for, counseling and psychotherapy. For example, mailing lists of its members are available from the American Psychological Association and a mail campaign, including reprints of this report, could be directed to them.

The General Public. Among the general public, the BRAIN SUPERCHARGER could be positioned as...

THE MOST POWERFUL TOOL FOR PSYCHOLOGICAL
CHANGE SHORT OF PROFESSIONAL PSYCHOTHERAPY.

This, or some similar positioning, would capitalize on the SUPERCHARGER's capacity for enhancing the personality, as suggested by this study, while avoiding any claims as a replacement for professional treatment.

Appendix B

Copy of Purchase Order from CIA for Brain Supercharger programs.

CIA Purchase Order

229

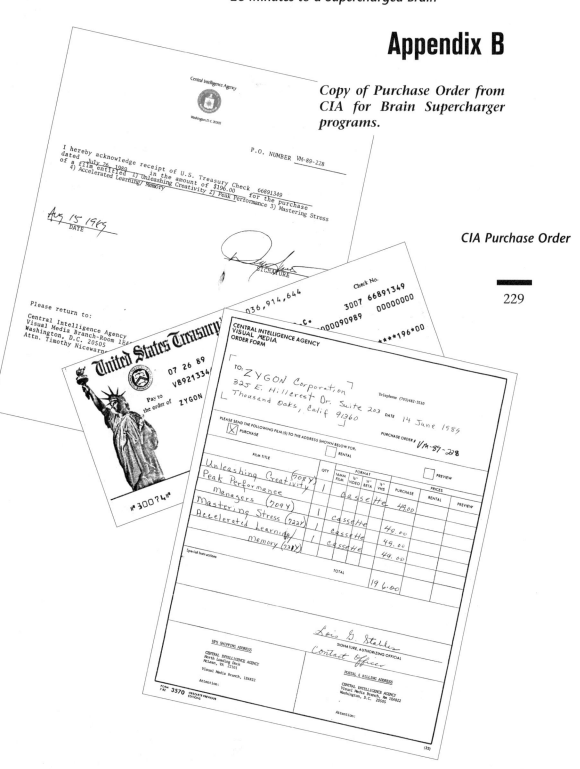

Appendix C
Bibliography

BOOKS

Belitz, Charlene and Meg Lundstrom. *The Power of Flow*. New York, New York: Harmony Books, 1992.

Bush, Carol A. *Healing Imagery & Music*. Portland, Oregon: Rudra Press, 1995.

Buzan, Tony. *Use Both Sides of Your Brain*. New York, New York: Penguin Books, 1991.

Capra, Fritjof. *The Tao of Physics*. New York: Bantam, 1975.

Cameron, Julia A. *The Artist's Way*. New York, New York: G.D. Putnam's Sons, 1992.

Campbell, Don. *The Mozart Effect*. New York, New York: Avon Books, 1997.

Casteneda, Carlos. *Journey To Ixlan*. New York, New York: Simon & Shuster, 1968.

Csikszentmihalyi, Mihalyi. *Flow*. New York, New York: Harper Perennial, 1990.

Dhority, Lynn. *The ACT Approach: The Use of Suggestion for Integrative Learning* Philadelphia, Pennsylvania: Gordon and Breach Science Publishers, 1992.

Dodd, Vicki. *Sound as a Tool for Transformation*. [n.p.] [n.d.]

Evans, Christopher. *Landscapes of the Night*. New York, New York: The Viking Press, 1983.

Ferguson, Marilyn. *The Aquarian Conspiracy*. Los Angeles, California: J.P. Tarcher, 1980.

Gardner, Howard. *Frames of Mind*. New York, New York: Basic Books, 1983.

Gardner, Kay. *Sounding the Inner Landscape*. Stonington, Maine: Caduceus Publications, 1990.

Goldberg, Natalie. *Writing Down the Bones*. Boston, Massachusetts: Shambhala, 1986.

Goleman, Daniel. *Emotional Intelligence*. New York, New York: Bantam Books, 1995.

Koestler, Arthur. *The Act of Creation*. New York, New York: The Macmillan Company, 1964.

Hutchinson, Michael. *Mega Brain: New Tools and Techniques for Brain Growth and Mind Expansion*. New York, New York: Ballantine Books, 1986.

Lozanov, Georgi. *Suggestology and Outlines of Suggestopedy*. New York, New York: Gordon and Breach, 1978.

Lozanov, Georgi & Evalina Gateva. *The Foreign Language Teacher's Suggestopedic Manual*. New York, New York: Gordon and Breach, 1988.

May, Rollo. *The Courage to Create*. New York, New York: W.W. Norton & Company, Inc., 1975.

Murphy, Michael and Steven Donovan. *The Physical and Psychological Effects of Meditation*. San Rafael, California: Esalen Institute, 1988.

Ostrander, Sheila, Lynn Schroeder and Nancy Ostrander. *Superlearning*. New York, New York: Dell Publishing Company, 1979.

Popcorn, Faith and Lys Marigold. *Clicking*. New York, New York: Harper Collins Publishers, 1996.

Prichard, Allyn and Jean Taylor. *Accelerated Learning: The Use of Suggestion in the Classroom*. Novato, California: Academic Therapy Publications, 1980.

Rose, Colin. *Accelerated Learning*. New York, New York: Bantam Doubleday Dell Publishing Group, Inc, 1985.

Schafer, Murray. *Turning the World*. [n.p.] [n.d.]

Schuster, Donald H. *How to Learn Quickly: An Introduction to Fast and Easy Learning*. Ames, Iowa: Research Into Mind, 1987.

Schuster, Donald H. *The Mind*. Ames, Iowa: Research Into Mind, 1985.

Stockwell, Tony. *Accelerated Learning in Theory and Practice*. Liechtenstein: European Foundation for Education, Communication and Teaching, 1992.

Suzuki, D.T. *Essence of Buddism*. Kyoto, Japan: Hozokan, 1968.

Weston, Denise Chapman & Mark S. *Playful Parenting: Turning the Dilemma of Discipline into Fun and Games*. New York, New York: G.P. Putnam's Sons, 1993.

Wycoff, Joyce. *Mind Mapping*. New York, New York: Berkley Books, 1991.

PERIODICALS

The Journal of the Society for Accelerative Learning and Teaching (SALT): Volume 1, Nos. 2 (two copies), 3. 1976.

Volume 2, Nos. 1,2,3,4. 1977.
Volume 3, Nos. 2,3,4. 1978.
Volume 4, Nos. 1,2,3,4. 1979.
Volume 5, Nos. 1,2,4. 1980.
Volume 6, Nos. 1,2,3,4. 1981.
Volume 7, No. 2. 1982.
Volume 8, Nos. 3,4. 1983.
Volume 9, Nos. 1,2,3,4. 1984.
Volume 10, Nos. 1,2,3,4. 1985.
Volume 11, Nos. 1,2,3,4. 1986.
Volume 12, Nos. 1,2,3,4. 1987.
Volume 13, Nos. 1,2,3,4. 1988.
Volume 14, Nos. 1,2,3,4. 1989.
Volume 16, Nos. 1,3. 1991.
Volume 17, Nos. 3,4. 1992.
Megabrain Report: The Journal of Mind Technology; Volume 1, Nos. 1,2,3,4.
Megabrain Report: The Journal of Mind Technology; Volume 2, Nos. 1,2.

Appendix C

ACCELERATED LEARNING: CORPORATE

Gill, Mary Jane and David Meier. "Accelerated Learning Takes Off." <u>Training and Development Journal</u> January 1989.
Meier, David. "Imagine That." <u>Training and Development Journal</u> May 1988.
Meier, David. "New Age Learning: From Linear to Geodesic." <u>Training and Development Journal</u> May 1985.
Reid, Gerry. "Accelerated Learning: Technical Training Can Be Fun." <u>Training and Development Journal</u> September 1985.
Robinson, Anne Durrum. "How To Have a Safe Trip to the Cutting Edge." <u>Training and Development Journal</u> May 1985.

ALPHA THETA MIND STATES

Herbert, R. and D. Lehmann. "Theta Bursts: An EEG Pattern in Normal Subjects Practicing the Transcendental Meditation Technique." <u>Electroencephalography and Clinical Neurophysiology</u> 1977. 42: 397-405.
Hoovey, Z.B. and O.D. Creutzfield. "Inter-Hemispheric 'Synchrony,' of Alpha Waves." <u>Electroencephalography and Clinical Neurophysiology</u> 1972. 32: 337-347.

ALTERED STATES

Don, Norman S. "The Transformation of Conscious Experience and its EEG Correlates." <u>Journal of Altered States of Consciouness</u> Vol 3(2): 1977-78.
Gellhorn, Ernst and William F. Kiely. "Mystical States of Consciousness: Neurophysiological and Clinical Aspects," <u>Journal of Nervous and Mental Disease</u> Vol 154, No. 6: 399-405.
Glicksohn, Joseph. "Photic Driving and Altered States of Consciousness: An Exploratory Study." <u>Imagination, Cognition and Personality</u> Vol. 6(2): 1986-87.
Ludwig, Arnold M. "Altered States of Consciousness." <u>Arch. Gen. Psychiatry</u> Vol. 15, 1966. 225-234.

BIOFEEDBACK

Brown, Barbara B. "Stress and the Art of Biofeedback." Harper & Row Publishers; New York, NY. 1977.
Budzynski, Thomas. "Tuning in on the Twilight Zone." <u>Biofeedback & Self-Control</u> Chicago, Illinois: Aldire Publishing Company, 1977/78.
Budzynski, Thomas H. "Some Applications of Biofeedback Produced Twilight States." <u>Biofeedback & Self-Control</u> Chicago, Illinois: Aldire Publishing Company, 1977/78.
Green, Elmer. "Biofeedback for Mind-body Self-Regulation: Healing and Creativity." The Varieties of Healing Experience: Exploring Psychic Phenomena in Healing. A Transcript From the Interdisciplinary Symposium of Oct. 30, 1971, Academy of Parapsychology and Medicine.
Nideffer, Robert M. "Alpha and the Development of Human Potential." <u>Biofeedback & Self-Control</u> Aldire Publishing Co. 1977/78.

CREATIVITY

Martindale, Colin. "Creativity, Consciousness, and Cortical Arousal." Journal of Altered States of Consciousness; Vol 3(1) 1977-78.
West, Stanley A. "Creativity, Altered States of Awareness, and Artificial Intelligence." Journal of Altered States of Consciousness; Vol 2(3) 1975-76.

HEMISPHIRIC DIFFERENTIATION

Joiner, Elizabeth G. "Listening From the Inside out." <u>Foreign Language Annals</u> 17 No 4, 1984.

HYPNOSIS

Blum, Gerald S. "A Conceptual Model for Hypnotic Alterations of Consciousness." <u>Journal of Altered States Consciousness</u> Vol 4(2) 1978-79.
Goldberg, Jeanne. "Mind Machines in the Hypnosis Office." <u>Journal of Hypnotism</u> September 1993.

LANGUAGE LEARNING

"Learning a Language Through Brainwashing." Impossible Human Center; Vol 4, No 3, 1990.
LeHecka, Charlotte F. "Rapid Language Learning: A Must for 21st Century." Innotech Journal; Jan-Jun 1992.
Palmer, Lyelle L. and Lynn Dhority. "The 636% Solution Paradigm: A Statistical Evaluation of the Extraordinary Effectiveness of Lynn Dhority's US Army Accelerated Learning German Class." Journal of the Society for Accelerative Learning and Teaching; Vol 18, Issue 3 & 4, Fall & Winter 1993.

MEDITATION

Goodman, Guruneel Singh Khalsa. "Effects of an Advanced Yogic Practice, the Doei Shabd Kriya, on states of Consciousness." Journal of Altered States of Consciousness; Vol 4(4), 1978-79.
Meditation and Electroencephalography, Collection of abstracts on this topic, plus bibliography.
Delmonte, M. M. "Electrocortical Activity and Related Phenomena Associated with Meditation Practice: A Literature Review." Intern. J. of Neuroscience; Vol 24, 1984.

MISCELLANEOUS

Jakimik, Jola and Arthur Glenberg. "Verbal Learning Meets Psycholinguistics: Modality Effects in the Comprehensive of Anaphora." <u>Journal of Memory and Language</u> 29 (1990).
Krippner, Stanley. "Soviet and American Perspectives on Hidden Reserves and Human Potentials." <u>Journal of Humanistic Psychology</u> Vol 26 No 4, Fall 1986.
Rosenthal, Robert. "Unintended Communication in Classrooms, Clinics, and Courtrooms." <u>MWERA Researcher</u> Vol 1 No 2.
Swets, John A. and Robert A. Bjork. "Enhancing Human Performance: An Evaluation of 'New Age' Techniques Considered by the US Army." <u>Psychological Science</u> Vol 1, No 2, March 1990.

MUSIC

"Brain Music of the Hemispheres." <u>Discover</u> March 1994.
Browne, Malcom W. "Mozart Makes the Brain Hum, a Study Finds." <u>The New York</u> Times 14 Oct 1993.
Dominguez, Dora. "Developing Language Through a Musical Program and its Effect on the Reading Achievement of Spanish Speaking Migrant Children." Western Michigan University, 1991.
Harding, Judy Ann Hove. "The Relationship Between Music and Language Achievement in Early Childhood." doctoral thesis, Montana State University, Apr 1989.

Hotz, Robert Lee. "Study: 10 Minutes of Mozart Sontana Music to the Mind." <u>Saint Paul Pioneer Press</u> 14 Oct 1993.

Jocobs, Tom. "Can Music Make Kids Smarter?" <u>New Age Journal</u> Jan/Feb 1994.

Mandelblatt, Marjorie. "Mostly Mozart." <u>MENSA Bullitin</u> Dec 1993.

Marple, Hugo D. "Short-term Memory and Musical Stimuli." Psychology and Acoustics of Music: A Collection of Papers, Edward Asmus, Editor.

"Music Therapy." <u>Creative Alternatives Newsletter</u> Vol 4 No 4, 1990.

Rauscher, Frances H., Gordon L. Shaw and Katherine N. Ky. "Music and Spatial Task Performance." Nature; Vol 365, 14 Oct 1993.

RELAXATION

Humphrey, James H. "Teaching Children to Relax." Charles C. Thomas, Springfield, IL. 1998.

Moon, Charles E. and Gary F. Render. "Relaxation and Educational Outcomes: A Meta-Analysis." Journal of the Society for Accelerative Learning and Teaching, 1988 13(3).

Poppen, Roger. "Behavioral Relaxation Training and Assessment." Psychology Practitioner Guidebooks, Pergamon Press; Elmsford, NY. 1988.

SOUND/LIGHT MACHINES

Harrah-Conforth, Bruce. "Alpha and Theta Response To The Mind's Eye Plus." Indiana University.

SUGGESTOLOGY

Bancroft, W. Jane. "Foreign Language Teaching in Bulgaria." <u>Canadian Modern Language Review</u> March 1972.

Bancroft, W. Jane. "Suggestology and Suggestopedia: The Theory of the Lozanov Method." <u>Journal of the Society for Accelerative Learning and Teaching</u> Vol 1 No 3, 1976.

Belanger, Bagriana. "Suggestopeadia and Teacher Training," from the symposium of the International; Association for Accelerated Learning; Jan 1985.

Eggers, Paul. "Suggestopedia: An Innovation in Language Learning." Media & Methods; Vol 21 No 4, Dec 1984.

"History of Accelerated Learning, Lozanov & SALT."

Marcum, Karen. "Lozanov's Suggestopedy: A Psycholinguist Analysis of its Theory and Praxis." Georgetown University; Jun 23, 1987.

Moon, Charles E., et al. "A Meta-analysis of the Effects of Suggestopedia, Suggestology, Suggistive-accelerative Learning and Teaching (SALT) and Super-Learning on Cognitive and Affective Outcomes." <u>Journal of the Society for Accelerative Learning and Teaching</u> 1988, 13(3).

Morrissey, Brian. "Suggestology & Suggestopedia: 14 Years After, The Advent of New Brainwave Technologies Makes a Rebirth Likely."

Palmer, Lyelle L., Michael Alexander and Nancy Ellis. "Elementary School Achievement Results Following In-service Training of an Entire School Staff in Accelerative Learning and Teaching: An Interim Report." <u>Journal of the Society for Accelerative Learning and Teaching</u> 1989, 14(1)

Stanton, H.E. "The Lozanov Method for Accelerating the Learning of Foreign Languages." <u>Babel: Journal of the Federation of Modern Language Teachers Association</u> Nov 1978.

Push-Button Meditation

The Ultra-Meditation System for Transcendence

Learn the secret of how meditation manipultates the energies of consciousness provoking the mind-brain to operate at higher levels of awareness. Use the companion Ultra Meditation CD to experience profound meditative states & ultimately plug your mind into the blissful esctasy of transcendence and pure consciousness. (Book + 1 CD)

ISBN 1-892805-23-5 • *Available Summer 1999*

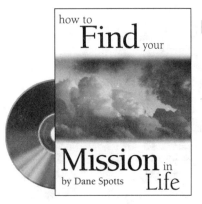

How To Find Your Mission In Life

Discover your passion and follow your bliss. The special CD workshop not only teaches you how to discover who you are, your passions and ultimately what you should be doing with your life, but takes you through a very insightful "dream discovery" session where using a powerful 3-step process of meditation and guided imagery you meet your future self and discover your life's purpose. Very powerful and revealing. (Book + 1 CD)

ISBN 1-892805-06-3 • *Available Summer 1999*

The Secret of Living a Perfect Life

5 key principles guide you to a revelation that will instantly transform your life. Once embraced, these principles expand your possibilities and give you everything you need to live a perfect life. The "secret" that will be revealed to you is a simple but profound truth that will shape every aspect of your life from that moment forward. (Book + 1 CD)

ISBN 1-892805-05-7 • *Available Summer 1999*

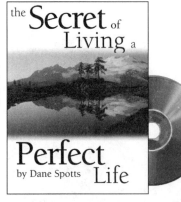

Mind Power Secrets

Teaches you how to access the hidden powers of your mind to create the future you desire. Using a remarkable mind control technology called "visioneering" it focuses the creative powers of your unconscious to make your dreams come true. Millionaire's and peak performing athletes use it to achieve success and you can too. (Book + 1 CD)

ISBN 1-892805-07-3 • *Available Summer 1999*

12 BRAIN SUPERCHARGER "MINDSCRIPTING" SOUNDTRACKS

Get the complete *Brain Supercharger* Mind Lab which includes 12 different titles (each about 28 minutes in length—recorded onto 6 CDs) incorporating the "Supercharger" technology. Different flavors if you will...each designed to train and relax your conscious mind...while opening a doorway into your inner mind.

12 Mindscripting Titles To Experiment With

As reported in Chapter 4, this mind technology has been used to help reprogram negative beliefs and self-sabotaging behaviors. How? Researchers believe the "alpha-theta" mind-state opens a window into the unconscious. Similar to hypnosis, once a channel is opened, it's possible to transfer positive programming. You'll learn to use the mindscripting technique for rewiring your belief systems and how you see yourself and the world. This is very empowering. Because your mood, emotions, and self-concept result from the way you think. By rescripting your internal dialogue you can shape your perceptions and transform your personal reality. How will you know if it's working? The only way to know for sure is by measuring your personal feelings. The purpose of your Mind Lab (the 12 *Supercharger* titles listed below) is to give you the raw tools to experiment with on yourself. Follow the instructions and keep track of your progress in your journal and prove the results to yourself.

Note: Each *Brain Supercharger* is loaded with powerful mindscripting™ affirmations embedded into the audio matrix. These unique soundtracks have sold for as much as $50 each, which gives the Mind-Lab a potential value of $600. As a reader of this book you can receive all 12 titles for half of their original cost...

1. Ultra Success Conditioning	7. Super Memory & Learning
2. Perfect Body Image	8. Sports Performance
3. Project a Winning Self-Image	9. Soaring Self-Confidence
4. Mastering Stress	10. Improve Love Relationships
5. Unleashing Creativity	11. Attract Wealth & Prosperity
6. Healthy Mind/Healthy Body	12. Enhanced Psychic Functioning

Brain Supercharger Mind Lab™..$299.95 [US]

TO ORDER 800-657-8646

CUSTOMER SERVICE 425-643-9939

or visit our web page at www.mind-tek.com

Ultra Meditation Transcendence System

The Ultra-Meditation 5-Level System for Transcendence was developed to open the mind's gateway to greater levels of awareness by driving your consciousness inward and feeding the brain with a steady flow of psychic energy. As described in Chapter 3 it is, "The ability to faciliate whole-brain synchrony entirely through sound...by applying the use of certain musical harmonics and sound frequencies mood can be shifted, "right brain" awareness activated, and whole brain synchrony promoted. 5 CDs are included in the special boxed set, each with a different audio matrix designed to promote transcendence and peak experiences.

Ultra Meditation I - The Beginning
Powerful beginning tool for exploring the possibilities of the "theta state."

Ultra Meditation II - Transformation
Complex audio matrix designed to drive you into a deeper more powerful meditation experience.

Ultra Meditation III - Awareness
Very subtle but powerful sacred sounds that connect you to an aboriginal dream-time meditation.

Ultra Meditation IV - Cetacean Mind Link
Connect your consciousess to the audio world of whales and dolphins.

Ultra Meditation V - Near Death Experience
Take your consciousness beyond & back to explore the 5-step process of a near death experience.

The Ultra Meditation 5-Level system for transcendence is the ultimate mind expanding audio experience.

Ultra Meditation 5-Level Transcendence System™..................................... $199.95 [US]

TO ORDER `800-657-8646`
CUSTOMER SERVICE `425-643-9939`

or visit our web page at www.mind-tek.com

The MindQuest Meditation Computer

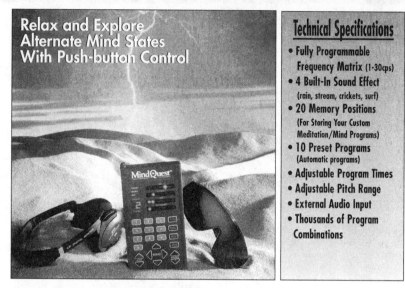

Relax and Explore Alternate Mind States With Push-button Control

Technical Specifications

- **Fully Programmable Frequency Matrix (1-30cps)**
- **4 Built-In Sound Effect** (rain, stream, crickets, surf)
- **20 Memory Positions** (For Storing Your Custom Meditation/Mind Programs)
- **10 Preset Programs** (Automatic programs)
- **Adjustable Program Times**
- **Adjustable Pitch Range**
- **External Audio Input**
- **Thousands of Program Combinations**

MIND MACHINE BREAKTHROUGH

After a hard day at the office, you owe yourself a good mind massage, so you plug in the *Thunderstorm* soundtrack into your MindQuest™ meditation computer. Punch in the code for a heavy duty relaxation session, and instantly launch your consciousness into another time and place. After only a few moments, you're sucked into an amazing virtual dream-state. Images, colors, and patterns are created on the insides of your closed eyelids while off in the distance you hear the rumblings of a great thunderstorm. The mental imagery is so strong it feels as if your mind and body are one...being pulled into the eye of the storm.

Amazing Light/Sound Effects

The powerful light/sound matrix stimulates your imagination like nothing you've ever experienced. And because it's computer controlled, you can experiment with thousands of different frequency combinations. Plus there are four incredible mind-blowing sound effects (rain, mountain stream, crickets, and surf) actually built into the on-board computer chip along with adjustable time parameters and pitch range. The programmable frequencies give you amazing push-button control over your meditation. The size of a pocket calculator the MindQuest is completely portable so you can use it to meditate and relax while traveling too.

Incredible Mind Journeys

Using proven light/sound sensory technology, the MindQuest allows you to experiment with different audio and light stimulation effects designed to unfold profound relaxation and unleash the powers of your imagination. A spectacular light show is orchestrated within the sound matrix and projected into your mind's eye. The result? Your consciousness is automatically launched into an incredible inner universe. Experience the ultimate meditation and dream machine, and take your mind on the ultimate mind journey.

Bonus Soundtracks Included—FREE

Each kit includes computer, headphones, light-pulse glasses, AC adapter, and four virtual dreamscape soundtracks.

MindQuest™...................**$199.95 [US]**

TO ORDER 800-657-8646

CUSTOMER SERVICE 425-643-9939

or visit our web page at www.mind-tek.com

WARNING: For Experimental Purposes. The MindQuest Uses Powerful Light/Sound Technology That Can Potentially Induce Seizures in Susceptible Individuals, Including Those With No Prior Seizure History.

Want To Join The Club?

WE ARE VERY INTERESTED in what you think of the ideas and technology presented in this book. And we'd like to hear your opinions and comments. On the following page is a brief questionaire, which you can fill out and return to us (or if you like you can visit us on online at www.mind-tek.com). Your comments will be kept confidential unless you give us permission to use them.

If you do us this favor of providing your feedback, we'll automatically enroll you in our *Mind Warrior's* club. A group of like-minded individuals who connect online to share their experiences and are working toward the evolution of their consciousness and the consciousness of our planet. As a member/subscriber you'll be able to participate in our online/web conferences and link up with others on a similar path.

In addition to the web conferences, there are plans to offer online workshops and teaching forums on emerging mind development technologies and related subjects of interest. It's something you'll want to be a part of as we cross over into the new millennium.

visit our web page at www.mind-tek.com/forum

Registration Card

Name_____

Address _____

City/State/Zip_____

What is your email address _____

How did you learn about this book? _____

❑ recommended by a friend   ❑ received ad in mail
❑ read book review   ❑ saw in catalog
❑ saw in bookstore   ❑ recommended by store clerk

Where did you purchase this book? _____

Please check the top two factors that influenced your decision to buy this book.

❑ cover   ❑ price   ❑ ideas presented
❑ author   ❑ the bonus CD   ❑ other

Would you like to be placed on our preferred mailing list? ❑ yes ❑ no

❑ **Yes, I would like to see my name name in print.** You may use my name and quote me in future products and promotions. My phone number is _____

Comments: _____

_____

_____

_____

_____

_____

Fold Here

- -

Attn: Book Projects Group
LIFEQUEST BOOKS
P.O. Box 1444
Issaquah, Washington 98027